Dear Mother,
I am the only one left!

The story of Civil War soldier Charles Shepard
— Told through letters to his family —

RUSS VANDERVOORT

Waterford Town Historian
Registered Historian with the Association of Public Historians
New York State

Dear Mother, I am the Only One Left
Copyright © 2023 by Russ Vandervoort

All rights reserved. No part of this book may be used or reproduced in any form, electronic or mechanical, including photocopying, recording, or scanning into any information storage and retrieval system, without written permission from the author except in the case of brief quotation embodied in critical articles and reviews.

Book design by The Troy Book Makers
Printed in the United States of America
The Troy Book Makers • Troy, New York • thetroybookmakers.com

To order additional copies of this title,
contact your favorite local bookstore
or visit www.shoptbmbooks.com

ISBN: 978-1-61468-855-6

*This effort is dedicated to
John and Helen Anderson
and the families who can trace
their heritage to Charles Shepard.*

CONTENTS

Prologue.. 1

Chapter 1: AFTER THE PANIC, A CHANCE ENCOUNTER........ 5

Chapter 2: THE CANAL SEASON OF 1863 COMES TO A CLOSE.... 17

Chapter 3: FOR THE SHEPARD FAMILY.....THE WAR BEGINS.... 33

Chapter 4: THE LETTERS START TO ARRIVE................. 43

Chapter 5: THE CANAL OPENS, CHARLES IS IN THE FIELD..... 71

Chapter 6: A HOMECOMING OF SORTS....................... 97

Chapter 7: THE BABY AND
THE MEETING AT THE MORGAN HOUSE 117

Chapter 8: THE BABY ARRIVES 127

Chapter 9: THE DARK DAYS BEGIN 141

Chapter 10: DOES ANYONE KNOW WHERE THE LOVE OF GOD
GOES WHEN THE WAIT, TURNS THE MINUTES INTO HOURS?.. 149

Chapter 11: THERE ARE NO FACTS, ONLY INTERPRETATIONS... 157

Chapter 12: PERHAPS A VISIT IS IN ORDER 163

Chapter 13: INFORMATION ARRIVES
IN A MYSTERIOUS MANNER 171

Chapter 14: INTO THIS HOUSE YOU'RE BORN,
INTO THIS WORLD, YOU'RE THROWN. 177

Chapter 15: A RETURN TO THE MORGAN HOUSE
.....AND ETHAN ALLAN. 183

Chapter 16: EATHEN ALLEN AND
THE VANDERWERKEN FAMILY. 189

Chapter 17: A STORY POORLY TOLD?. 193

Chapter 18: A DAY IN THE LIFE 197

Chapter 19: ....HURRY UP & WAIT 203

Chapter 20: .....THE WAITING IS THE HARDEST PART. 209

Chapter 21: .....HOW DOES IT FEEL?
TO HAVE NO DIRECTION KNOWN. 219

Chapter 22: .....AND IN THE END, THE LOVE YOU TAKE 225

Chapter 23: .....MY FRIENDS IN THE PRISONS ASK UNTO ME,
HOW GOOD, DOES IT FEEL TO BE FREE? 231

Epilogue 239

Letters & Battle Summary 247

Bibliography/End Notes 341

PROLOGUE

"Storytelling is an obligation to the next generation. If we don't honor that obligation, we are doing a disservice to our children and their children. Give something of meaning to your audience by inspiring, engaging, and educating them with stories." (1)

This book has been a work that has spanned a decade in its research and presentation. I feel a need to inform the reader how this story came to be told and why it took so long to tell.

Previous efforts have resulted in five books. The first was the *One Hundred Year History of the Hudson Valley Volunteer Firefighters Association* in 1989. That was followed by *Canal Canaries and Other Tough Old Birds* in 2010. A book concerning my family's canaling experiences. In 2014, I was a contributing researcher/writer on Richard Herzog's book *Images of America, Waterford*. In the last two years, I have contributed articles to the books *Saratoga County Stories and More Saratoga County Stories*. These efforts were all of investigative research and the subsequent retelling of the historical facts uncovered in a proper format.

This book is a bit different. The reader should be informed of its genesis.

When *Images of America* was being produced, Richard Herzog assembled a group of interested Waterfordians to work on this project. Included in this group were four classmates from the Waterford Schools who had graduated in 1965. One of my classmates was Helen Anderson, who furnished several articles for the book, plus a fair amount of historical memorabilia. One of those articles was the wallet of a man who owned a long ago Waterford business. Her family had acquired the property of the business many years ago. The wallet was discovered on the property. It was Civil War Era memorabilia that was not Waterford related. I was able to research the contents and determine that the Civil War Soldier listed on the paperwork was a member of the Vanderwerken Family. This family was well-known in the area and influential. However, the soldier in question, although a Vanderwerken, was a native Waterfordian; his portion of the family was years removed from Waterford. There was also a train ticket stub in the contents. We were able to reasonably determine that the soldier had won an inspection award during the Civil War, which earned him leave time. The Vanderwerken who owned the wallet was determined to be his uncle. The destination of the train ticket proved to be the location where his nephew was now on leave. Helen was thrilled to learn of the meaning of the wallet's contents. She then inquired if I would be interested in any Civil War Letters. I quickly answered in the affirmative. She supplied me with thirty - eight letters written by her husband's ancestor, Charles Shepard. Contained therein was the story about which you will soon read. The family did not know the full story, only how it ended. They did not know the circumstances under which the ending played out.

I was pleased and satisfied with the story that was able to be reconstructed through research. I had no previous experience in conducting Civil War research. I was amazed at the material that is available to be researched concerning the Civil War and those that were engaged in it. Through letters, diaries, newspaper coverage, Regimental Histories, and a seemingly unending amount of researchable material, one can realistically document a soldier's military experiences. I have since researched two others whose families were quite pleased with the results.

At the conclusion of my research and writing, I felt like I actually knew Charles; it was a good feeling.

This book is a milestone for me. All others have been straight historical reporting, based on fact, with no emotion or editorializing.

I labored over how to best present the material that was discovered and how to give Charles' short life more meaning and respect his legacy. My choice was to present a fictionalized account of his story. Fictionalized, I think, is a poor word choice. All the events that occur in this story are real. All the people that are mentioned throughout the book are real. For the sake of the storyline and to highlight some of Waterford's History during this time period, liberties have been taken with the conversations held between John Shepard, Charles' father, and anyone with whom he is alleged to have conversed. Obviously, any thoughts expressed by John are the thoughts of the author.

Let the story begin.

Chapter 1

AFTER THE PANIC, A CHANCE ENCOUNTER

John Shepard had been a canaller now for some time. Relocated to Waterford, New York, from Massachusetts, he had moved in 1838 to seek work in an area that was rich with opportunity. Just 20 years of age then, everything was an adventure. Now twenty-five years have passed. John is contemplative about his life, especially in the current times. As the canal season of 1863 is coming to its annual conclusion, he thinks of the good fortune that has been his companion in this journey through life and his journeys on the towpath leading the mules that towed the canal boats. The canals played a curious role in John's life. The bank failure in Massachusetts during the Panic of 1837 caused him to remove to Waterford. Part of the reason for the Panic's negative effects on the Massachusetts area was due to the banks overinvesting in Maine forest lands. The lack of an inland navigation system or a canal made the lumber produced in Maine expensive to transfer to market. As a result of the success of the New York State canals, other areas of the country were investing in canal building on borrowed money, and not all canals were as successful as the canals in New York State. (2) This overinvestment by his home commonwealth and other states, coupled with economic factors that John would never understand, was the cause for him to move to Waterford, seeking the work that was available because of the canal. He was amused that the financial success in one location, attributable to canals, could lead to a troubled financial situation elsewhere. In any regard, John thought it was a curious twist of fate. In 1836, the Bank of England decided to tighten the loaning of credit both domestically and to foreign parties to help increase dwindling reserves of monetary value held in the banks. (2)

The tightening of credit from European parties led to many unfinished and unfunded infrastructure investment projects in the United States. Canals in Pennsylvania and Maryland were unfinished, along with many railroads in the Midwest. Southern banks soon failed, and bonds were unable to be paid back in full across the country. Pennsylvania and Maryland borrowed heavily from European sources to fund canals connecting their ports to the Midwest, and both could not make the interest payments early in the 1840s due to the Panic of 1837. (3) Historians have attributed this panic to poor real estate investment and erratic banking policies. Northeastern forests were the most overvalued holdings. In Massachusetts, Nahant Bank and Boston's Oriental Bank fell victim to these speculative investments when their assets became dangerously concentrated in unimproved Maine land far from navigable waterways. An 1838 survey confirmed that this property was overvalued, and both banks failed. Developments in banking compounded the crisis. The money supply swelled when the Bank of the United States lost its charter, and each of the nation's 850 banks could, once again, issue their own banknotes with little restraint. This paper money rapidly depreciated when President Jackson mandated payment for government land in gold or silver. Ten months later, banks refused to redeem their banknotes in species, bringing commerce to a standstill. (4)

Waterford, New York, was known as the head of sloop navigation on the Hudson River. There had been much-established trade and commerce there since the late 1700s as the northernmost navigable point on the river. The Mohawk River joined the Hudson at this point, and the Mohawk could be harnessed to provide water power for several industries. In 1823, the Champlain Canal became the first of New York's Canals to be completed and operating. This created a passageway between Lake Champlain and Canada to New York City and the world. This was followed in 1828 by the opening of the King's Power

Canal, which provided a more reliable power source to create the power needed for a growing industrial community.

The single greatest contribution to Waterford's industrial development was King's waterpower canal, built around 1828 by John Fuller King. King performed a real engineering feat for those days by running two dams across the northern or fourth branch of the Mohawk River. The largest extends to Peebles Island. After holding back this water, King released it through his canal, running parallel to the river fully a one-half mile. The water fell back into the Mohawk with a drop of sixteen feet. Along the 53-foot wide canal were built dozens of factories which turned out an almost unprecedented variety of goods.

King and his group had a vision. They advertised their surplus power on New York's Wall Street as equalling "Thirty run-of-mill stone." The canal became known locally as King's Ditch. Each establishment had its own sluice gate to run the water through and turn its wheels. This power canal greatly influenced Business Development in Waterford; utilizing the great water power in a convenient form for general use led to the establishment of about twelve manufactories. The manufacture of fire engines was started in 1831, and they have done an extensive business, turning out some of the time $60,000 worth of work a year. (5)

Coupled with that twist of fate event, John remembered, was an encounter soon after his arrival in Waterford with a young girl from his new home village. While he was waiting with his team above the side cut locks for his tow to come out, this girl, as yet unknown, was talkative, and she had asked him if he had been anywhere interesting on the canal. He thought everywhere was interesting in its own right. Then he recalled Brown's Cash Store and the biggest store on the canal. Young lady, there is a right smart place out towards the west. You can buy anything there, from an anchor to a vest. The young girl's eyes grew big with disbelief when she said, "Why sir, that's on the canal near my hometown in Fort Hunter." They were both surprised by this exchange and shared a laugh. Before she went on her way, she told him her name

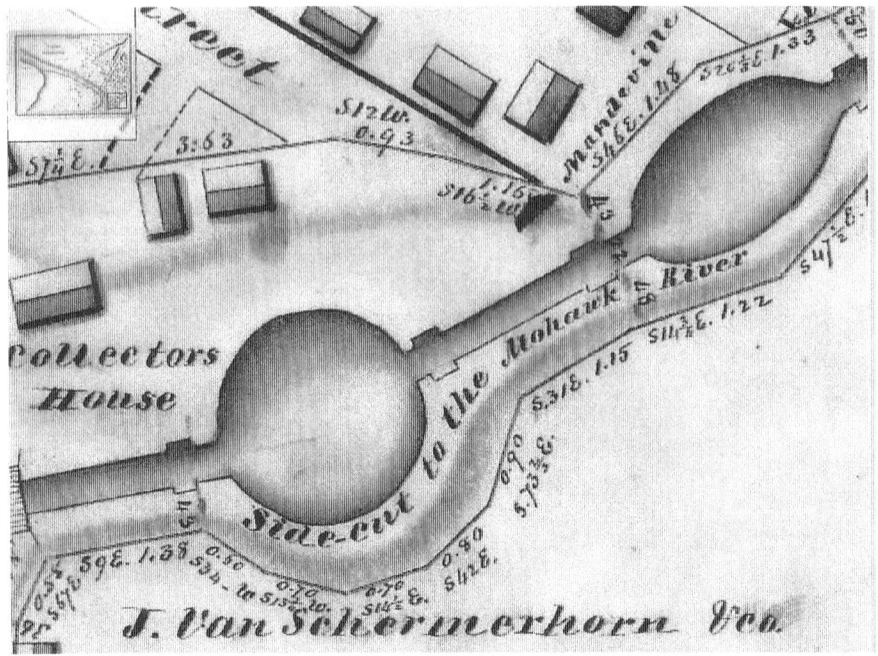

P01 Original Side Cut Locks were in operation at the time that Harriet and John had their encounter there. This was located in the approximate area of today's Lock 2 on the Erie Barge Canal. They were enlarged and replaced in the 1860s by these locks, still in use today as a spillway for Lock 2.

was Miss Harriet Kennedy, and she had recently moved from Fort Hunter to Waterford to join the family. Soon their chance encounters became more regular. Fate and the canals sure do have their way.

John fancied himself a part of something much greater than a mule driver. The wealth of the area, the state, and the country, John thought to himself, is largely dependent on all the canallers, whose work and lifestyles help to make this canal a great thing in a great country. Despite the current rebellion of the Southern States, the country is expanding in area and wealth. John took pleasure in his own estimate of the role he played on the canal. John had worked in earnest to achieve the role that he had enjoyed now for the last decade or so. He owned six mules and did not, any longer, although he had, in the early years, do any long-distance towing on the canal. His

P02 The Side Cut Locks after the 1860's enlargement.

thoughts could wander as he walked the towpath leading his team; this day was pleasant, and he became reflective. He had achieved a measured amount of success and owned a nice home just 137 steps from the Champlain Canal. His family was well. Harriet Kennedy, now his wife, was an industrious helpmate, and his son Charles had done well in school. He was doing quite well as a local peddler for a young lad, just 15 when he began the trade. He had grown into an accomplished agent at 18. His daughter, Rebecca, was an active, obedient child of 14 and a help to her mother. John's thoughts would come quickly during serene trips on the towpath. His thoughts, as comforting as they were, would unintentionally turn melancholy when he would remember his daughters Mary and Harriet. At this point, these poor sisters were John's only haunted area of regret in his life. Mary was their youngest child, who the Lord had seen fit to call home early. Mary did not see her second birthday, and Harriet was less than six. John considered himself a religious man, as most canallers did, and despite the loss and sadness over their early deaths, John considered himself and his family quite blessed.

John was approaching Lock 4 on the Champlain Canal. It was a river or guard lock. The towpath was on the east side of the canal in Waterford. The canal will cross the Mohawk River here. The Fulton Street change bridge would enable the teams to change sides, enter lock 4 and continue a westward journey on the Erie or continue south to Albany and the Hudson River. To effect this crossing, the mules must change from the left side to the right side. The change bridge would allow the mules to change sides, never removing their tow lines or crossing them. (See Diagram)

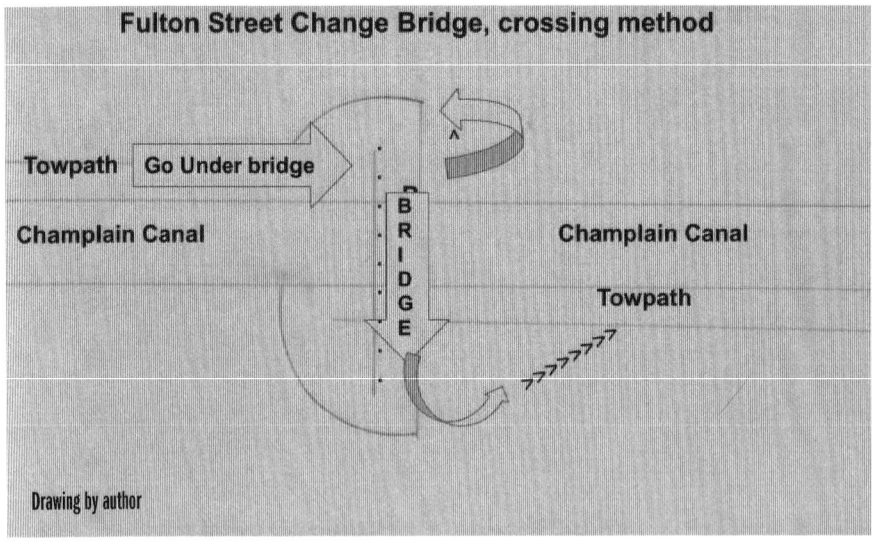

At most locks on the canal, a boat would either be raised up or lowered down to the next level. At a river lock, if the level of the river and the canal was the same, John and his team could tow right through. This was not the case today. John was told by the locking agent that the river was up today and a lock-through was necessary.

After crossing the canal with his team at the Fulton St. Change Bridge, the canal boat is headed for the Mohawk River crossing. The towpath has been on the Mill side; it now changes to what had been the berm side. The mules have walked under the Fulton Street Bridge on the Mill side, continued left up a ramp to access the bridge, and crossed the canal. When they come down the ramp to continue on the towpath, it is a completed operation with no need to disconnect the towlines. This is needed to access the towpath bridge over the Mohawk River.

Once through the lock, John and the mules would follow the towpath as it wound further to the right pulling the boat out of the lock. At this point, John would lead the mules up the ramp of the Cohoes Bridge Company. First built in 1795, rebuilt in 1806, and by 1823, it was incorporated as a part of the towpath. This allowed the mules to walk across the bridge to tow boats across the Mohawk River and into lock three on the Champlain Canal. (6) John thought how this event, the crossing of the Mohawk at Waterford, was the only time he felt sorry for his mules. He often smiled to himself to hear some people speak of the mistreatment of mules. John owed his economic well-being to his mules, and like most teamsters and drivers, especially the owners of the mules, he cared for his mules.

They were an essential part of his life. Unlike many other drivers, he did not name his mules. John felt the mules recognize his voice and his tone. They were well cared for and responded to his commands. That's all that had to exist between a driver and his animals. The mule's most strenuous work was in getting the towed boat moving; once achieved, the tow itself was rather easy. Until the crossing of the Mohawk. The Mohawk was crossed three times in a short distance in this area, once here in Waterford, by the damming of the Mohawk below the Cohoes Falls to create slack water and use the bridge as a towpath extension. This linked the Champlain to the Erie Canal. When traveling on the Erie, above the Cohoes Falls, the Mohawk was crossed two more times in a distance of about fifteen miles at Crescent and Rexford by means of aqueducts. Mules towing through the aqueducts had an easier time than those towing the dammed-up Mohawk at the Waterford crossing, especially when the Mohawk was high. The length of the tow line employed, the fluctuation in water levels, and the current from the falls and the dam could cause a tricky and laborious job for the mules, the driver, and the steersman on the canal boat. Even more so if there was opposing traffic. John hadn't ever witnessed one of these events, but he was present when it was resolved. Two years ago in August, news had spread up to the side cut locks of a boat over the lock 4 dam. John had gone over out of curiosity and to offer help or at least be in support of the victims. The greatest times for possible trouble would be when the Mohawk would be high, with the water flowing freely over the Waterford - Cohoes dam. The power of the river current would force the canal boat towards the dam. The mules, their driver, and the canal boatman would need to act in concert to keep the boat off the dam. The mules not only had to provide the power to move the boat forward but also to keep it away from the dam. The helmsman would need to steer a course in agreement with the mules, and the driver must keep the mules interested. All these efforts would be for naught if the tow line failed. John had learned that this was often the case when a problem occurred; it would be a line failure; oftentimes, the tow line would simply fail from the effects of trying to move the boat forward and, at the same time, holding it off the dam. If the mules were to make a successful tow and crossing under these conditions, it could be very tiring. If the towline were to snap, it would be very hazardous to all involved; all participants would be in danger of injury.

The following is from the Troy Times, August 16, 1861.

In this article the original reporter was confused between the Cohoes Falls and the canal dam and falls on the Mohawk River between Waterford and Cohoes.

A CANALBOAT GOES OVER THE COHOES FALLS
NARROW ESCAPE OF TWO WOMEN AND ONE MAN

There was a terrific scene at Cohoes yesterday. While an attempt was being made to bring a canal boat across the canal just above the falls, the tow rope snapped asunder, and the boat was quickly carried over the falls. On board the vessel were two women and one man. The scene was a fearsome one. Everyone expected to see the boat dashed to pieces and the unfortunate souls on board sent into eternity. The boat, however, struck right upon the rocks and was only slightly damaged. Those inside made their appearance on deck in a terribly frightened condition. News of the affair spread rapidly and soon the banks were thronged with spectators. Steps were immediately taken to save those on board, small boats being sent out to effect rescue.

P03 Although a 2017 drone photograph, it demonstrates a fair representation of this area during the 1860s. Starting from the bottom, we see the Cohoes - Waterford Dam. The reporter has confused this with the Cohoes Falls, visible at the top right corner. The dam's construction materials of the 1860s were much different than what is seen here. In the center is the new Cohoes - Waterford Bridge during construction. To the right or Waterford side of the bridge, one can still see the towpath that led to the bridge towpath that John Shepard would have used. Notice the concrete wall to the right that follows

Dear Mother.....I am the Only One Left 13

the shoreline. Between that wall and the shoreline, far right, center, one will notice water. That is the original Champlain Canal, Lock 4, and the Waterford Museum and Cultural Center are located there. Leaving Lock 4 and crossing the Mohawk River to Lock 3 under ideal conditions, the canal boat would be closest to the bridge and furthest from the dam.

John's thoughts cleared; we are over the bridge, and his breathing became a little easier. He was beginning to notice how involved with his thoughts he was becoming. Maybe it is his age, he thought, a young man, like Charles, doesn't think about something, they just do it. There were three more locks in Cohoes to link the Champlain Canal to the Erie Canal. John would lock through two more to complete this journey. Later that day, John would see his workday come to an end. He had delivered one of the Rock Island Flour Mill canal boats to the Weigh Lock in West Troy. It would be towed from there to the West Troy Side Cut Locks and join the Cornell Tow to New York City by another driver with a new team. The Cornell Steamboat Company was started in 1847 by Thomas Cornell. Thomas Cornell operated his business from Rondout, where he repaired and maintained a fleet of 62 tugboats that towed barges of materials, including coal, to New York City and other ports. Thomas Cornell built repair shops along the creek to provide full service to the boats and fixed rail locomotives as well. Thomas Cornell was an astute businessman who used his increasing power to expand his control over the river traffic. Eventually, Cornell had a virtual monopoly of towing on the Hudson River and employed over 450 employees on their boats and in their workshops along the Rondout Creek. At one time, he owned the largest fleet of towboats in the country. (7)

The Rock Island Flour Company of Waterford had one customer in New York City, they owned their own canal boats, and two times each week, John would make this same delivery and pick up a Rock Island light (empty) boat for return.

The day would start at daybreak for John. First, he would take a quick walk down to Grogh Street from his Sixth Street home, where his mules were stabled. (**Author's note: Grogh Street was located be-**

tween Broad Street and the present-day Erie Barge Canal. Grogh St. ceased to be a thoroughfare in 1858, but the barns were still known as the Grogh St. Stables through 1905)

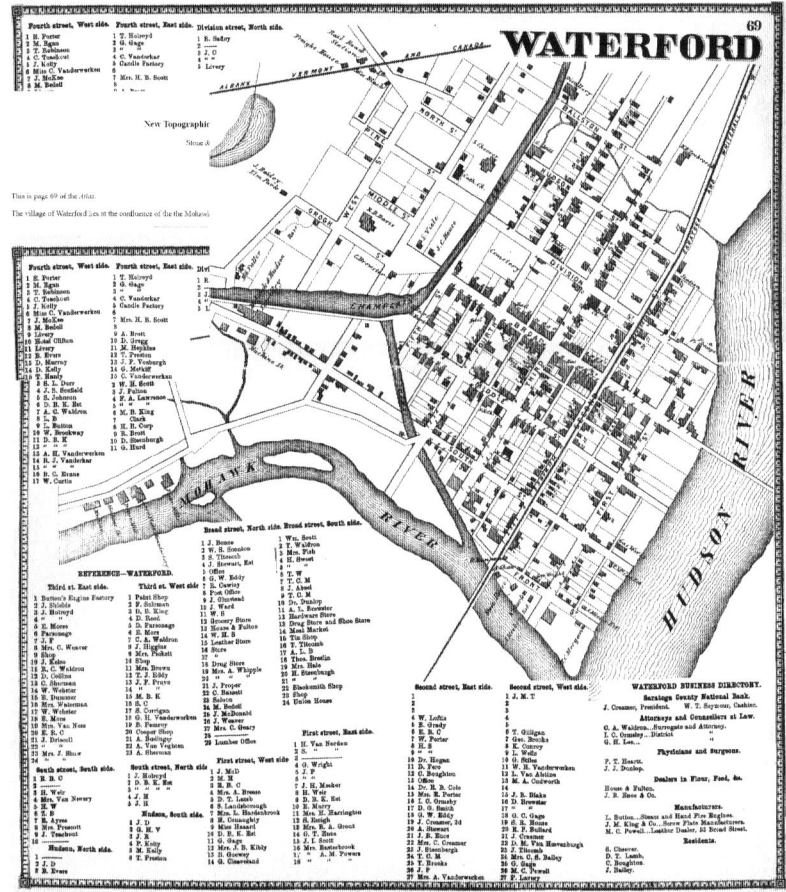

P04 This 1863 Beers Map of the Village of Waterford shows the Grogh St. Barns at the intersection of Grogh and West Sts. Today West St. is 7th St. John lives at the house on 6th St. next to the vacant lot at 6th and Division. 6th St. appears to be unnamed, and Pine St. would later be where Middle St appears on the map. This may be mislabeling or the real names prior to the Barge Canal construction of 1903 - 1918, which caused the relocations, creations, and renaming of many streets in the upper village area. Beers Maps were very reliable, but to a modern-day observer, Middle St. just seems to appear in error. The full map shows two Middle Streets in a small village with no connection or even close proximity to each other.

Dear Mother.....I am the Only One Left   *15*

There he would ready his mules for the day. Owning six, he would switch mules every day, or in very busy times, he would employ another driver if business warranted. On the two days each week that he towed for Rock Island, he would usually return home by 6 p. m. The other five days would depend on the towing jobs available. Those days John did not know when they would end, but each was most the same. Return the mules to the Grogh Street stable and care for the mules, then return to Sixth Street to Harriet, Charles, and Rebecca.

These were dynamic times for Waterford, the Canal, and our very lives, what with the war and all that was about. There were many changes taking place on the canal. A couple of years back, the side-cut locks to enter the canal had been enlarged, improved, and moved a few hundred feet nearer the village's main street. Last year the dam for Lock 4 had been raised to provide more water, and this year a new Weigh Lock was opened just north of our home. These were major improvements to the canal and provided teamsters like John, who liked the short trip, more opportunities to tow locally.

P05

Chapter 2

THE CANAL SEASON OF 1863 COMES TO A CLOSE

John was pleased with himself, the canal, and his station in life. The same could not be said about John's feelings for the state of the nation. In 1863 it was completing its second year of the Civil War. John kept abreast of its activities in Harper's Weekly and the sacrifices and sufferings of John's friends and neighbors.

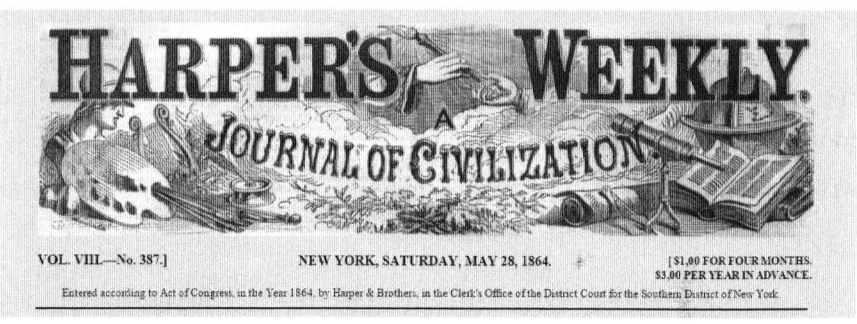

Harper's Weekly, A Journal of Civilization, was an American political magazine based in New York City. Published by Harper & Brothers from 1857 until 1916, it featured foreign and domestic news, fiction, essays on many subjects, and humor alongside illustrations. It carried extensive coverage of the American Civil War, including many illustrations of events from the war.

The Halpin boy from Pine Street, just around the corner from John, the Vanderwerken boys, the Vandercars, and Lawrence Higgins came to mind immediately. John knew firsthand of the torment of Lawrence Vanderwerken over the loss of his first son and had even saved the public article of thanks from the Waterford Sentinel. That Lawrence had posted after his son's funeral.

To The Officers and Members
of the Knickerbocker Engine Co. #1

Gentlemen,

Your kind attention and care, shown in the management of the funeral of you former associate and my son, John H. Vanderwerken, deserves acknowledgement, which I herewith render you, on behalf of myself and family. I pray that the time when you shall again be called upon to officiate at such a ceremony, may be far distant, and remain with much respect to you as a company and well wishes as individuals.

Yours respectfully,
Lawrence Vanderwerken
Waterford, July 24th 1862

The Waterford Sentinel was started on May 18, 1850, by Dr. Andrew Hoffman, now of Albany. In 1858 it was sold to J.H. Masten. He sold it to Wm. T. Baker. Baker continued it for two or three years until 1870 when it was sold to Haywood & Palmateer. This partnership ended in 1871 with the death of Mr. Haywood. (8)

"I pray that the time when you shall again be called upon to officiate at so sad a ceremony may be far distant."

John Shepard found empathy with these words, particularly from John Vanderwerken's writing to the Knickerbockers. John Shepard knew both Lawrence Vanderwerken and his son John. John Vanderwerken was 11 years older than John Shepard's son Charles. Lawrence was a farmer; John was one of several sons. He had enlisted in December of 1861 at age 26, and by the end of July 1862, he had fallen victim to typhus. Camp Fever had taken him, the number two killer, of deaths by disease. He never saw a battle. The loss somehow felt greater with the knowledge of death resulting from disease rather than on the field of battle. It just seemed more of an unfortunate loss than an honorable sacrifice for the greater good of one's nation and beliefs. But, a true loss, nonetheless. By this time (October 1863), Waterford families had suffered the loss several times.

John Vanderwerken had been a member of the Knickerbocker Engine Co. #1 of the Waterford Fire Department before enlisting in the Army, joining his brother James already a member of the Knicks.

March 1, 1847, with 22 members present, it was resolved that James Vanderwerken be accepted as a volunteer and John Higgins & W. Ferrell as members. Farrell & Vanderweken receiving 20 votes, 19 for Higgins (9)

The Vanderwerken family was one of the oldest in Waterford. They are said to be the descendants of Roelof Vanderwerken, who had purchased much of the land in Waterford from Annetie Lieuwens in 1686 for 126 beaver skins. A day credited to be the founding of Waterford. (10)

John Shepard had great respect for the fireman in Waterford. He had moved to Waterford in 1838. In 1841 Waterford experienced the largest fire in its history. The fire occurred about 3 o'clock in the afternoon on Sunday, July 11, 1841. It had been an especially hot July; many said the temperature at Waterford that day had been recorded at 98 degrees in the shade. John did not witness the fire. Early that Sunday, he had contracted with a local canal boat owner to tow him to Stillwater. News of the fire traveled fast on the canal; those traveling north on the canal would tell the lock tenders, and they, in turn, informed all going south of the fire. There was concern among the canallers headed south on how far they could continue. As bad as this fire was, it sounded even worse as reports came in from those who had traveled through. Upon his return home, after comforting Harriet, who had grown quite concerned and alarmed over the situation, he toured the scene. John's home on 6th Street was spared any actual damage from the fire. Geographically, it was downwind from the reported north-by-northwest wind that was blowing that day, and the Champlain Canal separated their home from the fire area. John remembered the devastation that day, as well as Harriet's fears and worries about the safety of their many friends who lived in the ravaged area. He recalled seeing that at least two churches had been destroyed, the County Bank, nearly all businesses, and so many homes. There were some injuries but no loss of life. John thought I had moved to a community that now lies chiefly in ruins. He was thankful that his home and neighborhood had been spared, quite certain that his livelihood was still intact, but could Waterford recover from this event? Would his new neighbors and friends rebuild, or would they relocate? Although John did not witness it himself, he heard the stories, told by the many who did, of the activities of the firemen of Waterford, Lansingburgh, Troy, Cohoes, and West Troy. These brave firemen, John thought, were able to put a stop to this fire and save a good portion of the village, even if much of it lay in ruins. He would always think of these two events together, The John Vanderwerken funeral with the Fire Department officiating and the Great Fire of 41.* Why he could not separate the two, he did not know. *See the New York Tribune below.

> *Excerpt from the Strachan Diary July 1841. Went to church this afternoon & I witnessed the fatal (?) fire that took place there immediately after the Divine Service. By this dreadful conflagration, the best half of Waterford is laid in ashes. The Episcopal Church, the bank, the District Schoolhouse, the mansion house, and a great many private dwelling houses and stores are burned to the ground. Among others, the excellent new brick house. Dr. Porter's Office, which belongs to me and is valued at $3000, on which there is insurance of $1500.* (11)

The Troy Daily Whig July 13, 1841
Disastrous Fire - Waterford Destroyed

A fire broke out at 4 o'clock on Sunday in the Village of Waterford, Saratoga County, four miles above Troy on the Hudson River and Northern Canal, which was almost entirely laid to ruin. It raged with the greatest fury for three hours, and consumed nearly the whole of the business part of the town, including the Town Hall, the Saratoga County Bank, Episcopal Church, the academy, the Mansion House, nearly every store in the place and about fifty dwelling houses - about seventy to eighty buildings in all, among which were the most valuable in the town. The fire caught at 4, P.M. in a small building. It burned for three hours and was finally arrested by the exertions of the Troy and West Troy firemen who arrived on the grounds at half past five. We were on the ground then and remained there until the fire was extinguished, and can safely say that we have never witnessed such a scene of confusion, devastation, and distress.

The whole village was covered with furniture, goods and articles of every description. Every house seemed to be emptied of its contents and the inhabitants of the village and the adjoining towns, together with hundreds from Troy, crowded together in the neighborhood of the fire. At one time the destruction of the bridge over the river seemed inevitable, and nothing saved it but the exertions of the Troy and West Troy firemen. Waterford having but one fire engine and that being almost useless. The fire was finally stopped at the home of John Stewart, a brick building a few rods west of the bridge. The books of the Saratoga Banks were saved, the specie in the vault survived, some $10,00. By this destructive confalgration the prosperity of Waterford must be seriously impaired, and it is doubtful if she will ever recover from this loss. It is by far, the most serious calamity that has occurred in this section of the state since the Great Fire in Troy of 1820.

John's thoughts turned to his amusement on a day in 1847, the Knickerbockers and the Saratoga County Fair. There are just some events that always bring a happy thought and a satisfied smile, and this was one of those. The Knickerbockers were attending the Saratoga County Fair in the City of Mechanicville just north of our fair village. They had contracted with Jerry Green of the packet Plattsburgh to provide transit to the fair. I told Mr. Green that, in honor of our fireman, I would provide the team for the tow. What a grand event it was. The boys from the Knickerbockers were known to make a grand presentation at events such as these. They were quite adept in marching drills and accustomed to bringing home the prize. This was to be no exception. Packet Master Green and I awaited the Knicks at Broad Street, above the Side Cuts. What an arrival it was. Thirty-Six strong in full uniform, both the engine and the hose cart were festively adorned in a bed of flowers. They arrived with the accompaniment of the Washington Brass Band. They had marched through the streets of the village with a proper contingent of citizens and young lads following along and cheering. They halted at the packet, boarded, and then we conveyed to Mechanicville. After their exhibition march at the fair, where they won second prize, They reboarded and had a pleasant trip back to Waterford. I'm told the festivities lasted late into the evening at the Morgan House.

A committee was in place to secure the band, secure band transportation, decorate the cart and engine, procure transportation to and from the fair, and make arrangements for dinner at the fair. To procure some person to act as pioneer * on the occasion and furnish a cap for him and to see that all suits are filled for the Company. R. Savage is to prepare the machine and cover it in flowers. The Company met pursuant to adjournment when in full uniform and with their machine and hose cart decked and trimmed in a most gorgeous manner, they marched through the streets of the village after the martial music of the Washington Brass Band and finally halted upon the Packet Plattsburgh, Jerry Green Commander which conveyed us to Mechanicville where the fair was being held. Upon return to the house of the Company, having spent the day pleasantly, a special meeting was held at the Morgan House. Resolutions expressive of the thanks of this Company to the ladies of the village for their efficient services in aiding us to trim our machine and cart and the flowers and bouquets presented were offered and accepted unanimously. Three Cheers and a Tiger was called for throughout the evening. The Company then engaged themselves in a stag dance and adjourned as they got drunk weary. *The Pioneer was the Drill Master.

The Knickerbockers were well known throughout New York State for their drill proficiency from this era until the turn of the century and won the State Championship in Rochester in 1886. The local press in Rochester put forward the claim that these were not firemen; they were West Point Cadets. (12)

I wisely settled the mules in and returned home. But what a pleasant, colorful, and exciting day it was. The kind of day that stays with a man for an extended period. John had been invited to attend the Special Meeting at the Morgan House, but he thought it best not to be in attendance; later, he regretted not attending. Of the many "Three Cheers and a Tiger" that evening, one was for John and the mules.

John's thoughts were beginning to confuse him. A man's thoughts can run their course with no restriction of a map or conscious guidelines to control the mind's thoughts. John truly felt his life was good and rewarding. Why can't I just remember the good and forgo the bad? Today is October 27, 1863. A day we will remember, and it should be a happy day. The mules had been prepared, John was ready for today's work. I will look for one or two tows today, maybe two tows to lock 4 or one to lock 5. Today is Charles's wedding day. I must get the mules stabled and be ready for this evening's ceremony. The minister will come to our house. Rebecca and Harriet are beside themselves with anticipation.

John had established himself on the canal and in Waterford over the past quarter-century of towing that he, like many other locals, would pick the transient jobs of local towing. Yes, the pay was less in some respects. A teamster could make $25 in three days on a long haul, but that same teamster could make $20 - $25 making several local tows from the Waterford Side Cut Locks to Mechanicville, north or to the West Troy Weigh Lock going east. John preferred the comfort of being home each evening with family and amenities. On a long haul, you might take shelter for the night on the boat you were towing, sleep with the mules or seek a boarding house. These options were no longer appealing to John, and they diminished his profits. John had grown accustomed to the canaller's life of working the season, usually April through mid-December. He enjoyed the freedom of not working the winter months in the northeast. Of course, to enjoy this freedom, John worked, or at least tried to work, every day during that season. A season could be interrupted, and most were by inclement weather and breakdowns of the canal system.

Rarely was there a shortage of work, but from time to time, that would happen. Many canallers had an additional trade or would seek some employment in the off-season. John was fortunate that he never had to engage in off-season employment. This pleased him. He liked that time with Harriet, Charles, and Rebecca. Now Charles was to be wed. Charles and his bride were to become part of our household. Charles and I both have thoughts on the empty lot near (See previous Beers Map) us on 6th Street for their future home. Emma, who is to become Charles's wife, this evening, is Emma Thompson from Schaghticoke in Rensselaer County, just across the Hudson River. We don't know too much about Emma. She was born in Niverville, N. Y., in Columbia County. She and Charles are close in age. We have made her acquaintance, she seems a pleasant girl, but I see a sadness in her eyes. Harriett's and Rebecca's eyes always seem so happy. The only times I ever saw sadness in Harriett's eyes was during the fire in 1841 and our shared loss of young Mary and poor Harriet. Of course, my girls are always happy to see me and comfortable in my company; perhaps Emma had apprehensions upon meeting me. I hope I don't give her cause for concern.

Later when we got to know Emma, we learned of her troubled childhood. Her parents had both passed away at an early age, her father when she was just three, and then her mother at age four. She was then taken from Niverville to Schaghticoke to live with relatives that she did not know. In her seventeen years, she would now be with her fourth family. The first was her parents, who died in her fourth year, and the second was the Niverville family, who cared for her until the arrangements could be made for the move to Schaghticoke. The Schaghticoke family and now the Shepard family. I hope we can do well with her. We respect Charles's preference. The ceremony that evening was a pleasant affair with a few friends and Emma's Schaghticoke family. Harriet and Rebecca prepared a fine meal. After a few toasts of good wishes, the guests returned to their homes, and all the Shepards, old and new, retired for the evening.

In the days leading up to the canal season's end for 1863, there is the usual flurry of activity. It is not the best time to increase your year's profit. The steamboat operators on the Hudson River are in great demand now. Many owners of canal boats desire to return to their homeport for the winter. Some have off-season jobs there, some just have a family to live with, many want to get their children into school over the winter months, and there is much traffic traveling south on the Hudson. John feels lucky that his main client, the Rock Island Flour Mill, will want to make their final run to the Port of Albany before the season closes. This will provide John with much-appreciated and needed season-end revenue. It will also leave John with his much-desired solitude time walking the towpath. The one-mile level from the Waterford Side Cuts to Lock 4 will be much quieter than usual. There will likely be no opposing traffic. The only potential bottleneck would be the Juncta Lock in Cohoes, where the Erie and the Champlain Canals become one. Many of the western boats that work the Erie will stay out west, but a great number will still be seeking access to the Hudson River at Albany, seeking a tow to the Erie Basin in the New York/New Jersey area. John was well known to the lock tender's at the Waterford and Cohoes Locks; they would work with him, if possible, to expedite his passage. John, of course, had learned over the years that a little offering to the tender could enhance your chance of a quick and safe lock-through. As demonstrated in the following Newspaper story.

NY Times October 6, 1890.
THE BANDITS OF THE LOCKS

In the town of Lockport there exists an organized band of brigrands in the shape of lock tenders who in a systematic way levy tribute on the boatmen passing up and down this waterway. The boatmen may ply the canals of this state from end to end and no human being has a right to demand of them one cent for the privilege of passing a lock. Yet here stand those fellows on the Lockport locks and exact 25 cents from every Captain who will pay it, and if the stories told by the boatman are true, most of them permit themselves to be thus robbed. It is idle to talk of this as a gratuity. Men do not demand gratitudes or take revenge upon the expected givers if they fail to get them. This is what a Times correspondent saw a tender on the Lockport Locks do. It is a misdemeanor for this activity to take place. The boatmen state they are willing to be bled this way because they will suffer if they don't. Many report damage to their boat, their lines and their cargo if they don't pay. Similar activity has been reported at the "six-teens" in Cohoes, though not so openly as observed in Lockport.

Author's Note: Although this is an 1890s story, it could have been written anytime during the Mule Era. The "sixteens" were the Cohoes Locks.

As John waited for the boat he was to tow that day to be readied, he thought about how his life was changing. Today, December 10, 1863, is the last day of the canal season. Charles and Emma have made the announcement that Harriet and I will become grandparents in the summer. Rebecca is pleased to have a sister in Emma and to be becoming an Aunt. Christmas is upon us, the working season is ending for three months, and there is great joy in the Shepard house. John's earlier assessment of his family being blessed was correct. But, every time John allows himself to think in this state of imaginary grace, his thoughts always return to daughters Mary and Harriet, who were taken so young. Would they be sharing in the joy of Christmas and the excitement of becoming an Aunt? One would think so. I wish my happiest thoughts didn't usually end with thoughts of the girls.

Perhaps they are guiding our family, and this is why they return me to reality. It is well that Mary and Harriet have stopped my thoughts. I see our tow is ready; we will soon be off. This will not be a normal Rock Island tow. *The Rock Island Flouring Mills*, J. B. Enos & Co., were established in 1847. They are run by water power from the King's canal. They contain eight runs of stone and manufacture superior quality flour by what is known as the new process of grinding. The mill does no custom work. It has the capacity for making about two hundred and twenty-five barrels a day of the flour described above. They could make about four hundred barrels the old way. The number of men employed is about twenty. The firm owns canal boats, shipping their own product by them direct to New York. They also own a large elevator and storehouse on the Champlain Canal in the village. (13)

John would normally tow to the West Troy Weigh Lock and return a light boat. (a light boat is an empty boat) Today there is no light boat, and John will tow all the way to the port at Albany. He will return to Waterford late, but he has a special stop. John is headed for Pease's Temple of Fancy on Broadway in the City of Albany.

It is John's intention to purchase something elaborate for the family to commemorate this special holiday season with all the good things that are happening, something that the family may cherish for years to come, to remind all of the great joy of this holiday. season. It is his hope to find something that may be displayed on every Christmas Season to remind all what a joyous season it was in 1863. The Temple of Fancy must have something fitting.

P06 Pease's Great Variety Store was located in the Temple of Fancy at 518 Broadway in Albany. From the 1840s to the 1860s, Pease's store was something of an upscale "five and dime," The building still stands at the corner of Broadway and Pine Street. Richard H. Pease and (later) Harry E. Pease were proprietors of the store and also noted printers. They printed the first Christmas card in America in 1851 (only one of which exists, at the Manchester Metropolitan Museum in England), and they also produced the hand-colored lithographs of fruit for Ebenezer Emmons's book Agriculture of New York State, published between 1846 and 1854.

John found an ornate and detailed engraving there that portrayed the spirit of Christmas with just the proper amount of solemnity, respect, happiness, and gaiety, all displayed in a seasonal way centering on the birth of a child as a path to salvation. Once again, John was pleased. This would be a Happy Christmas. John caught himself short, and again the happy thoughts were going to be tarnished by the sadness of his remembrances of the girls. But, no, not this time. John was just too happy with all that was about. I think Mary and Harriet guided me to this fine store. I would never have found the Temple of Fancy; thank you, girls, for helping father. Yes, John was truly pleased.

It was a long walk back to Waterford that evening. There was a winter chill in the evening air, and it was dark. John didn't usually carry a lantern as he would depend on the boat he was towing to have lanterns if needed. John kept lanterns in the mule barn but had gotten out of the practice of carrying them as he rarely worked late in the evening. The Night. John's thoughts turned to something that he had just read; where he read it escaped his memory, but the theme was now at the top of his thoughts. In the Middle Ages, the night was seen as a sort of anti-time, the very negative of day, when all things bad happened, and only people with evil intent were found on the street. Ah, but the canal was a friendlier place, and this isn't the middle ages. It is the Lord's time, and sweet Mary and Harriet were watching over him this evening; all would be well. He had set out that day at 6 a.m., and yes, it was morning twilight. He knew it would become brighter. It did. But. John did not plan this trip well. The boat wasn't ready until 7 a.m., but he was able to make good time to Albany. He had to stable his mules at a public stable in Albany and walk up Broadway to the Temple of Fancy. He was quite taken with the city and spent a great deal more time there than he had anticipated. After making his purchase at Pease's Temple, he treated himself to lunch in one of the many inviting shops on Broadway before heading back to retrieve his team. He hadn't realized the lateness of the day. He had hoped to find a canal boat heading north out of the port to tow to Cohoes or Waterford, but there were none. This meant he would not earn any towing fee, and he would have no light. This walk will probably take three hours. I didn't tell Harriet of my plans; I hope my lateness won't cause concern. John's concern for the darkness was unfounded. There was good light and still a fair amount of traffic, and indeed John was fortunate to find a tow at the West Troy Side Cuts going to Waterford. Now he would earn a fee, have the company of the boatman, who was William Cole from Waterford, an acquaintance, and a lantern. They spoke briefly at their departure in Waterford. John inquired as to William's nephew, George, from Halfmoon. John was aware of George's capture in September of '62 at Harper's Ferry but had learned no more. John knew that General

McClellan was in charge at Harper's Ferry when many were taken prisoner there, along with William's nephew. He had heard many complain that McClellan was drunk that night as he had been at Bull Run, a Battle that had taken the lives of several Waterford boys and injured others, Including Ralph Savage. Ralph had been aboard with the Knickerbockers on that Mechanicville trip some years back. William explained that he had been shortly paroled and was now in Florida. In the spirit of the season and in the happiness of John's mood, he elected to take no fee from William, as he had provided great safety and comfort for John on this journey; Yes, the girls were at his side today. This was a good ending to the 1863 canal season.

Author's Note: Civil War Military record for COLE, GEORGE D. Age, 21 Enlisted August 9, 1862, at Halfmoon, mustered in as private, Co. H. captured in action, September 15 and paroled September 16, 1862, at Harper's Ferry, Va. wounded and captured in action, February 20, 1864, at Olustee, Florida., paroled, October 18, 1864, mustered out, May 2, 1865, at Foster Hospital, N. C. (14)

The season ended with no fanfare. Funny, John thought, how the excitement level is so high in mid-April in Waterford as the canal boats are towed up the river to Albany, West Troy, and Waterford to begin their journeys on the Erie and Champlain Canals. The very air in Waterford seems alive with excitement and anticipation.

The river will be so full of canal boats that you could walk across the river to Lansingburgh and not even use the bridge; you could just walk from boat to boat. John flashed back to a time several years ago in West Troy when he saw one of the men there perform such a stunt. In 1855, the number of canal boats at upper locks with those moored to the Troy docks extended so far that the tow from Albany passing up the channel between formed a bridge and Captain James Oliver (known as Dutch Oliver) crossed from West Troy to Troy, utilizing boats of the tow to perform the trick. (15)

See below, the river full of canal boats.

P07 The river itself could become a floating city for many days waiting for the canal to open. There could be as many people living on the canal boats in the river as there were residents of Waterford, or so it seemed. (According to New York State and Federal Census reports from this era, the population of Waterford was in the 3,500 - 4,000 range. It was documented that canal boats could number in the hundreds waiting to enter the canal, but there weren't enough people onboard each one to equal the normal population. But, still a great number.) There was excitement and people everywhere. It didn't matter how many seasons you were involved; it was always exciting. The season's end just came, and it was over.

Chapter 3

FOR THE SHEPARD FAMILY
.....THE WAR BEGINS

The off-season could be very peaceful and relaxing. John had come to look forward to it, perhaps this year more so than others. There was much to be done. First, John would bring his mules to Reverend Bush's farm. (behind present-day 8th Street) For a small fee, the Reverend's family would see to the mules' needs so that they would be ready come spring. John couldn't help but notice that many of the mules who worked the line would return in the spring looking slightly underfed.

> "Well, come wintertime, nobody had much use for them mules then, ya see. So they'd winter them out. Old Quackenbush Farms up in Stillwater used to take in a lot of those mules. They used to charge $1.00 per week, per mule, for the winter. Some of them mules would get pretty skinny over the wintertime. They wouldn't feed 'em so good, you know, then they would fatten them up come Spring." (16)

The Reverend's family were good keepers of John's mules. This winter, John and Charles were going to devise a plan to purchase the nearby lot for Charles and Emma to build a home and raise their family. John was concealing a hope that Charles would take an interest in towing instead of peddling. Lord knows towing has been good to John and his family. He had hoped this winter to suggest that Charles get involved. John had two teams and would sometimes hire someone to tow with the other team. John was a trusted, dependable teamster, and being well-known could help Charles to establish himself with good clients.

Of course, Harriet, Rebecca, and Emma would all have the excitement of the new baby's arrival to keep them making plans during the winter months. It would be a busy time.Christmas of 1863 was observed in fine fashion. We all truly felt blessed and had much to be thankful for. The feeling would best be described as giddy. In truth, this was a new feeling; we weren't often giddy. We always enjoyed Christmas Time; this year, it was just better. We had temporarily forgotten about the war. The giddiness was short-lived. On December 27th, Charles made the announcement that he had enlisted in the New York State 4th Brigade Heavy Artillery and would be entering the Union Army on the 29th.

John had anticipated and feared that this day would come. He and Harriet had never discussed it. Harriet wanted no business with the conflict, and talk of it was not welcome in our home. John had followed the conflict. Almost everyone thought for years it would come to this. John's thoughts went back to 1858, and the talk around town and on the canal was of slavery, leading to discussions on separation by some of the southern states. Two years later, many of the slave states were threatening to secede if the Republicans won the presidency. Mr. Lincoln's victory set things in motion. By Inauguration Day, it was apparent what would be next. The rebels had seized many forts and arsenals in the south. The army only held Fort Sumter in South Carolina and some forts off the coast of Florida. It was April 12, 1861, when the rebels opened fire on Fort Sumter. These were exciting and nervous times in Waterford, the state, and the North. No one could speculate what the price in young lives lost would be before this conflict was to be resolved. In Waterford, we held confidence that the Rebels would never get anywhere near NYS. Hell, they wouldn't get out of the South; they would be put down in short order.

John felt that the North would persevere and be successful in preserving the Union. Like many others, he thought it would not take this long to suppress the uprising, return our nation to peace and end the enslavement of our southern friends. Our Southern Friends, John, always liked that term. Our Southern Friends was a term used for the runaway slaves. Waterford and the Champlain Canal were utilized by groups of abolitionists who assisted the contrabands, as the runaways were often labeled, in their journey north. John never actively participated in this endeavor, although he morally supported it. There were many mornings when John would notice very anxious Southern Friends taking refuge in the Grogh Street barns. Many Southern Friends would be stowed here, awaiting the canal boat that would conceal and transport them as they made their way north. John was aware of and sympathetic to their plight. He felt a part of it just by pretending not to notice it was occurring. Most people on the canal were aware of this activity; slavery had been illegal in NYS for many years.*

*Excerpt from The Evening Post, March 23, 1826.

> A portion of the Senate of the United States have wasted, irreverably we fear, three months in reiterated efforts to delay what from the beginning they knew it would be impossible to defeat. The confirmation of this mission. Most strangely, too, the great objection made to the mission is, that the southern Republics have wisely provided for ultimately ridding themselves of the acknowledged evil of negro slavery. This was the burden of Mr. Randolph's speeches, and he only talked out more plainly what his coadjutors felt and acted upon; and in this coalition in favor of perpetual slavery, we find Mr. Van Buren, from this free state! Shame on Mr. Van Buren, for New York is a free state. New York has abolished slavery.

The Dutch Reformed Church in Waterford worked with others in Troy and Albany to affect the transportation of the Southern Friends to northern NY and Canada. John liked the term Southern Friends better because, with his friendships in the Fire Company, he had heard the fireman tell of fires in the Nigger's Nests.** John was just more comfortable with Southern Friends. Everyone knew that a "Nigger's Nest" was a safe house that was used in the wintertime when it was too cold to use the canal to transport our Southern Friends; they may have to wait longer for safe overland transport, they couldn't wait in the barns, they had to have real shelter. No one ever reported the homes or the people involved, so the practice was generally accepted. John would also find amusement in the story he had read earlier in the Troy paper about the Troy House. The Troy House was a large hotel in the city just across the Hudson River.

P08 The Troy House *Source Hart Cluett Museum, Troy, New York*

A long-ago freed slave, Peter Baltimore, operated a barbershop on the first floor of the hotel. A reporter for the paper once commented, "One would do well to exercise caution in attending to the services offered in this little parlor. Many men are seen to enter, but few are ever witnessed leaving." He was, of course, referencing the Southern Friends who from the Troy House would next find themselves on a canal boat headed west on the Erie or north on the Champlain for a new life of freedom.

**Friday Morning 9 O'Clock 12 January 1849 Thermometer 15 degrees below 0 or 47 below freeze. (sic)Fire Co. called out by an alarm of fire when the church bell rang Proved to be a chimney fire which stirred up the Niggars Nest in the house of Mr. Leronis. No damage done to the building, but great consternation among the darkies Quinctius, Cincinnatus, Delematius, & Salivitus,

Records of Knickerbocker Engine Company 1849 (17)

P09 The "Nest" and the fire was thought to be one of the two homes shown to the left of the enlarged Side Cut Locks.

With Charles' enlistment, John felt pride, fear, and honor all at the same time. When the conflict began, Charles was just sixteen; he wouldn't be called on then. Two years have passed, the war continues, and reports do not bode well for success; Charles is now eighteen. If he doesn't enlist, he will likely be drafted. But, if Waterford fills its quota, no draft will be necessary.* Charles did not want to take that gamble. If he were to enlist, he would receive a bonus and receive more pay. (New York State had the highest quota of 28 Regiments and 60,000 men. It has not been discovered what the quota was for Waterford.) (18)

The solution on how to staff the military was a general call-up of more men under the new militia law. On Aug. 4, Lincoln called up

300,000 men for nine months of service, on top of the 300,000 he had already requested in July for three years. The militia call-up was General Order No. 94:

> Ordered:
>
> I. That a draft of 300,000 militia be immediately called into the service of the United States, to serve for nine months unless sooner discharged. The Secretary of War will assign the quotas to the States and establish regulations for the draft.
>
> II. That if any state shall not by the 15th of August furnish its quota of the additional 300,000 volunteers authorized by law, the deficiency of volunteers in that State will also be made up by a special draft from the militia. The Secretary of War will establish regulations for this purpose.

Some confusion about this draft may spring from the fact that both the entire call-up of 300,000 militia and the subsequent filling of the deficiency in that call-up by conscription is called a "draft." This was not something that had been done in the lifetime of any of the men in the government, and their terminology was not always clear. Yet Lincoln unambiguously writes of "drafting" in reference to the filling of the quotas by conscription in many places [e.g., letter to George P. Fisher, Sept. 16, 1862; telegram to McClellan, Oct. 27, 1862, etc.]

Like the earlier call, this one was apportioned among the states relative to their populations. But this time, the government said it would draft men into service from any state that did not meet its quota. Specifying that the call-up would be for nine months and calling the troops "militia" gave it the power to do so.

The War Department order gave each state until Aug. 15 -- a mere two weeks -- to meet its quota or face a draft. Indiana's quota was about 21,000; little Rhode Island's was less than 3,000. New York's quota of almost 60,000 men was the highest. Wisconsin's was just under 12,000. The governor there pleaded for more time since it was an agricultural state and the fall harvest was approaching, but the War Department only gave him another week, until Aug. 22.

On Aug. 9, the Secretary of War issued General Order 99, detailing how the conscription should be handled. It directed the governors to enroll all able-bodied men aged 18 to 45, and the wheels of the draft began to turn. The process passed down the line, from the federal government to states to counties to the smallest unit of the local municipality. The legwork was done by the county assessors, the men who usually collected tax data. They copied the names of each eligible man into record books, noting those already in service and any obvious physical disabilities. The Pennsylvania enrollment officer in one township evidently hadn't appreciated the random nature of the draft, or else couldn't resist adding editorial comments on some of the men he registered -- "Ran and hid, refused to give age;" "Ought to be taken. Bad influence at home or he would volunteer," "Not healthy ('So they say)," "claims weak eyes," "Saucy & loafing about at home," "Make a first-rate soldier, not worth much for anything else," and so forth. *General Order No. 94:* (19)

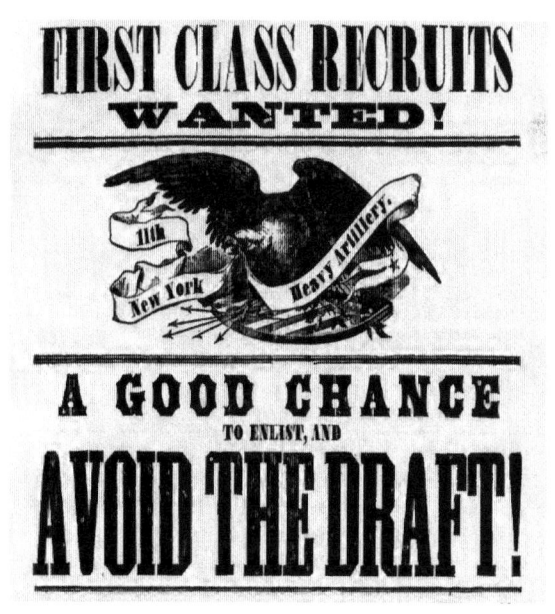

P10 Example of common enticements to recruits to enlist. An enlistment would reduce the quota. The incentive was a signing bonus.

Charles thought this would be a good way to buy the lot we discussed. If Charles hadn't enlisted and Waterford met its quota, Charles would not be drafted. Charles said to me, what would people think if all the other boys went and I stayed behind? He was right. Little did I know then, this was the last Christmas, or for that matter, the last time I would ever feel giddy. Giddiness was not a part of John's lifestyle, perhaps as a youth and just this Christmas, but never again.

John remembered well the excitement everywhere after the firing on Fort Sumter. John thought to himself, was I giddy with excitement? No, some were, but giddy to John were times of great happiness and joy. Excitement was being keenly aware of and interested in the outcome of events. These events could take many forms and show many emotions.

John was taken by how quickly events unfolded, and a response was forthcoming. At this time, the Federal Army was small and mainly stationed in the West. The Virginia Militia was larger than the Federal Army. New York's Governor Morgan, the next day, drafted a bill supplying $3 Million and 30,000 troops to the Union Army. A general feeling of panic existed. Was the Capitol about to fall? Washington was said to be surrounded. President Lincoln called for 75,000 men. On April 21, seven days after the firing on Fort Sumter, Albany's 25th Regiment departed for Washington. Locally the War had begun. John was impressed by the wonder of it all. It will be over soon!

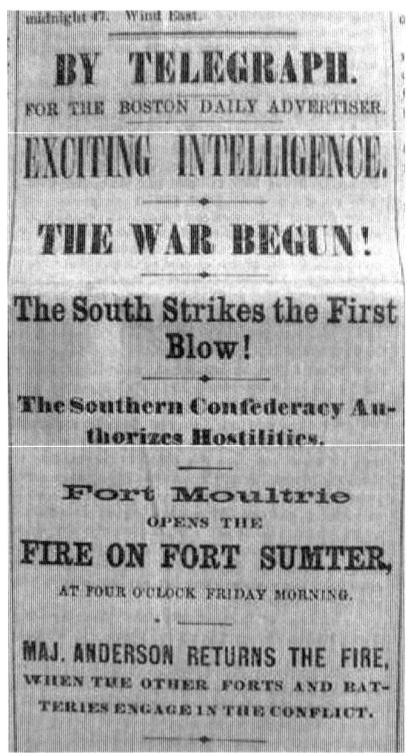

P11 A newspaper account of –the firing on Fort Sumter.

John also remembered attending some of the meetings held at the Mason's Lodge and the Breslin Engine Co. House to encourage our boys to answer the call. The Albany Regiment left for Washington on April 21st. Waterford followed on May 2nd, just 11 days later, with the 32 men raised for Company A of the 22nd Regiment of Infantry. How proud the Waterfordians were to send their boys off. John Cramer, the first Supervisor of the Town of Waterford and a financial supporter of our Company A, marched with the boys at the head of the line of march. John, 81 years of age at the time, marched with them until they reached Lansingburgh and met up with another Company. It was a grand day; everyone was so proud. Charles, just 15 at the time of this event, was wide-eyed with wonder and interest.

John Cramer was a United States Representative from New York. He was born in Waterford on May 17, 1779. He attended rural schools and graduated from Union College in 1801. He studied law, was admitted to the bar, and commenced practice in Waterford. He was a presidential elector on the ticket of Thomas Jefferson and George Clinton in 1804. Cramer was appointed a master in chancery in 1805 and served as a member of the New York State Assembly in 1806 and 1811. He served in the New York State Senate and was a delegate to the State constitutional convention in 1821. He was elected as a Jacksonian to the Twenty-third and Twenty-fourth Congresses (March 4, 1833 – March 3, 1837). He served again as a member of the State assembly in 1842. Cramer died in Waterford on June 1, 1870. His interment was in Waterford Rural Cemetery. (20)

For more than fifty years, he dictated nearly every nomination made by the Democrats in this county and was concluded to be the Warwick of Saratoga. Although he always adhered to the Democratic party, when the rebels fired upon Fort Sumter, his patriotism at once arrayed him on the side of the Union, and he headed a subscription in the town of Waterford with the sum of $1000 to aid in raising volunteers for the war. When the company from that town was organized under Captain Yates and marched for the camp at North Troy, John Cramer, on foot, marched at the head of the column, although then upwards of eighty-two years old.

The Waterford send-off was symbolic of the early response to the conflict. Many speeches were given, prayers were offered, and the band played; it was very exciting to see the men march off. By the time Charles departed, it was from the City of Cohoes with much less fanfare, just a few speeches, a blessing, and the hopes for a safe return. They left Cohoes for Elmira by train. Charles wanted to have our words at home and did not want us to accompany him to Cohoes. Mother was quiet and concerned but hopeful. Rebecca seemed more excited and inquisitive than concerned. I thought that Emma's eyes seemed even sadder. She had lost her mother and father after four years, she and Charles have been married, but sixty days now, he is off to war. All reasons for sad eyes. For the first time in a long while, I was without thought. I trust in the lord; it is in his hands; if Charles is to return safe, his wisdom will prevail. He implored Mary and Harriet to look after their brother, but his thoughts, as well as his hopes, he admitted to himself, were quite lacking.

Chapter 4

THE LETTERS START TO ARRIVE

An explanation of the letters is needed in order to proceed. These are the typewritten transcripts of the letters of Charles W. Shepard dated from January 13, 1864, up to August 25, 1864. Jack Walther, the great-grandson of Charles of North Carolina, transcribed them in about 1960. At that time, they were nearing one hundred years old. They were handwritten, and they were in poor condition. To the best of anyone's knowledge, the originals no longer exist. The originals at the outset, January 13, 1864, through April '64, are written on real paper, usually letterhead paper from Fort Ethan Allen. Charles was at Fort Marcy, which was a part of, although not attached to, Fort Ethan Allen. The rest were written on whatever was available. Some were scraps of paper, others were the backs of old used envelopes, and at least one was on stationery provided by the Sanitary Committee. They are written to Father, John Shepard, Mother, Harriet Shepard, Sister, Rebecca Shepard, and Wife, Emma Shepard. Sometimes, due to age and condition, some words just could not be transcribed. They are usually followed by ( ) Jack Walther, Charles' great-grandson did not feel comfortable guessing at a word. Leaving the interpretation of the missing word/words to the reader was his decision.

The United States Sanitary Commission (USSC) was a private relief agency created by federal legislation on June 18, 1861, to support sick and wounded soldiers of the United States Army during the American Civil War. It operated across the North and raised an estimated $25 million. To support its cause, they enlisted thousands of volunteers. (21)

P13 Letterhead stationery of the 4th N.Y.

P14 Example of stationary provided to the soldiers by the Commission.

Author's Note: All letters published here have been transcribed for clarity and presentation. Like Jack Walther before me, I have elected not to change any of Charles' spellings, word choices, punctuations, expressions, etc. Hopefully the reader will be seeing the same as the family saw in 1864.

Charles left Cohoes on the 29th of December 1863. Fifteen days later, Mother received her first letter.

Washington, Wednesday, January 13, 1864

Dear Mother,

I left Elmira Monday morning at about 3 o'clock in the morning and I couldn't send my money home. I had to wait 'till I got to Washington. I got 125 dollars and I sent 110 dollars home by Adams Express Company. I ain't got no time to tell you what I have seen. I am well and fat as a hog. Give my love to all and don't write 'till I write again. I will write as soon as I get to my regiment, so goodbye.

Your truly son,
Charly W. Shepard

How happy Mother was to receive her first letter. Charles did not write much, but what was written was very uplifting in the Shepard household. The letter was read by the entire household several times and, for such a short letter, discussed in depth by all. Harriet kept the letter with her in her apron and was noticeably relieved and seemed relaxed for the first time since Christmas.

The Camp at Elmira is mentioned in this letter

P15 The site was selected partially due to its proximity to the Erie Railway and the Northern Central Railway, which crisscrossed in the midst of the city, making it a prime location for Union Army training and muster point early in the Civil War. Most of the 30-acre Union installation, known as Camp Rathbun or Camp Chemung, fell into disuse as the war progressed, but the camp's "Barracks #3" were converted into a military prison in the summer of 1864. (22)

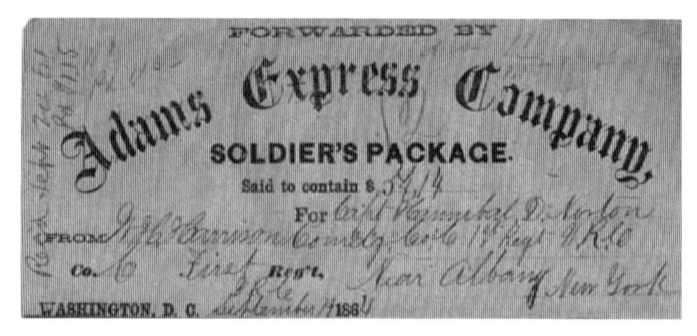

P16 Charles mentions Adams Express in his first letter. Sample of a ticket on a soldier's package home utilizing the services of Adams Express Company.

Adams Express became a household (and battlefield) name during the Civil War. In 1845 the government ruled that only the U.S. post office could carry letters for a fee, but Adams shipped just about anything else through its offices or those of its southern subsidiary, Southern Express Co. Both armies expressed money to pay the soldiers. Arms, uniforms, and flags were shipped from factories and supply depots. Soldiers sent packets of money home for family upkeep, and bodies of fallen soldiers were even expressed home.

Adams Express was such an integral part of a soldier's life and to the war itself that many battle area field offices would be built where needed. Interestingly, the Company served as paymaster for soldiers on both sides during the bloodiest war on American soil, serving the Union soldiers through Adams Express and the Confederates through Southern Express. And Company lore has it that at least one slave, known as Box Brown, was packed in a box and shipped to freedom via Adams Express. (23)

It was a long winter's week until the next letter was received.

Author's Note: This is one of only two saved letters to his wife, Emma. There is reason to suspect that more were written but did not endure the passage of time.

Fort Marcy, January 20, 1864

Dear Wife,

I received your kind letter and was glad to hear from you. It did my heart good. I am well and enjoying myself. You don't know how good I felt when I received yours and mother's and father's and sister's letters. I threw up my hat. I bet I have the itch back. I am all over it. No one knew it except the doctor and myself. I told the doctor that i would try to make it alright with him if he would try his best to cure me and he took more pains with me than he did the sick, so I gave him two dollars and he would take ten if I gave it to him but I gave him two. Too many! When Mother told me to read the Bible I could not keep from crying but I feel happy as a lark. I will be home in the summer for the war will be over. The Rebels are coming in our lines by hundreds every day. When you see your Mother give her my love. I get paid every two months and maybe longer. I can't write you much this time. Give my love to all. So good-bye.

Your truly husband

The rebels are coming in our lines by the hundreds every day. These weren't just encouraging words by Charles. John was happy to read these words, even more so when these claims could be substantiated in Harper's or other papers. Confederate Soldiers were becoming disgruntled at the "rich man's war and the poor man's fight." There were occasions when "whole companies, garrisons, and even regiments decamped at a time. At critical times in the war, the extent of desertion prevented the South from following up victories or half-victories in the field; it was both the cause and effect of lowered morale. (24)

Dear Mother,

I received your kind letter and was happy to hear from you. I am well and in good spirits. I have a good bed to sleep on and a good house to sleep in and good food to eat and dry clothes to wear and I am good and fat and hearty as ever. Dear Mother, I try to keep rid of bad company. The room that I am in they are all

good men. We have Church every Sunday here and we have a piano in the church and we have tracts sent to us to read. We have good times. Mother, pray for me that I may be a good boy. So good-by. Give my love to all.
Your truly son,
Charly Shepard

From this letter, Charles makes his situation sound quite pleasant with good food, a good house, and dry clothes; John begins to wonder if perhaps Charles is experiencing some temptations being away from home. He has read in Harpers about soldiers writing home, with disgust, about the lack of morals that could exist in camp. Prostitution was a huge problem. In Washington, D.C., there were said to be over 7,000 prostitutes. Many soldiers were writing home. complaining about swearing, gambling, and other vices. Evidently, for some soldiers, too much free time was a bad thing.

Dear Father,
I received your kind letter on the 20th and was glad to hear from you. I am well and hope this letter finds you the same. Father, I don't see much war around here. Mosby made a raid about two miles from the Fort the other night and the pickets came running and we were all ordered out but we didn't go. He went back. I would like to get a pop at him. I bet he would (................) a might smart shot. I reckon they thru the guns every day and the shells go thtough the air a humming. I must now close my letter so good-by.
Your Truly Son,
Charly Shepard
You all must excuse my letter

John took comfort in this letter. It is only the 20th of January, and Charles has only been gone about three weeks, but at this time, there is no cause for concern. He does mention Mosby in this letter.

Author's Note: known by his nickname, the "Gray Ghost," he was a Confederate Army cavalry battalion commander in the American Civil War. His command, the 43rd Battalion, Virginia Cavalry, known as Mosby's Rangers or Mosby's Raiders. (25)

P17 John Singleton Mosby

Dear Sister,

I received your letter and was glad to hear from you. I am well and hope these few lines will find you well. It is a nice place here. The sun is hot here and the grass is green and the birds sing and it is a pleasant place here on the hills of Georgetown. I want a pair of boots. Go to Mires and he will know what I want and put a box of blackon and a brush in it. I will write some more the next time. Tell him to make it larger in the instep. So good bye.

On January 20th (1864), all received a letter from Charles. He tells us how warm and nice it is in Virginia. The birds are singing, and the grass is green; it is a pleasant place there. John finds it is too cold to venture out today in Waterford, New York, and it is snowing. Charles seems well and happy. I guess Charles is still peddling. I see Rebecca must provide some boots.

In the 1860 Federal Census, Charles's occupation is listed as a Peddler. His enlistment in the army appears to have widened his market to sell shirts, boots, tobacco, and other products, according to his letters.

P18 Charles is now at Fort Marcy in Fairfax County, Virginia, and staying inside the Fort.

Now that we have received letters from Charles, we are adjusting to the fact that he is away, and we agree that we do feel closer to him. We have been sharing our letters after we read them. Rebecca thinks it would be fun for each person to read their letter to the others as soon as we open them.

January closed with no further news from Charles. We didn't know when to anticipate news from Charles. It could take a few days for a letter to be answered and received. No one ever really said it, but as much as we had anxious anticipation of the receipt of a letter, there was usually dread, at least on my part; what would this letter contain?

I wasn't sure of Rebecca's want to not read our letters alone before sharing with the rest, but everyone else thought it would be great fun.

John knew of the Mud March to close out the Army's efforts at Fredericksburg as 1863 drew to a close. Lincoln replaced generals again, this time Burnside with Hooker. Union Army morale was said to be low. John could only judge by what he could read. How old was the information, and was it true? At least there wasn't much fighting going on. Charles should be safe for the time being. John could overly concern himself with thoughts during the winter months. Most winters, he was relaxed and content with his well-being. These were new feelings of real fear for his only son's welfare. He wished the canal was open. He wished Charles was home.

Fort Marcy, Monday, February 1, 1864

Dear Sister,

I now take the pleasure to inform you that I am well and hope that this letter will find you and Emma and Mother and Father the same. It is a rainy day here and it is very muddy here. I am going to Washington on the 10th and will go to the capitol and the Whitehouse. I saw the capital when I came to Washington. It is a big building. I will tell you. I suppose you will get a letter from a young soldier. You write to him. You know I would not tell you to write to a loafer. He is a nice young fellow. He told me this morning he wrote to Waterford. He lives in New York when he is home. Dear Sister, I am in Church writing this letter. We have from 8 o'clock in the morning to eight o'clock in the evening to come and write and read. Dear Sister, it is almost dinner time and I must close, pleasant dreams.

Rebecca was eager to put her plan of action into effect; she was the first to excitedly read her letter from a handsome soldier friend of Charles who wanted to write to her. We found Rebecca's excitement a refreshing change. It was indeed uplifting to hear laughter and excitement in our home again. We hadn't realized how much it was lacking. Charles liked to joke and tell stories. I hadn't realized how lacking in laughter we were without Charles until just now.

Dear Father,

I received your kind and most welcome letter and was happy to hear from you. I have just come from breakfast and we had a cup of coffee a nice piece of meat and bread and butter. You would hardly know me. I am getting so fat my cheeks are as big as a cow's bag. I am going to Washington the 10th of the month and I will shake hands with the President. I bet. I wish you were here in my room and could see some of the men. Some are writing, some are playing cards and some are reading the Bible and some are blackening their boots and some are getting ready to go on guard. I was glad to hear you got that lot. Now we can all live alone, I bet. It was a blustery day here Wednesday. Today is a pleasant day here. We think we will go down to Bull Run in a Fort in a few months. Bull's Run is about 17 miles from here. This Fort is in Fairfax County, Georgetown Heights Georgetown is about three miles from here. The Chain Bridge is about a half mile from here. There have been 50 cases of smallpox taken from headquarters. There has been one taken from our Company. How are you? 50,000 men drafted! You say that Waterford has filled their number. I am glad Waterford has. I will be home in less than 9 months. I bet. The soldiers are in good spirits. Mosby is about 5 miles from here. The Pickets have a brush with him every night. You will hear fun when the Spring opens, I bet. I saw the house that the Rebel General Lee lived in. It is a splendid place, I tell you. They use it for the headquarters of this regiment. Oh, we have everything needful in this regiment. Dear Father, it is a hard looking place in the country. I ain't seen a fence since I left home. I must close my letter. For it is almost time to drill. Good day and good luck to you.

    From your son

    Charles W. Shepard

    Company H 4, Reg. H

    Washington D.C.

 Well, if nothing else, Charles seems well-fed at this point. He seems happy that we were able to obtain that lot for him and Emma, and he is living inside the fort, which gives us comfort. Comfort, however, was not the word to describe John's thoughts about the mention of Bull Run. The Waterford boys of the 22nd hadn't fared well there. Young Charles Bace, one of our drummer boys, was taken prisoner there, as well as Samuel Johnson. The Battle of Bull Run was in July of 61. We still don't know if they are safe or not. That Battle was the first after Fort Sumter, and we lost. It started to set in then, but we either didn't recognize or, perhaps, chose to ignore the fact that this was not going to be a short war. 1st Lieut Hiram Clute was wounded at Bull Run and died from the effects of that wound. Patrick Hussey suffered a wound, Joseph Harriman lost an arm, and Ralph A. Savage was wounded at Bull Run, and so far, he is the only one to return. All fine Waterford boys from good families.

Charles writes of smallpox in the camp and in his Company. Makes me remember poor John Vanderwerken and his loss to typhus earlier. I hope my reading of this letter out loud did not convey what my thoughts were on Bull Run and disease. The words of Lawrence Vanderwerken that John carried in his billfold came back to him. "I pray that the time when you shall again be called on to officiate at so sad a ceremony may be far distant." I pray as well, Lawrence; I pray as well.

It also appears that Charles is busy and in the company of good men. He is getting to see things like the Capitol. I doubt that he will shake hands with Mr. Lincoln. I don't know what to make of Charles's comment about Waterford meeting its quota. That means if Charles hadn't enlisted, he would not have been drafted, at least not this time, but likely still in the future. I still agree with his decision. He was right to have made it. I am proud of him, just so very concerned. I don't like it. Charles mentions Mosby, the Gray Ghost, again. I don't like that either.

Dear Mother,

The first one I think of is home when I wake up in the morning thinking how I would like to see all of your faces. Dear Mother, I am sorry that I don't know where that old man is. There ain't no old men in my Company and if I did know where he was I would go see him. Mother, you know how I hurt my finger in the shop the nail is coming off. I have got a very sore finger but it will get well in a few days. Oh Mother, I wish blackberries were as plenty there as they are here. We can go out in the Spring and pick our hats full in a little while. About my boots, I got 5 dollars and another pair for them. I am going to have my gun in a few days. I ain't got all of my other suit yet. Don't send me the New York paper for we get them every day. Send me the Waterford paper. I wish you could see our room. How nice and clean we keep it. They don't allow spitting on the floor. Dear Mother, tell Emma to take a squint at the lot every day. Oh, I don't know hardly what to write. I see the same every day. I must now close my letter. Tell Becks not to sit up late nights and wipe her nose and don't play on the cupboard. Pray for me, your son. Pleasant dreams, good day. Give my love to all.

Your son, I am well,
Charles Shepard

Harriet did well reading her letter to the rest of us. She pines for Charles's letters, yet she is full of apprehension once they arrive. She did well and smiled a few times at the things Charles would write.

She did have to take a pause at the closing; Pray for me, your son.

None of us were surprised to hear that Charles had sold the boots he wanted from Mires. Mother was surprised by the spitting-on-the-floor reference. You can't do that at home either, Mother said as she read the letter.

Author's Note: The old man that mother is looking for is Henry Sitterly. Henry is 42. He enlisted the day after Charles in Cohoes, but he transferred to Co. I in January. Apparently, when Henry transferred from Company H to Company I, he and Charles were separated early and had not known each other prior to their service experience.

> For Beck and Emma
> One of the canons of St. Paul's being in company with some ladies let fall a handkerchief and in stooping to pick it up again he happened to break wind backwards. Bless me ladies he cried out, I believe it is His Majesty's Birthday for I think I hear one of the canons at St James. "No Madam" answered another lady then present. "I am sure it is not so far off as St James as I can smell the gunpowder."

(On the back of the joke card was this note)

> About those shirts, the men want them to wear. Send ten pair. You send them and the men will pay the expense on them and will pay me for what they cost and a little more. They make them at Smith and Gregory factory. I believe that's the one.

This note was still in Rebecca's envelope and not discovered until later. It is a joke for Emma and Becks and an order for shirts that he will be peddling in camp. I don't think Charles will be interested in the canal when he returns. He does like to sell things.

> Dear and loving Mother,
> I received your kind and loving letter and was happy to hear that you were well. I received the box and everything alright. My boots fit me to a Tee. I can get them on with a paper of tobacco in one side and a bottle in the other. I guess they are large enough. Mother, that old man you spoke of, I don't know

how he is. If I did I would go and give him some of my cake, but there were some sick men in my room and I gave them some of my cake and they thanked me for it. It pleased me to do a favor for a sick man. The folks in Georgetown try to poison our soldiers. One of the Company soldiers came from Georgetown the other day and he stopped in Georgetown to eat some dinner and they tried to poison him. The soldiers threaten to burn it down if they ever do it again. Georgetown will be burnt in the dust. The Rebels, they need hanging every one of them. Mother, I try to do what's right. I must close my letter for tonight. I want to read a Chapter in the Bible tonight before I go to bed. Then, good night. I guess I won't go to church this morning. I will finish my letter. Before I went to bed last night I read two Chapters of Romans and this morning I read 10 of Romans. Mother you read those two Chapters. I suppose Emma has gone to Scaghticoke. Mother, I will close my letter for I want to write some to Father and Becks.

Mother was pleased with her letter as she began to read it but felt some discomfort with Charles' report of the dangers in Georgetown and his thoughts that all the rebels should be hung. (*) She shook her head at Charles not attending church service but was pleased with his continued attention to the Bible. (Mother read from those same passages later that evening) She read the letter quite slowly and seemed to be at peace. Emma was in the habit of sometimes living with us and sometimes in Schaghticoke. I didn't understand. I think she may be uncomfortable with us. Mother will hear no discussion on the matter.

(*) *One day, a man with very strong anti-Union sentiments was caught putting a villainous compound into the spring from whence the regiment obtained drinking water. On being remonstrated with, he said he meant to poison the Yankees! After shaving his head and applying molasses and flour, the men amused themselves by chasing the poor wretch back across the bridge into Washington.* (26)

> Dear Father,
> The soldiers are in good spirits. We received our guns from the government Saturday. I ain't done no duty yet. You will hear some fun in a month or two. You will find out this war ain't gonna last forever. I bet, the folks in Georgetown tries to poison our soldiers. The soldiers threaten to burn it down. They were half scared to death. I guess they will find out the soldiers won't stand no such as that. This regiment is about all enlisted over. They are all gone home. I was out in the country today and had a good dinner. Chicken pot pie, sweet potatoes, mince pie and applesauce, coffee, ham and meat bread and butter. Maybe I didn't eat! No, no, I made the table suffer, I bet. It is a hard looking place about two miles from the Fort. The ground is all dug up and the woods all cut down and left laying. I am in first rate spirits at present. I received a very good letter from Mother. It was a good one. Well, Father what are you towing now? The men use their horses rough here. It makes me feel sad to see the men run their horses. Well Father I must close for I want to write a few lines to Becks.

John found this letter reassuring from Charles and helped to allay some of his fears for his well-being. He was certainly getting enough to eat. John thought the comment on towing was a bit strange. Charles should know there is no towing taking place in February. Maybe because the weather in Georgetown is spring-like, that is causing him to be thinking about towing. I'm glad that he is thinking about towing. Also, he should know that I haven't used horses for towing in quite some time. I learned that mules were better animals for work than the horses. With the war continuing, it is difficult to find a horse. They are mostly going to the Army. John recalled thinking about how he had made the right decision to replace his horses with mules in the 1850s. There had appeared in one of the local papers a report on some 250,000 horses needed for the army and that 1,000 had to be replaced daily. John liked to discover things he could take comfort in. When one makes a good decision, it encourages other decisions to be made. Charles mentions that he is in particularly good spirits, which is good to hear. Printed reports in the papers tell of low morale among the troops. There is talk in the Town that two of our boys from the 22nd, George Bennett and Nicholas Nelson, have been reported as deserters. We hope this report is not true; perhaps they are just missing. There are too many concerns for a father whose son is off to war. If only the canal would open soon. I need the familiar excitement of the canal.

> Dear Sister Beck,
> I received another letter tonight. I am well and I hope that these few lines find you the same and parents, Be a good girl to Father and Mother. Kiss them for me. I suppose that Em has gone to Scaghticoke. I hope she won't stay long. I am going to write a letter tonight to her. I got a box and it was full of stuff. I thank Miss Stiles for those pickles and give her my love. That fellow is a nice young fellow. I guess he will send you his likeness. Well Sister, I am tired, I have written so much.

I will close, good-bye, pleasant dreams.

Your Brother,

Charles Shepard

The fellow referenced in this letter is the one that Beck is now writing.

Smith Judson A 4th Regiment, New York Heavy Artillery Company H, Sergeant

Dear Father,

I now take the pleasure to write to you. I am well and enjoying myself and I hope this letter will find you the same. I was out in the country Sunday and I had a good dinner and I went out to Falls Church and its a hard looking country old trees cut down in the road to block the Rebels. The Rebel Mosby is about ten miles from here. This regiment is on the Georgetown Heights about 6 miles from Washington. It is a nice place, The Fort I am in is a big one. There are about 18 canons, 5 20 pounders, 8 30 pounders and 2 100 pounders. That is a peacemaker. I tell you it would make things hop. All the soldiers are enlisting over because they thing the war will be over in the summer and I think so myself because the Rebs are about starved out and licked out. I have just been out to drill and I am all sweat. It is a hot day here. I ain't had hardtack yet. The boys tell me that I am as fat as a hog and I think so myself. When I wake up in the morning I can hardly get out of bed. We have to keep our clothes clean and our boots blacked up

our hair combed up and our necks clean and our guns so bright that you can see your face in them. I thought I would be put into another Company but I was a lucky man. It was a lot of Cohoes Boys. My Company is in the Fort the others are all outside the Fort. The Fort is made up of large logs and there are 4 rooms and they are numbered 1 2 3 4. I am in room 1 and they are all nice men. We have Church in the morning and at night. I think by the talk that we will go to Tennessee in about two months but we can't tell everything about it. I would like to stay here all the time for it is a nice place. We have to drill twice a day but we don't have to do any duty yet. Send me the Waterford paper every week. If you send me a pair of boots put a brush and some blackon with it. I don't think I will get paid for two months. I must now close my letter. Give my love to all.
  Your truly Son
  Charles W. Shepard
  Co. H, 4th Reg Heavy
  Artillery, Washington

John was to learn later on that Charles' description of the fort was very accurate. The Gray Ghost is mentioned again, but other than that, all is well. Good food, and good lodging, may go to Tennessee in a couple of months. This is a good letter. Maybe we are growing more accustomed to Charles' absence, where he is, and what he is engaged in. I have come to terms with it. He sounds settled in. He has the good fortune to be in a room inside of the fort, and he wants the newspaper every week. I feel better about Charles after this letter.

P19 This was Charles Regiment drilling at Fort Marcy. The Company is unknown. 1863.

Dear Mother,

I received your kind and welcome letter on the 27th and was glad to hear from you. I was on guard for the first time and I caught a cold. I got a sore throat, but I will be over it in a few days. There are a lot of men going home on furloughs tomorrow. It snowed here yesterday about all day. Today is a pleasant day here. There have been about 50 new men come into this Company since I have been here. Mother, it doesn't make any difference to me what color just as you think best. Make it so it will button all the way up. I just had 2 good crullers a man gave them to me. They were fresh, just came out of the spider. You asked whether I wanted some meat. I would care for a little dried beef. Well Mother I will now close. I don't want anything else now, I will write a few lines to Father. I hope this letter will find you well. So good-bye a long kiss.

      Your Son, Charles Shepard

This was an easy letter for mother to read before the family. It seems we are all coming to grips with being able to more confidently handle Charles being removed from us. Charles had two good crullers; they were fresh, just come out of the spider.

P20 Fresh out of the Spider. This cooking apparatus was referred to as the Spider. It only had 6 legs but it reminded them of a spider.

Dear Father,

I received your most kind letter of the 27th and was happy to hear from you. I am well, all but my throat is sore but getting better. I have met three that I know. One is Tom Morley, the one that works for Brown, Ghrome Wheeler in Washington and you know that man that was boss over the mud digger. He had a fight with Bob Brott, I can't remember his name. There ain't much news here. The soldiers laze all around the room enjoying

Dear Mother.....I am the Only One Left 63

themselves. I will send you a Washington paper tomorrow morning. I see the same every day. I will now close my letter, so good night and may you have good luck.

     Your Son Charles Shepard

How about them shirts? I want one like Em got me in Cohoes and one check shirt.

Charles mentions Judson Smith again to Rebecca. It appears as though she may have misaddressed a previous correspondence.

     Fort Marcy, Tuesday, February 15, 1864

Dear Sister,

 I received your most kind loving letter and was glad to hear that you are well. It snowed here yesterday. it is all melted off today and it makes it muddy. There have been 2 or 3 deserters in my Company and if they catch them they will shoot them. I feel sorry for a farm boy, he saw tough times. Judson A. Smith that is that fellows name. He is a sergeant. He is a nice fellow. I saw a letter you sent him. Dear Sister, you must send me your likeness. I will send you mine as quick as I can. The wind blows hard, we had beans for dinner. I have been quite sick but I am well now and enjoying myself. My pen ain't good for anything. I must now close. Good-bye and a kiss,

     Your Brother C. Shepard

Charles is anxious to establish this writing tryst with Rebecca and Sergeant Judson Smith. Judson is Charles Sergeant, Charles, always the peddler, probably feels that it could be in his best interests to have his sister involved in this letter-writing relationship between her and Judson. I can't say I disagree. Charles speaks of deserters from his regiment. This war is hard on everyone. We are pro-abolitionists; we agree that there should be no slavery. Does not everyone hold these beliefs, and even some wonder if it is worth their son's life? I can understand the young northern boys who might be encouraged to leave by desertion. I don't believe that Charles would be tempted. He keeps telling us that the war will be over soon. Those are such good thoughts, and Charles usually has a little joke in most of his letters.

Author's Note: Charles mentions he will be sending home an image of himself soon. If he did, it has either been lost to time, or perhaps a family member has it somewhere and doesn't even know who it is. I have been searching for a picture of Charles with no success for many years.

Fort Marcy, Sunday, March 5, 1864

Dear Sister,

I received your letter and was glad to hear from you. I am very well. I have been out in the country today and got my dinner. I had ham and eggs and two cups of tea, cabbage, cake and pie. We have everything that is good down her by paying a good price for it. That is cheap. Becks when you write to that fellow again, direct it Judson A. Smith. That is his right name. Where I had dinner today, I had an introduction to a young lady. Her name was Rebecca Mark. She took quite a shine to me but it will do her no good. She was pretty good looking but she can't come in. When I was on guard duty the other night I came across two boys by the name of Shepard. I ain't had no tobacco for eight days. I stopped once before for 12 or 14 days. When I get home-

sick I take a chaw to pass away the time. I don't chew a paper a month. I can't chew much in this part of the country. It makes me sick. Kiss Mother and Father for me. Give them my love. My love to all. I will now close my letter, so good-bye, a long kiss.
Your Brother, Char Shepard

Author's Note: Research bears out a very strong likelihood that these are the two boys by the name of Shepard that Charles came across.

SHEPHARD, WILLIAM. Age: 21. Enlisted January 24, 1862, at Port Richmond; mustered in as private, Co. A, to serve three years; re-enlisted February 9, 1864, and reported missing in action since August 25, 1864, at Reams Station.

SHEPHERD, GEORGE H.—Age, 21 years. Enlisted, December 26, 1863, at Granger; mustered in as private, Co F, December 26, 1863, to serve three years; captured, May 6, 1864, at the Wilderness, Va, no further record.

After this letter, Rebecca agreed that we should read our letters first and then present them to the rest of the gathered family. Charles is still too young, innocent, and trusting in his ways. As his father, I am sure that Charles had no real interest in the girl in this letter. Likely the connection was that the young lady's name was Rebecca. I am sure it was innocent. He should have kept that story to himself. I think that Emma's eyes suddenly look sadder.

Dear Father,
I did not hear a word from you but never mind you were downstreet when Mother and Beck wrote the letter. We think we will stay here this summer. The soldiers are enlisting at a great rate. The Great War will be over this summer. That's what's the

matter and that's what the soldiers think too. I will now close my letter, so good-bye.

Give my love to all who inquire about me.

More optimism from Charles. It is time to start preparing for the next season on the canal. Perhaps, I will visit Reverend Bush's family and see about the mules.

Author's Note: "You were *downstreet*" from the letter. Waterfordians often refer to being downstreet if they are visiting the business district. To the canaller, it usually meant one of the local taverns. A local term well over 100 years old. Charles is quick to excuse his father from writing because he is "*downstreet.*" He could be on family business, or he could be taking on a load of "wet goods," another Waterford/Canal colloquialism for visiting a local tavern. In either case a legitimate excuse.

Dear Mother,

I received your letter and was glad to hear that you are well. I am well at present and enjoying myself. Where is Emma? Is she to Schagticoke, or is she home? I sent to her in Schagticoke and one to home. Mother, I have often thought since I left home what good parents to advise me and tell me what's right and wrong. I have looked back and see now what a bad boy I have been to my Father and Mother. Now it makes me feel bad. I will try and be a better boy. Don't forget me in your prayers. I want to write to Father. You must excuse these few lines. I don't know whether Emma is at home or not. If she is give her my love. So good-bye.

Your Son, C. Shepard

We haven't seen Emma since that letter about the young serving lady named Rebecca that Charles said took a shine to him. I wish that Emma was better known to me. Mother is silent on the issue. I would like to speak with her and tell her my thoughts. Mother says if Emma doesn't return soon, she will visit Schaghticoke and have a talk.

Fort Marcy, March 11, 1864

Dear Mother,

I received your most kind and welcome letter on the 10th and was glad to hear from home. I am well and hope this letter will find you the same. If you send me a box send me a pipe and some smoking tobacco. I have stopped chewing tobacco. Smoking is the best thing a person can do. It keeps away sickness. I ain't chewed no tobacco in two weeks, it makes me sick to chew in this part of the country. We have just raised a flag pole in the Fort. It is a nice one. It is about 60 feet high. We have got a nice flag to put on it. Mother, send me two dollars. We will get paid in a month or so. Mother, I must close my letter. So Good-bye, a long kiss.

We are no longer reading our letters to all. We have decided it was best for each of us to read our own letter and then share the contents of the letter with the rest. Emma is with child now, about three months. Mother is thrilled. Emma is over Charles's writing of the Rebecca he mentioned in Virginia. Emma is living sometimes with us and sometimes in Schaghticoke. I have come to believe that she is confused and lonely.

Dear Father,

I received your letter last night and was happy to hear from you. The Army is all a moving now. We were inspected yesterday by General Barney. We were inspected to go away in a month or so. Send me a pipe and tobacco when you send my box. The men are all crazy to move. There ain't nothing new in camp. How did you like the paper? Send me two dollars. I will now close these few lines, so good-bye.

Your Son Charles Shepard
Fort Marcy

I found Charles' letter amusing in that he requested two dollars from both Mother and me. The men are all crazy to move, says Charles. I would be happy if they stayed put longer. He mentions an inspection by General Barney; I wonder what that means?

In 1862, after the American Civil War raged for a year, Barney joined the 7th New York Militia Regiment (Company F) as a Private for 90-day service. In October, he joined the 68th New York Infantry Regiment (Company G). At the time present, the 68th Infantry was part of the Army of the Potomac's XI Corps and, in the brigade of Alexander Schimmelfennig, was posted in the Washington defenses. A month later, Barney, who was listed in some rosters as John Barney, was commissioned a 1st Lieutenant.

In February 1864, Barney was promoted to Captain and assigned to the staff of General Rufus Saxton. He functioned as an Assistant-Adjutant General to the forces. At twenty years of age, he was breveted to General. As such, he would inspect troops in preparation for battle. (27)

Chapter 5

THE CANAL OPENS, CHARLES IS IN THE FIELD

Dear Sister,

I received your letter on the 10th and was happy to hear from you. That fellow is well and will give me his picture in a week or so. I must go and clean my gun, so good-bye.

Your Brother, Charles Shepard

This set of letters was very short. It seemed like Charles' mind was on something else. He was interested in tobacco, money, inspection, and his gun. Mother and Rebecca offered no outward display of interest or emotion over these happenings. Maybe it is just something a father would observe while others would not notice. I think I will take a walk down and see how the river looks today. Maybe we can get that canal open soon.

The winter of 1863 - '64 saw less snow than usual; as a result, the river achieved a level safe for navigation and opened to traffic on March 11, and canal boats were starting to arrive. The river would soon be full of boats between Waterford and Lansingburgh. The excitement level, as always, would be very high, and it is always infectious. Nearly all involved are taken up by the activities surrounding our annual rebirth, with the openings of the river followed by the opening of the canals. This had been a very long winter. With Charles away, every day was full of concern for his fortune. I would wait impatiently for his next letter and news of his well-being. The relief of receiving a letter would be followed by the anxiety about what this letter might reveal. After reading a letter, now there was a matter of interpreting the spirit of the message that Charles was attempting to convey. A parent always desires to help his children, even when they have matured or moved on to a stage in life where that help is no longer needed, that desire does not wane. When the child is engaged in war, the parent is left in a state of helplessness, sorrow, and confusion. You want to do all that you can, but at the same time, you realize, what can you do? You feel the sorrow of the other families, like the Vanderwerkens and others. You realize your sorrow, at least at this time, is only of absence and fear and not the total loss of a child who has been called upon or volunteered to engage himself in this struggle. You wonder, is my child needed in this endeavor? Must his life be endangered and be dependent on the winds of fate on a daily basis? Why must a family worry so? Yes, it was a long winter. It will be good to be back in the comfort of the canal.

John had looked in on his mules at Reverend Bush's family farm towards the end of March. Not surprisingly, he had found them in good order, in health, and in fitness. After meeting with the family for a time, John settled up accounts with them for their lodging and caring for the mules. They exchanged family pleasantries, Mrs. Bush inquiring as to Charles' wellbeing and assuring John that Charles was in their nightly offering of prayer to the soldiers. Upon departing her company, John announced he would return in a few days to retrieve the mules to place in their Grogh Street stable.

As busy and as hectic as the opening days of the season could be, John had grown accustomed to the fact that the first few days of the season sometimes weren't that kind to him for finding business.

There were just so many boats waiting to get through the Side Cut Locks and gain entry to the canal, and quite often, not enough mules were available to provide tows. The results could be unexpectedly bad for John's type of operation. John liked to tow local.

When mules became in short supply announcements would be published in Waterford and Whitehall newspapers among others. This one is from the Waterford Times in March 1905. Although it is a 1905 submission it is indicative of an ongoing issue.

WANTED
100 teams on opening of Champlain canal
To tow boats from Waterford to Whitehall.
Rates Waterford to Whitehall $25 and
Whitehall to Waterford $20, Inquire of R. B.
Vaughn, Waterford, or H. G. Noel, Whitehall.

He usually liked to hold out for tows to the Juncta or maybe something to Mechanicville. At the beginning of the season, he was dependent on what was arriving at the top of the Side Cuts and what their destination was. As the newspaper ad demonstrates, oftentimes, at the beginning of a towing season, there could be a shortage of mules. As a result, some mule drivers would raise their rates of tow. John did not, however, if an owner were to petition to accept an above-normal tow rate, John might be tempted if the situation met his needs. He had a reputation for being a fair dealer and wished to keep it. John would deal most times with those he had towed for in the past, no written contracts were necessary, and he could see no reason to raise his rate just to make more money. It was not his way.

John could walk the line down along the battery where the boats lined up awaiting passage to solicit business, but he would be at the mercy of when his tow would transport through the Side Cuts. He could line up business, but it might be the next day before they got through.

Fortunately, he had the Rock Island Flouring Mill job, and they were ready; John would have an opening day tow, almost the same one he had to close out last season. How pleased John was at the close of last season. It would be but the time of two weeks before Charles would release his plans involving the 4th Brigade of Artillery. How John's world had changed from days of joy to a disparaging winter of emotion. It will be good to be towing again. There will be a lot of news.

Our local Sentinel is good, and Harper's has much information, but the news that comes from the canallers seems more dependable and often tells a better story. It was one of the things John really liked about the canal, hearing the views of people who had visited many places and what they had seen or heard. The stories they told were somewhat different than what one might read, but they offered a perspective not available elsewhere. And so it was, opening day, 1864; John felt vibrant and happy for the first time since Christmas as he roused his mules to life ahead of the Rock Island canal boat. The season has started. Another new beginning. The canal opened on April third, and perhaps fittingly, Charles had written letters that day.

Camp near Culpeper, April 3, 1864

Dear Father,

I now take pleasure to inform you where I am. This Regiment is in the 2nd Corps. We are a Brigade today but I don't know what Brigade nor what Division, I will know in a few days. We are in 3 miles of the Rebs. We can look upon Pinney Mountain and look into the Rebel Camp. We moved from General Meade's headquarters, Friday, April the 1st. And marched about 5 miles in mud up to our knees. Our Siege Guns have come to the Regiment. Our camp is right by the Blue Ridge. I tell you they are big mountains. It is awfully muddy here at present. This is a hard looking country. You can bet the Rebels are coming into our camp in flocks, coming every day. They say that any that wants to fight can stay. There ain't many that wants to fight. They are hard looking men. They look at our soldiers and say, " A right smart lot of men." I reckon we are going to be paid off in a few of days. You must try and read this. I ain't got any ink, so

I had to write with lead. I must close now I ain't got any good place to write. My love to Em, Mother, Sister and all the rest, so good-bye. I am well and hardy.

Your Son, Charly Shepard

This letter has caused me much heartache at a time when the canal, as expected, had given me new hope. Charles is no longer in the Fort. It is a longer letter than the last one. He says he has no pen and no place to write. I am afraid that Charles is now beginning to become a part of the war. My mind is sad. I am afraid that any feelings of happiness or pleasure are gone from our lives. It is just so difficult to separate your thoughts. Concern for the welfare of Charles is on everyone's minds at home, yet no one speaks of it; you can just feel it in our relations with each other. It is something difficult to express in words, yet we all share in it, knowingly, without expressing it.

Author's Note: The following is a field report from a newspaper reporter assigned to the 4th Heavy Artillery. It is interesting to note how keenly aware and up-to-date Charles is regarding the 4th's activity and where they are. The date of the report is after the letter but covers the same period.

HEADQUARTERS ARTILLERY BRIGADE NEAR BRANDY STATION, VA. May 1, '64.

MR. EDITOR—SIR:—It was a fine morning on the 27th day of March last when the 4th N.Y. Art. was drawn up in line, with knapsacks packed, awaiting the final order to join the Army of the Potomac. At 10 A. M., every being in readiness to move, the regimental brass band announced the hour of departure by playing Yankee Doodle. The whole regiment, 2400 strong, filed out of the fort, bidding adieu to the defenses of Washington by uproarious cheering for Gen.

Grant. We soon reached Alexandria and, at 3 P. M., got aboard the cars. Our band played a lively air while hundreds of people gathered around to bid us farewell. At 7 o'clock in the evening, the iron horse gave a few snorts, and we were soon underway for the front. I took one parting look at the dome of the Capitol and the numerous forts erected for the defense of the city, then fell asleep and did not wake until we reached our place of destination. We got off and lay on the ground until morning when our march was resumed and at 9 P. M. on Monday, we halted about three miles north of Brandy Station and pitched our shelter tents, but before we had finished, it commenced raining and continued for three days. There were no woods to be found inside of two miles, and our men suffered greatly from the effects of the cold rain. So great was the fall of water that our tents were no more of a protection for us than brown paper. After it ceased storming, we received orders to join the 2d Corps, and again it commenced raining, but we soon reached the Artillery Reserve, three miles south of Brandy Station. It rained for about two days, but I was fortunate enough to find a number of the 126th N.Y. boys, so I remained with them until the storm was over. It cleared off, however, fine and pleasant, and the sun again shone with brilliance over the mass of troops composing the Union army. In a few days, the ground was dry, and everything went off pleasantly.

Our regiment has been assigned to three different corps. The 1st Battalion to the 6th, the 2nd Bat. to the 5th, and the 3rd, in which I am in, to the 2nd.

Our Battalion was present at a brigade review by Gen. Hancock near Stevensburg and also at the grand review of the 2d Corps by Gen. Grant, at which 50,000 troops were present.

Last week an order came for our company to join the 1st Bat. 6th Corps and Co. L. to take our place, so we packed up and marched there and pitched our tents on the ground formerly occupied by Co. L. The day after we arrived in the 1st Battalion, details of ten men out of each Company were made to drive teams, &c, five men, with me, were detached to Brigade Headquarters for a permanent guard. There were also six men detached from each of the other Companies in our Battalion for the same purpose. We draw our rations from the Brigade Quartermaster, and when the army moves, we go as the advance guard of the Brigade. We have good times—no drill, no roll call or inspecting, but every member of the guard is expected to keep his gun and equipment in good order, and we are the boys that can do it. Our uniform is new, and we make a fine appearance, whether on duty or otherwise.—Col. Tompkins is in command of the Brigade. The Headquarters is located in a beautiful pine grove about two miles north of Brandy Station. It is a beautiful place, the whole being surrounded by a fence made of pine boughs, with several entrances extending to the General's quarters.

Since I have been detached from the company, 20 more men from each Com. in the Battalion have volunteered to join Light Batteries, and now our Bat. is quite small. —What will become of the rest, I don't know. All the Regiments about here are in readiness for marching orders, and the first battle of the campaign will soon take place—perhaps ere another week passes by. It is getting late, and I must close. My best respects to all my friends.

          Your obedient servant.
          Chas. E. Rorison. (28)

Dear Wife,

   I got paid yesterday and I sent $25 to you. I got paid $40 and they took out $8 for clothes and that I overdrew and paid the Sutler $4 for eatables that I got since we came out to the front. We don't get enough to eat sometimes and I kept 6 for myself. Em. I don't spend no more than I can help. You be close. When I return home we will want all the money we can get. Well, Em dear, I ain't got any more time to write at present. I am well and hope that these *few lines will find you the same. Some of these poor soldiers didn't have no money to send home to their wives who have children. I will get paid next month again. Kiss Mother and Father for me. We marched 6 miles today. We are in Culpeper now and will stay there. We are going to do Provost Duty in Culpeper. Well, Em dear, good night. My love to all. As soon as I get settled again I will write. Kiss, Your Husband Chas. Shepard*

Author's note: It is interesting to note that Charles' math does not add up. It may be a 1960s transcription error. As a peddler, one would think he was good with the numbers.

This letter was received on April 11th. There is some pleasure in this letter in the fact that Charles is showing interest through Emma; she is living with us in Waterford again, in saving money towards their future life together on Sixth Street. The sutler mentioned in this letter is a person who follows an army to sell food and supplies to its soldiers. Charles' claim to be doing Provost Duty in Culpeper is encouraging. Provost Duty was similar to being the police force in captured areas. John felt that this would be safer than being involved in battlefield activities. Maybe Charles will be held safe.

Author's Note: This is the last known letter to wife Emma. She appears to be splitting her time between Schaghticoke and Waterford. There were likely others that were just lost to time.

Dear Sister,
I received your most kind and welcome letter. I hardly know what to write to you. Well, I said I didn't know and then a nice young fellow told me to send his best respects to you and he is a gay

young fellow. I wish I had your face to look at once in a while, Beck. I don't hear Mother to call me up in the morning, but, I have a good bed to sleep in good grub to eat and lots to eat. I see more niggers every day than you can shake a stick at and the poor bucks, their lips stick out a foot. I suppose I have seen more than three thousand niggers since I left home. I am down on the buggers. One big buck nigger comes to me and said you are a nice sort of fellow. I reckon you don't see no white women here. Once in a while you will see one but they are almost as black as a nigger. Well how did the black mare do? Did she win? I bet. I wish you would send me your likeness in the next letter. You would laugh to see the men jump up and take their hats off. When an officer comes into the room we have to jump up and take our caps off. Well, Sister, I ain't got nothing more to say at present, so good-bye.

My love to all

Again being the father, I think I can recognize outside influences on Charles. We have long referred to our Southern Friends as "niggers"; to us, it was identification. In this letter, Charles just seems so taken with the word; I *bet*, as Charles would often state in his letters, that the writing of Charles is being influenced by the men he is living with. He also tells Rebecca that he doesn't know what to write. Charles was a very talkative boy and could ramble on. I think this is Charles rambling on while writing.

Dear Father,

I received your most kind letter and was happy to hear from you. I am well as ever, thank God. I am down here where you can look into the Reb's camp. We had a heavy skirmish at Robson's Ford the other day. Some part of the Army has been ordered to pack their knapsacks with hardtack to be ready to march at a minutes warning. Culpeper is a hard looking place. Some of the buildings are all to slivers. There is hardly a home in Culpeper that window left in them all knocked out by our soldiers. It looks like war down here. I tell you. There is more soldiers around Culpeper than you can shake a stick at. Well, there won't be quite as many by next winter, I think. You will see them walk right through the Rebels. Culpeper Court House is full of Rebels and they send them away every day. You must try and read this letter because I have no place to write. We are in camp at an orchard. It is a nice place. I received them postage stamps and the Waterford paper. Well, Father, there ain't any extra news today so I will close for this time. I must read some in the Bible. So goodbye, pray for me. My love to all. Good morning.

                              Your loving son, Charles W. Shepard

Author's Note: The skirmish mentioned in the letter involved the Rapidan River. The divisions were back across the Rapidan by 2 a.m., with the Confederates reoccupying their entrenchments immediately afterward. Union casualties totaled 262, while the Confederates lost sixty. Due to a Union deserter who revealed the Union plans to the Confederates, Butler never made an attack on Richmond, while Lee never requested reinforcements from the city. The I Corps also failed to cross the river, never getting closer than a mile and a half from Raccoon Ford.

After the battle, General Hays was accused of being drunk during the battle and of acting irrationally. However, many officers, including several in his division, attested that Hays was sober throughout the engagement. All of the accusations about Hays being drunk at Morton's Ford came from the 14th Connecticut, which suffered nearly half of the Union casualties in the battle and may have felt resentment against Hays because of it. (29)

Culpeper, April 17, 1864

Dear Sister,

I received your kind letter and was happy to hear from you. You must forgive me for not writing before. You know when I write a letter home I mean it for all. You say your friend Smith don't write anymore. Well Beck, he ain't much anyway. How did you like Westover's letter? It was a good one, I got it. I had a letter from Julia Thayer the other day and she is well. Well I am on my way down in Old Virginia, far away from home and I would really like to have your likeness, Mother's and Father's, and Em also. I wish you could look in my tent and see how we live. Charlie Westover is asleep and another boy with the mumps is very sick. Poor boy, no one to take care of him but us and we do the best we can. I have got to be quite a cook. I cooked dinner today and I will tell you what it was. It was bread fried in grease. That's all. That was bully for us. Well Beck, the soldiers have to take it hard sometimes. You write to Westover he's a good fellow. He writes a good letter. Well, Beck. I will close for this time. Westover sends his respects to you and says he would like to hear from you. So, good-bye kiss.

Your Brother Charly Shepard

When I read Rebecca's letter, I found my thoughts on Charles' letter writing to Rebecca concerning Judson Smith were wrong. *"You say your friend Smith don't write anymore. Well, Beck, he ain't much anyway."* I thought that Charles wanted Rebecca to write to strengthen his relationship with the Sergeant. He now wants her to write to Charles Westover, we know Charles, he is a nice boy.

It is a long five weeks before we hear from Charles again. Business was good on the canal. Rebecca and Mother kept busy with their gardening at home on Sixth Street. Mother always likes to do a good amount of canning come autumn so we would have enough to get through the winter. Together with Emma, excitement about the forthcoming baby would grow with each passing day. We seldom spoke of Charles; we just couldn't; there were no thoughts that anyone cared to share out loud. Each night we all prayed for Charles. Each day with no mail from Charles was beginning to take its toll. Harriet's eyes, usually bright and cheerful, with that certain, young-eyed look, were no more. She began to look as sad-eyed as Emma. Rebecca, somehow, seemed unaffected. Perhaps due to her youth, she was somehow above it all. The wait was intolerable.

Sunday, May 22, 1864

Dear Mother,

I take the pleasure to write to you a few lines to inform you that I am still among the living. I have been in a battle. I came out alright. There was a great many killed. It was an awful sight. We shove the Rebels so they did not come back again. Well, Mother about ten o'clock in the night we came out of the battlefield to the rear and rested. In the morning we went on to the field and threw up breastworks. We got the breastworks done. We was ordered to report to Ginney Station (Guinea). You look that up on a map and see how far it is from Vernia Courthouse to Ginney Station. Well, it was an awful hot day. Some of the men got sunstroke. I was so tired when we stopped that I laid down in the road and went to sleep. Then as soon as the army stopped we was sent out on reconnaissance. Well, Mother, an order just came to move so I must stop.

Mother was never the same after this letter. Anytime a letter was received, she would have me read it first and then only tell her favorable things. I would leave the letters out so that she could read them at her will. I don't know if she ever did. They were never discussed. We don't know what has happened in Charles' life between April 3rd through May 22nd. It was a long period of wonder and worry. This letter did little to ease our burden. However, Charles's attempts at humor, *"I take the pleasure to write to you a few lines to inform you that I am still among the living."* failed to bring us any comfort. After worrying for the eternity of five weeks about his welfare and now facing the realization that our son is in a war zone and lucky to be alive has, at the same time, temporarily lifted our spirits and caused us even greater concern for his future safety. *"I have been in a battle; I came out alright. There were many men killed; it was an awful sight."* I don't think that Charles is trying to be poetic here. I do wonder how a man participates in these events, knowing that his life is at stake and that to survive, he may have to take another's life. John could not come to grips with this type of survival. He wondered if Charles could. Charles says he is at Ginny Station. I tried to find it on a map. I think he means Guinea Station. That has been in the papers. Charles is in Hancock's 2nd Corp. (30)

Author's Note: As dawn broke over Guinea Station on May 21, the lead elements of Hancock's Second Corps arrived in full force. Although a small stop on the Richmond, Fredericksburg, and Potomac railroad, Guinea Station was a vital supply point for the Army of

Northern Virginia when it was based along the upper Rappahannock River. Quartermasters and medical personnel had once swarmed this quiet spot, but the Federal advance into the Wilderness and Spotsylvania had forced them to withdraw south to Milford Station.

I would only report to Mother that Charles was well and where he was. She asked few questions. It is not well that Harriet has isolated her feelings; I don't know what pain she is fostering. I will respect her wishes, but at some point, she must involve herself. This is a great burden to bear alone, no matter what the outcome.

> *Camp on the Banks of the Ann River near Hanover Courthouse.*
>
> *Dear Mother,*
>
> *We have marched all night and all day. We have got to the Ann River near Hanover Courthouse about 25 miles from Richmond. Yesterday we was in a fight with Hill's Corps. They tried to drive us in the river but they got slipped up on it. We took a great many prisoners. Well, Mother, the army is in good spirits. They go along singing and full of fun. Well, Mother, you must excuse my letter this time. Maybe the next time you hear from me I will be in Richmond. Try to read this. I will write to Em and Beck the next chance I get if the Lord spares my life. May the Lord bless you all. So goodby. My paper is rather dirty and so am I. I will send you the likeness of a little boy I found on the battlefield.*
>
> *Your Truly Son Charly Shepard*

Charles mentions, "My paper is rather dirty, and so am I." We hadn't been discussing Charles nightly around the dinner table or in our parlor afterward. Early on in January and February, our night's entertainment and activities would often center around our opinion of, what's Charles doing now? Almost everyone would have some scenario involving mischief, gaiety, merriment, and sometimes even mayhem, all attributable to Charles. After the letter of April 11th, everyone lost interest in our nightly discussion of Charles's potential activity. An aura of solemness had permeated our family parlors, much like that feeling when you enter a home where someone is being waked. I introduced after dinner, perhaps as a result of having had a particularly good day with old friends on the canal on such a splendid afternoon, some of the topics of Charles' letter; his dirtiness and the walking along singing. After the discussion, in which everyone took part, Mother was a little reluctant at first but later joined in; we decided; Charles didn't mind getting dirty, but he did like to clean up. We came to the realization that our soldiers in the field, where Charles has been now for almost two months, have no regular access to water or to a clean change of clothes. We all decided that Charles was uncomfortable with this. We wondered what kind of songs the men would be singing as they made their way. It was a good evening; everyone felt better. I think for the first time since Charles left in December that we all retired for the night, relaxed and ready for a good night's sleep.

Author's Note: This is the Report of Captain Augustus Brown. He was Captain of 4th Brigade Company H, which was Charles Company. John Shepard had no access to these reports.

CAMP IN FRONT OF HANOVER JUNCTION
May 25, 1864

MR. EDITOR:—I take the liberty, inasmuch as I am not acquainted with their address, to convey through your journal to relatives and friends the sad intelligence of the casualties in my Company.
   On the 19th instant, two companies, "H" and "K," were posted as pickets on the extreme right of the Union lines in front of Spotsylva-

nia Court House, Co. D being in reserve, with orders if attacked to hold the position as long as possible. Lt. Edmondston commanded the left of the company line and took up his quarters in one of three old houses a little in advance of the pickets, posting a small force in each of the buildings. These houses stood in an open field, bounded on three sides by woods and dense underbrush, and occasionally a rebel could be seen for an instant, dodging about among the leaves.

About 4 o'clock P. M. firing commenced, and at once became general along the line of Co. K and the left of H. Soon the woods about the houses spoken of were alive, with rebel skirmishers pouring their fire from front and flank upon the brave boys posted there, and it was returned with equal vigor and effect. Co. D immediately came to our support, and each of our small company reserves was sent to reinforce the left of our line. Scarcely had this been done when the rebels advanced in two lines of battle in splendid order from the woods upon our simple picket lines, threatening our complete annihilation or capture. We knew we had no line of battle to fall back upon and that a valuable supply train was then coming up the road a few rods in our rear, and we were determined to hold the rebels in check, at all hazards, until reinforcements should arrive. This we did for more than three-quarters of an hour until the 1st Maine and 2d and 8th N. Y. Artillery came up and went in with a will. Our line, except a few men on the extreme right, who were flanked and cut off, formed with these regiments, and the rebels being driven back remained on the field during the night.

The fighting ceased about 9 o'clock P. M., and we learned to our surprise from prisoners taken, that the whole of Ewell's corps was gaged in the attack. The rebel dead strewn over the field the next morning showed how fearfully that corps must have suffered in its attempt to flank us and capture our supplies.

The list of killed, wounded, and missing of Co. H is as follows:

KILLED.

Sergeant Judson A. Smith, shot in the right leg, died in hospital the next morning; Artificer Goold R. Benedict, shot in the head and killed instantly; Private Wm. R. Mead, shot in the groin, lived but a short time; Private Joseph Housel, Jr., shot near the heart and died soon after, being carried from the field.

WOUNDED.

Corporal Samuel L. Harned, both legs severely. Privates— Chas. E. Abbey, face, severely; Erastus D. Adams, foot, slightly; Levi C. Brockelbank, arm, flesh wound; Charles M. Butler, leg, severely; George H. Bullock, arm, flesh wound; Samuel C. Cole, foot, slightly; Albert E. Lyke, face, severely; Frederick A. Phelps, side, slightly; Charles F. Sanford, arm, severely; Allen R. Smith, leg, flesh wound; Charles M. Struble, hand, slightly.

MISSING.

Sergeant David B. Jones, Private Asa Smith.

The graves of the dead are marked, and the wounded are all sent to the hospitals at Washington, except Phelps, who is now with the company. Nothing definite can be ascertained concerning Sergeant Jones and Asa Smith; many reports are in circulation, but none are reliable, and I have the strongest hopes that they are safe, though they may be prisoners.

Time will not permit me to notice at length the character and services of those who have given their lives for the cause as I could wish.

Suffice it to say they were among the very best men of the company—their places in the ranks can never be filled. Surely "Death loves a shining mark."

Very respectfully, your obedient servant,
AUG. C. BROWN,
Capt. Co. H., 4th N. Y. Artillery. (31)

Author's Note (continued) This is the first battle for Charles Shepard. He sees his Sergeant and sister's pen pal killed. Charles Abbey, a good friend, was wounded, and his friend Asa Smith was reported as missing.

What a difference two days have made. I towed to Stillwater today and returned later than usual. It was a pleasant Spring Day, and at the locks in Mechanicville and Stillwater, I met up with several longtime canal acquaintances. We engaged in good talk; thankfully, no one inquired about Charles. Many of my out-of-town canal friends do not have intimate knowledge of my family. The talk is usually about business and local events. Of course, at the second lock in Mechanicville, you can't go through without old J.C. Rice telling how he was there in 1823 when the water was first let into the canal. To hear him tell it, no one was sure what would happen when the water came in. "Now you see, son, that was 41 years ago; ain't many around today that can member that!" It was always a pleasure to see Mr. Rice at the lock. A man can derive a lot of satisfaction from an anticipated common occurrence, like listening to old J. C. tell his familiar story. Although I have heard it oh, so many times, today, it was good to hear.

His story appeared in The Mechanicville Mercury in 1883

> J.C. Rice, of Mechanicville, N.Y. who is hale and hearty at eighty-four was present when the water was let into the Champlain canal and met the water from Lake Erie in the Erie canal, in 1823.

It was the first time in months that I was busy with friends and temporarily clear-headed. This was the perfect letter to come home to. I encouraged mother to read it herself, but she was not ready. The news of this letter was so much better than the one two days past that I felt renewed, some of the burden was relieved, and there is still hope for the future. "The army is in good spirits, and they go along the road singing and full of fun." I hope it is as good as Charles makes it sound.

Following the stalemate at Spotsylvania Court House, Grant was determined to continue his offensive against the Army of Northern Virginia. After a failed attempt to bait Lee out of his earthworks, he found the Confederates entrenched on the south side of the North Anna River, where Lee's "inverted V" forced Grant to divide his army into three parts in order to attack. On May 23, 1864, one of A.P. Hill's divisions assaulted the isolated Fifth Corps, which had crossed the river at Jericho Mill. After a bloody seesaw fight, the Federal bridgehead remained intact. On the other flank, the Second Corps seized the Chesterfield Bridge over the North Anna. On the 24th, an alcohol-fueled infantry attack by a brigade from the Ninth Corps was repulsed at Ox Ford. Hancock, meanwhile, advanced on the Confederate right. Lee hoped to strike an offensive blow, but he was ill, and the opportunity for defeating an isolated part of the Federal army passed. Once the threat of Lee's position was revealed, Grant withdrew both wings of the army back across the North Anna River. Grant outflanked the position by moving downstream and continued his advance on Richmond. Shortly after 6:00 p.m., an artillery barrage prefaced an infantry attack by Hancock's men, who scrambled up the Confederate defenses and chased the Rebels across the river. (Just as Charles says in his letter.) (31)

Wednesday, May 25, 1864

Well Mother, the morning has come again. Oh, how thankful we ought to be to the Lord. He gave us plenty to eat and drink. Oh, if we could only thank him enough for what he has done for me, Mother. Charles Westover told me to tell you he tries to do right. Mother, if you were here to look over the field and see the soldiers you would think that you were in a hornet's nest. Some a singing and talking, everything you can think of. On the night of the 23rd, about 5 o'clock in the afternoon the rebels came across the field in seven lines of Battle and drove our troops a little, then they turned around and stood their ground and the artillery opened up on them with grape and canister and oh, to see them go. It was awful. You could not see no more of the Rebels.

Seven Lines of Battle, we killed 900 Rebels on that one surge. Well, Mother, I must close for my paper is getting short, so I will close for the present, so goodbye, may the Lord have mercy on us all til we meet again. Give my love to all.

Author's Note: There exists the possibility that when these letters were transcribed that the date on this letter may have been mistranscribed as May 25 when in fact, it may have been written on May 23. When Charles writes of a battle, it is usually on the same day. The letter appears out of sync time-wise. Once again, Charles' writing is supported by historical facts, as seen below. Charles reports that at about 5 o'clock, the artillery opened up on the Reb with grape and canister fire.

After extricating themselves from a tremendous traffic jam, the lead elements of the Union army, Maj. Gen. Gouverneur K. Warren's Fifth Corps and Hancock's Second approached the North Anna River on May 23. Hancock moved toward Chesterfield Bridge over the river and a small redoubt manned by Col. John W. Hennigan's South Carolinian brigade. Despite sending repeated messengers to the rear as they watched Union skirmishers advance, Henagan received no reinforcements nor any orders of retreat. Shortly after 6:00 p.m., an artillery barrage prefaced an infantry attack by Hancock's men, who scrambled up the Confederate defenses and chased the Rebels across the river. (32)

Camp near Hanover Courthouse,
Virginia, Wednesday, June 1, 1864

Dear Sister,

It is so long since I got a letter from you. I often think of you and wish that I could see you but before long I think this cruel war will be over so the soldiers can return home to their friends. Dear Sister, I am about 9 miles from Richmond. I wish it was only one mile, I hope this month brings this war to an end, but I am afraid not. If you could be down here and hear the canons roar and the muskets, you would think the world was coming to an end. We got so nigh Richmond that they can hear the roar of the canon and we will be so nigh before long, they will smell the powder, I bet, or something else. Well, Uncle Smith is killed. He got killed the 19th of May. Charles Abby got wounded in the month. Uncle George got wounded at the Wilderness in the two day battle. Dear Sister, I must close I don't have time to write much. Write as often as you can. I am well and hope that these few lines will find you well. We are going to have a Siege Train, it is on its way to us now. Well I will close now, good-bye, God Bless you. May the Lord spare my life to meet you all again. My love to all.

Rebecca had become lax in her writing to Charles. She, too, had become disillusioned with the effects that Charles' absence was having on our daily lives. Having corresponded with Judson Smith, Charles's Sergeant, soon after Charles's enlistment and later being told by Charles that "he wasn't much anyway" had tempered her enthusiasm for the activities of the soldiers. She was writing to Charlie Westover, who was known to us. We could see changes in Rebecca. So many changes in her life. Her brother is away and obviously in danger. Her sister-in-law Emma will be giving birth soon. Rebecca is writing to soldiers, but she seems not to be as outgoing as she once was.

Author's Note: In John Shepard's thoughts about Judson Smith, he nor anyone else in the family is aware that Judson has died in battle. It is thought that Charles was attempting to shield Rebecca from the realities of war.

At 4:30 a.m. on May 12, 15,000 men of the Union Second Corps under Winfield Scott Hancock advanced Upton-style with bayonets fixed across a fog-shrouded field on Edward Landrum's farm, just as the Confederates were returning their cannons to their former positions. About twenty guns were captured—some without firing a shot. A few Confederate infantrymen tried to shoot, but damp powder from the mist prevented many guns from firing. In a short time, Hancock held a half-mile of the Confederate trench line and took nearly 3,000 prisoners, including Generals Edward "Allegheny" Johnson (a Virginian) and George H. Steuart, along with the remnants of the famed Stonewall Brigade.

May 19, 1864 - At the Battle of Harris Farm near Spotsylvania Court House, the Confederates under Richard S. Ewell encounter fresh Union troops pulled from the Washington, D.C., defenses. Ewell loses 900 men against the Union men who had never before seen combat. (Charles made that statement of 900 killed in his letter) (33)

When the armies left Spotsylvania Court House on May 21, many of the dead remained unburied. A Confederate cavalryman wrote that

> "The dead Yankees are heaped up in piles half as high as a man, in front of our Breastworks, and all around on the Battlefield, the dead Yanks are lying just as thick as they can be, and none of them burried [sic]," adding, "they will all rotten on top of the ground."

Another Confederate—an infantryman in Ramseur's brigade—remembered the ghastly upturned faces of the decomposing dead who lay between the lines. "Both parties seemed to be exhausted," he thought, "so much so as to prevent them from interring the fallen braves." A month after the battle, the First Maine Cavalry passed through Spotsylvania Court House and found "Federal and Confederate dead…lying around in all directions." The regiment halted briefly to bury the dead, but it could not have interred many, for by nightfall, it was at Guiney Station, fifteen miles away. (34)

Dear Mother.

I received your most kind letter and was glad to hear from you. I am well and hope this letter finds you the same. It does me good to get a letter from home. When a soldier gets a letter from home how good he feels. You will see his laugh and some don't get any. Some ain't got no friends to write to. Oh, how bad I would feel if I had no Mother or Father to write to. I would hardly know what to do. Thank God, I have lots of friends to write to me. That is all that keeps a soldier in good spirits. Well Mother, there ain't much fighting going on. We went in on a Flag of Truce today. You could see the Rebels on their breastworks and our men on theirs. Once in a while our men would go halfway and the Rebels would too and exchange newspapers and run back to their breastworks. The Rebel breastworks ain't only 20 yards from ours. My Company is back in the rear. Ain't been in any battle since the 19th of May nor ain't likely to go in any for we are an Artillery Brigade. Our Colonel is Chief of Artillery. Mother, there ain't much news, if any, so I will close. Charles Westover sends his love to you and wants you to pray for him and for me also. I will write in a few days again. Give my love to Grandmother and Grandfather and all the rest. May the Lord spare our lives until we meet again. Write as often as you want. Good-bye and a kiss.

   Charly Shepard

   Company H

   Heavy Artillery

I encouraged Mother to read this letter herself, and she did. Charles mentions Chas. in this letter, which is his friend Charlie Westover. We are all relieved to hear of a lull in the fighting.

There is some mild comfort to Charles' writing of the Artillery being towards the rear of the action. At least they are not in hand-to-hand fighting.

 Dearest Mother,

  I received your most kind letter this morning and was very happy to hear from you. It is Sunday and it is just the same as any other day here. Well Mother, I was reading the Bible when the Sergeant came and threw a letter in my lap. Oh, you better believe I opened it quick. I was up most of the night working on breastworks. We were in the works so I had a chance to write a little. Dear Mother, I have written 5 or 6 letters home. I don't know the reason you don't get them. Mother your letter found me well and I hope this letter will find you the same. There ain't much fighting going on now. Charles Westover sends his love, he wants you to pray for him and he will pray for himself. Oh, Mother sometimes I feel so happy when I try to do a favor for *some of the soldiers. Oh, if some of them would only read their Bibles and pray, how much better I would feel. I try to pray and read my Bible and do what's right. Dear Mother, there is a rumor in camp that we are going to march to Harrison's Landing. I must hurry up and cook some dinner. I will close. If we don't go I will write tomorrow again. Kiss Em for I will write her as soon as I can. Good-bye, my love to all. Tell Beck to send her picture and I will get it. Give my love to Beck and Father. God bless you all, good-bye.*

Your loving son
Charles Shepard
4th Artillery Brig
Company H

P21 The Tidball Charles mentions in his letter.

Another letter to bring relief to Mother and all of us. Charles and Charlie Westover seem to be spending a good deal of time together. Charles is keeping up his prayers and reading the bible. It sounds like Charlie W. needs someone to pray for him to pray for himself. An all-good newsletter does raise the family spirit, especially Emma and Mother. As pleasant and anticipated the event is of the approaching entry into this world of our grandchild, it would be more so if Charles were here to share it with us.

Upon the vacancy within the 4th New York Heavy Artillery, his other career champion, William F. Barry, wrote:

"The Regiment very much needs a Colonel who is not only a good soldier but who possesses sufficient artillery information and experience to instruct and handle the Regiment properly in this special service. I believe these qualifications can only be found combined in some suitable officer of the Regular Artillery of the Army of the United States. Should the vacancy which I now anticipate really occur, I respectfully present Captain John Tidball of the 2d Regt. U.S. Artillery as an officer in all respects admirably suited for the position… I am confident that (the 4th New York Heavy Artillery) will soon become… a credit to the State and models of their kind."

Upon his arrival to the 4th New York, Private James Hildreth (of Battery / Company F) was not happy, writing home that "the colonel is as mean now as he was good when he first took command. Everyone hates him, from the highest officer to the lowest private. He is the meanest man I ever see."

Hildreth later changed his tune, writing home again that

"Colonel Tidball is very strict but uses us better than Hall used to. He has always spoken pleasantly to me, and he makes the officers stand around more than he does the men; they fear him more." (sic) (35)

Chapter 6

A HOMECOMING OF SORTS

Today is June 17th, 1864. I have elected to take a tow to Stillwater. Mules for towing are in short supply right now. The owner being towed, Stephen Wood of the Seymour Lumberyard, offered to pay more than I am accustomed to. I knew Mr. Seymour and towed for him years back. Young Mr. Wood seems to be a fine fellow and desperate to have a tow. I have no regular clients needing a tow, so I will take this one. This means I will be late to arrive back at Waterford today. I hope Harriet will not be worried. She worries so these days, Charles and the war, Emma and the baby. Sometimes, I fear it is too much for her. She needn't fear, so for me on the towpath, I have never had any trouble. In these times, I feel safer and more content on the towpath than anywhere else.

John picked up Stephen Wood's light (empty) boat at the top of the side cut lock just below Broad Street. Towing a light boat, they would not have to be weighed at the new Waterford Weighlock.

During the summer of 1862, the dam across the Mohawk River at Cohoes was raised eighteen inches, thereby obviating the difficulties which had been experienced during low water, both in towing boats across the river and in maintaining the levels on each side of the river. The weigh-lock at Waterford was also completed this year, and it proved to be the most useful weigh-lock on the canals, being of great benefit to navigation on the Erie by relieving the West Troy weigh-lock of all the boats that came from the Champlain canal and permitting all boats that desired, to pass into the Hudson River at Waterford. (36)

A good tow was just what John needed. These days, it seemed, there was always too much on his mind. His attentions were drawn to this very day one year ago when the boys of the 22nd Regiment returned home.

Dear Mother.....I am the Only One Left   97

John remembered the excitement of the day when they departed for duty. What a grand sight it was, the speeches, the music, Old John Cramer marching with the boys as they marched into Lansingburgh, the wide-eyed expressions on the younger boys, and even some envy from those left behind. Charles was in wide-eyed wonder and curiosity that day, as John recalled, and now we are wild-eyed with curiosity about Charles's welfare. Ah, but this is the day that all have been waiting for, the return of the 22nd. One year later, I am much more appreciative of how splendid a day the return was. The entire town was filled with anticipation of the soldier's return. I dare say that all of Waterford lined all of the lower streets in the village to offer a welcome home. During the canal season, all canallers strive to earn a full year's earnings in however long the season may last. Usually late April through early December. Most canallers, especially those with families, would work every possible day of the season. I did as well. Most canallers would work through periods of ill health rather than miss out on an opportunity to enhance their pocketbook. But not today. I gave no thought to working today. I checked the mules, cleaned the barn area, left them food and water, and followed the building excitement in the village. All the firemen were out in full uniform with their engines and hose carts bannered in red, white, and blue; every woman and child in town was dressed like it was Sunday.

Many of the homes and nearly every business was Gailey strung with banners in a very festive display. The atmosphere was intoxicating. At about 2 p.m., the soldiers arrived. They were met by a brass band, local officials, and all the firemen and marched along to the wild cheering and adulation of virtually all. Charles was very taken by the whole proceeding as well as he should have been. Who among us had seen such a demonstration before? It was truly exciting.

From the Waterford Sentinel June 16, 1864

RECEPTION OF Co. A, TWENTY-SECOND REGIMENT.—Waterford presents a gala appearance today in honor of the reception of Co. A Twenty-second regiment, which will have a cordial welcome. Elaborate decorations have been prepared and the streets of the village are lurid with bunting and patriotic emblems. On the corner of Broad and Second Streets, a soldier's tent has been erected, filled with equipment, and over the door is the inscription, "Walk into my shebang." The different hotels, Porter's newsroom, and many private houses are ornamented.

According to the program, the company was to arrive from Albany, by the Saratoga railroad, at 1.40 P. M., today—when the bells would be rung.

WATERFORD.—The reception of Co. A Twenty-second regiment at Waterford yesterday did honor to the residents of that village and to the committee in charge of the arrangements. The procession which escorted the soldiers through the principal streets consisted of Knickerbocker Engine Co. No. 1, Hudson Engine Co. No. 2, Breslin Hose Company, and numerous citizens. We have rarely seen such a universal decoration of buildings. After marching through the principal streets, the volunteers will be welcomed by John O. Mott and partake of a collation at Morgan Hall under the auspices of the ladies. At the Morgan House, John O. Mott made a speech of welcome, abounding in patriotic sentiments. Lieut. Col. Strong made a rousing, soldier-like response. Mr. Mott stated that $6162 had been subscribed and $6145 expended in aid of soldiers' families in Waterford. After this reception, part of the soldiers proceeded to Cohoes, where another welcome was in store for them. (37)

Yes, it was a day like no other in Waterford, not since our move here in 1838, anyway. 1841 saw the Great Fire. The excitement that day was terrifying, and fear had its grip on the community. The fear that day was intense but fleeting and, in a way, brought a close community even closer and, to an extent, thankful that no lives were lost and that the devastation was not total. The excitement in '61 when the boys marched off was one of a kind, once-in-a-lifetime experience, but the feelings generated were short-lived. Soon, at least by September of 61, the excitement gave way to everyday life, and the realities of daily wartime life settled like a pall over the community. That was when we heard the first news of the loss of Timothy Vandecar to typhoid fever, and then in July of 62, the same report on John Vanderwerken. But this, this was the entire community in the sense of celebration, honor, thankfulness, and joviality of never before seen proportions. Displays of goodwill were universal. One had to witness it and experience it to truly understand the moment. Thinking back now, as we approach Lock 5, I remember how this village-wide celebration and the public's happiness and adulation of the 22nd's homecoming had affected Charles. You could see it in his expressions and demeanor. The only tears seen in public that day were tears of joy. Thinking of this event has lifted John's spirits. He is towing out of Lock 5, but Lock 6 lies just ahead, then a pretty good tow to Hewlett's Lock. Out of Lock 6 on our way to Mechanicville and then Stillwater, John's thoughts return to this day one year ago once more. With all the celebration, now thinking back, where was the family of Hiram Clute and John Murray? Both Waterford Boys of the 22nd wounded in battle and later died. Did their families share in this joy? What of Jonathan Porter and John Wright, both killed at South Mountain, were their families celebrating today? John knew the Clute family. He did more towing up their way (Crescent on the Erie) earlier in his towing career. I should get up that way and pay a visit one day. He knew he never would. John liked to work things out in his own mind. If he could arrive at a satisfactory conclusion without taking action and it did not influence his business or his family, he rarely followed through. He was satisfied that because he was sympathetic to the plights of the families who had lost so much, they would somehow find solace. Why John thought this, he could not explain to anyone, including himself, but still, it brought him comfort and, to some degree, a feeling of righteousness. It felt good for a while. Half the day has passed. We have arrived in the Village of Stillwater. I will visit one of the local taverns for dinner before the towpath walk back to Waterford.

Petersburg, June 20, 1864

Dear Father,

I received your most kind letter and was glad to hear that you are well, Well Father, I have seen some tough times since our march from Cold Harbor. I will give you a little description of our march from Cold Harbor. We started Monday night, the 12th, about 6 o'clock and marched until 7 o'clock the next morning. We were about a mile from the Ciahcahominy River. There we cooked our breakfast, such as we had, then we were told we had two hours to rest. We then marched all day and most of the next night. Then we were about four miles from the James River that we marched to the next day with good will. Then we was ordered to chop a road through the trees so the men could march through. That took us all day. Then we rested all day and night. The next day we went down to the river and helped load the boats with wagons, mules and artillery. We stayed a day and a night, then we marched up to Petersburg, here we are now. We gave the Rebels fits. The first time we came here, we drove them about half a mile. I hope this cruel war will end soon for it is awful. The Rebs will have to get out of the city or Grant will burn it down. We have got two of the railroads in our hands now. We will soon have the other and the city too. Well Father, I will close my let-

ter for this time. Send me a paper, when you send it put in a couple of papers of tobacco in it. They won't know the difference. Well, Father I will write in a few days again. So, good-bye, may the Lord bless you all. A good kiss to all.

Charly Shepard
Co. H 4th NY
Artillery Brigade

I have been trying to follow Charles' travels in the local newspapers and Harper's. It is not promising nor comforting what I see reported. It appears the 4th has been in battle the whole month of May, and they are on the move again. Charles writes, *"I hope this cruel war will end soon, for it is awful.* We find our family life is tense. We live day to day, pretending all is well. We really avoid discussing Charles, and our thoughts go largely unspoken and unshared. Our nights are long, lonely, and quiet. Mother prays much more than what was her custom. There is little joy in her life or in her demeanor. Emma's time is drawing closer; when there is a conversation in the house, it is among Harriet, Emma, and Rebecca. Rebecca's spirits are better than the rest, probably due to her youth. Still, she is not the joyous or mischievous child she once was. I am certain it is the concern for her brother, the seriousness of the family's situation, and the upcoming arrival of a niece or nephew.

JUNE 18, 1864 HARPER'S WEEKLY
GENERAL GRANT'S CAMPAIGN.

Meanwhile, Hancock had been no less successful in gaining the position he wanted. By noon he had pushed back a heavy skirmish line so close to their own works that Barlow's division planted Arnold's battery within 500 yards of a rebel battery. An artillery duel of an hour silenced the rebel guns first engaged but disclosed others right and left. During the evening, while Warren repelled an assault, Hancock made one. Barlow's division charged and carried a range of rebel rifle pits, thus advancing the left and center of the corps line equally with the right and cutting off an enfilading fire that might have troubled us. This advance was under cover of artillery fire of a dozen guns and eight Coehorn mortars.

Dear Mother,

I now take the pleasure to answer your letter. You see that I commenced this letter with ink, but my ink give out. Well, Mother I am well and hope that this letter will find you the same. I am most played out. It is awful hot down here and it is awful dry weather. We ain't had no rain for over a month and if we don't get some before long, I don't know what we will do for water, it is awful hard to get water now. Well Mother, I have been in another battle. The 18th of June we made a charge on a Rebel Works and got repulsed but we gained a half a mile in ground. The boys fell like hailstones all around me. I expected to go at any minute, but I got through clear. We lost 5,000 men in that charge. Oh, it was an awful sight. Well Mother, they talk about sending us back to Washington in the Fort, I hope they will. Well you must try and read this letter because it ain't wrote very good. I will write in a few days again. Send me the Waterford paper and put a couple of papers of tobacco in it. Well Mother, I will close for this time. May the Lord spare my life to meet once more. May the Lord bless you all. So, good-bye, a kiss.

Your loving son, Charles Shepard

Finally, some talk and discussion in our household. This letter awakened in us a sense that we needed to be able, once more, to let Charles back into our reality. For too long, we have sequestered our thoughts on Charles, and we were spiritually abandoning him. This letter when he can so easily relate; "The boys fell like hailstones around me, I expected to go any minute, but I got through clear. We lost 5000 men in that charge. Oh, it was an awful sight."* He then expressed to us his hopes of a future.

We all agreed that Charles was adjusting to his current situation, and if he could demonstrate feelings of hope, then it was our duty and obligation to share his feelings of hope within our family's activities.

Odd for such a letter that exposed, so vividly, the dangers and imminence of Charles's day-to-day life brought us some measure and understanding of his ability to cope with all that was about him. It is not possible for me to relate how our acceptance of Charles' current lifestyle has brought us peace as a family. We are talking and leading a normal life as a family, during these times, with a son in the military. We are not happy; we are all still very worried and concerned. We were not ignoring the situation; we were ignoring each other and our thoughts; this letter somehow brought us back together again.

Author's Note: This is the battle that Charles mentions in his letter.

June 18, 1864. With the arrival of Lee's two divisions under Maj. Gen. Joseph B. Kershaw and Charles W. Field, Beauregard had over 20,000 men to defend the city, but Grant's force had been augmented by the arrival of Maj. Gen. Gouverneur K. Warren's V Corps and 67,000 Federals were present. The first Union attack began at dawn, started by the II and XVIII Corps on the Union right. Hancock * began to suffer effects from his lingering Gettysburg wound, and he turned over command of the II Corps to Maj. Gen. David B. Birney. The men of the II Corps were surprised to make rapid progress against the Confederate line, not realizing that Beauregard had moved it back the night before. When they encountered the second line, the attack immediately ground to a halt, and the corps suffered under heavy Confederate fire for hours,

*On July 3, Hancock continued in his position on Cemetery Ridge and thus bore the brunt of Pickett's Charge. During the massive Confederate artillery bombardment that preceded the infantry assault, Hancock was prominent on horseback in reviewing and encouraging his troops. When one of his subordinates protested, "General, the corps commander ought not to risk his life that way," Hancock is said to have replied, "There are times when a corps commander's life does not count. During the infantry assault, his old friend, now Brig. Gen. Lewis A. Armistead, leading a brigade in Maj. Gen. George Pickett's division was wounded and died two days later. Hancock could not meet with his friend because he had just been wounded himself, a severe wound caused by a bullet striking the pommel of his saddle, entering his inner right thigh along with wood fragments and a large bent nail. Helped from his horse by aides and with a tourniquet applied to staunch the bleeding, he removed the saddle nail himself and, mistaking its source, remarked wryly, "They must be hard up for ammunition when they throw such shot as that. News of Armistead's mortal wounding was brought to Hancock by a member of his staff, Captain Henry H. Bingham. Despite his pain, Hancock refused evacuation to the rear until the battle was resolved. He had been an inspiration for his troops throughout the three-day battle. Hancock later received the thanks of the U.S. Congress for "… his gallant, meritorious and conspicuous share in that great and decisive victory. (38)

On Pickett in front of Perersburg, June 2, 1864

Dear Sister,

I received your kind letter and was glad to hear from you and to hear that you are all well. I am well and hope that

these few lines will find you the same. I was glad to get your likeness. It done me good, I tell you, I was eating my dinner and I would take it out almost every minute and say to myself, that is her. Now if I had Em's, and Mother's and Father's I would be a hunky boy. I showed it to some of the boys, and they said, "she is a good looking girl." Now let the rest send me theirs. I had hard work getting this paper. I can't get any more. Some of you must send me some and send in t some tobacco in the Waterford paper when they send it. There ain't much fighting now. Well Sister, it is most time to get supper, so I will close. I will write in a few days, Kiss Em for me. May the Lord bless and spare our lives until we meet again. Give my love to all. A kiss. Your Brother

Ch Shepard.

Just when we had come to terms with Charles and his war duties, we received this most welcome and comforting letter. This has been the greatest news in what feels like an eternity. You can feel a sense of relief in every room of our home. Our thoughts were open; most of the talk was on the anticipated arrival of the baby. Did I see some happiness in Emma's eyes? It is so hard to tell. We still don't know Emma. We try. These are not easy times. Charles is out of paper, but at least, *"They ain't much fighting now."*

Camp in front of Petersburg, June 29th

Dearest Mother,
I have got a half a sheet of paper and a poor lead pencil, so I will try and answer your letter. I was glad to hear that you

was all well. I am well and I hope this dirty paper will find you all the same. Suppose you will have a fine time up north for the fourth of July. I would like to be up there to enjoy it with you all but, I think I would hide myself in the cellar if they fired any firecrackers for I have gotten tired of hearing such noise. Well Mother, we are in summer quarters in the woods. It is a nice place.

We got a good chance to clean up. I am glad of it, I am so dirty that I hardly know myself. You can tell by this paper. I got Beck's likeness. It did me a great deal of good. Now, if I had Em's, and yours, and Fathers, I would be a hunky boy. Well Mother, I must close for my paper is getting short, send me some soon so I can write. Try and read this. God bless you, my love to all. I will write in a few days. I hope you will have a good time in New York. C. Shepard

These letters are making us more comfortable with each one's receipt. We had decided, even before receiving this letter, that the Fourth of July would be observed quietly by our family this year. Mother remembered how Charles and his friend Charlie Westover would love the crackers and candles on the 4th. (firecrackers and Roman candles)

Dear Sister,

It is with pleasure that I now take the pleasure to set myself on the ground in the woods to answer your most kind letter and was glad to hear that you are all well. I am well and fat and I hope this letter will find you all the same. Well Sister, I am putting a little extra in my letter. It is what I wear on my hat. It is the 2 Army Corp badge. It is called a club. Well, we are a club and a dirty one too, You would think so if you would see us. We look as if we had been drawed through a knot hole then rolled through the dust and put in a kettle and boiled. The weather is most hot. Every five minutes I take off my shirt and wring it and put it back on. All we have to do when we cook our dinner is put it out in the sun. In a little while our dinner will be cooked. Oh, talk about your comforts, you don't get it here. I had a bully breakfast this morning, soft bread, a piece of pork, had to pan it through the spider so the maggots would not run away with the fire and the spider. Had a coffee strong enough to kiss a nigger. Then to settle my breakfast took one of Uncle Sam's pills. Charlie Bandwell got sunstroke yesterday. Tell Em that Charles Westover is very sick and gone to the hospital. It is hard but it is honest, I have been a lucky fellow, had the Rebel bullet go through my hair. Oh, the varmint, if I could get a pop at him he would think that one of our nigger soldiers was after him. I saw the nigger corp pass yesterday. They was a good lot of soldiers. I saw your brother, he asked me how you were. I told him you were well, I showed him your picture and he said it looked just like you. Well Beck, I have written enough nonsense so I will close. There ain't much news of any importance in our front, but we expect to go to Washington for the Rebels are there. Well try and read this letter, give my love to all. I will write in a few days so good-bye. I took a dress from a Rebel Home, I will send it when I get back to Washington.

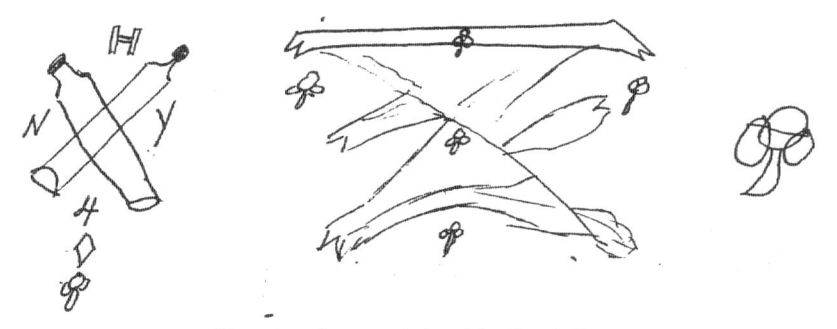

The drawing contained in the letter.

Author's note: This letter was in such poor condition that it was difficult to read during the 1960s transcription. It is thought that it was equally hard to read in the 1860s. They were written on dirty scraps of paper and stuck in an envelope. There are discrepancies in this letter. We usually don't see writing that leaves us to wonder. For example, he alludes to a rebel bullet passing through his hair and does not follow up with that story. He also makes reference to showing Rebecca's picture (likeness) to her brother. He is her only brother. Likely mistranscribed after the passing of 100 years. He also mentions a dress that he is going to send home. No one today has any knowledge of that happening. We also experience, for the second time, the overuse of the descriptive term" nigger." I strongly feel, yet have no way to substantiate, that this was a colloquialism rather than meant to be a derogatory term. When he alludes to the bullet incident. He mentions that if the shooter knew a nigger soldier was after him, he would be in trouble. He also states, "I saw the Nigger Corp pass yesterday; they were a good lot of soldiers." I have studied Charles for a number of years; I feel he used the terminology of the day to express his thoughts.

Petersburg, July 5, 1864

Dear Sister,

I now got a sheet of paper by trading my whiskey ration for it, so I will answer your kind letter and was glad to hear from you.

Dear Mother.....I am the Only One Left

I am well and hope this letter finds you the same. I suppose you all had a good time up north on the 4th. I hope you did. I had a good time in camp myself, hearing the firing of muskets and mortar shells at night. They go through the air at night. You would think it was a Roman candle. I don't like such Fourth of July's. I hope I will never see another in Virginia. Dear Sister if any of you want me to write, you must send me some paper. This is the last I will write until I get some paper for I can't get it for love or money. Charles Westover has gone to Washington, he is very sick. Tell Em, he fainted away. If he don't get good care, he will die. It is too bad, me and him and Charles Abby had always been together since we came out. Now Westover is gone and so is Abby, so I am the Lucky Boy. I have had good health. Well Beck, I think this outfit is going back to Washington when our hundred days are up and that is Wednesday the 7th. I hope we will because it has been the worst hundred days I ever had or ever go through again. I bet. Well, Mother has gone to New York I suppose. Well, I hope she has gone and will enjoy herself for she works hard and wants a good rest. She is a good Mother. Well Sister, I will close. Kiss Em and Father for me, my love to all, good-bye, Your Brother

Chas Shepard

We were aware that most battle units in the field would be relieved after 100 days at war. Charles was keeping track of the days, and we were too. Charles would have been surprised by the 4th of July celebrations now. Celebrations during the war were often lessened by the demands of battle. Crowds were smaller because most of the men were at war, and the firemen's processions were noticeably absent as well. Most in Waterford just could not identify a cause to celebrate. The atmosphere was more somber than usual.

An article in The New York Times described the July Fourth commemoration as akin to "the anniversary of a divorced couple's wedding."

John thought of the irony of the significance of the 4th of July. Naturally, the time-honored tradition of honoring our forefathers on this date in 1776, to the lesser-known July 4th in Rome, New York, in 1817, 50 years later of the event that would change his life. John was thinking back to that day on this 4th of July. It was on July 4, 1817, when the canal was starting to be built. Now 47 years later, John is completing some 25 years, a quarter of a century, of working on that canal. Largely, I have been successful, and we have looked forward to a bit of commemoration of the 4th. This year we will quietly give thanks that Charles is still safe and if when his 100 days of battlefield relief come due, he may remain so.

Petersburg, July 6, 1864

Dear Father,

I received the Waterford paper and some tobacco. You put on too many stamps, two was enough. Well Father, I am well and hope this will find you the same. It is very warm here today. We all lay in the shade, a panting away. Well Father, what kind of a time did you have up north? I hope a good one. I suppose that Mother went to New York and you and Em and Beck stayed home. Well I had the pleasure of being a Picket, shooting all day and once in a while a canon and at night mortar shells and the stars fall. That was my fireworks. Well Father, I begged this paper off one of the boys and had to do hard work to get it. Father, you get the Harper's Weekly Newspaper and look where the Handcock Corps is crossing the James River it looks just like it. You will see Handcock in a chair just as he sat in that chair by the riverside, and the Battery that you see, my Company built that Battery. The picture looks as natural as you were there yourself. You will see a Rebel Soldier in a corner of a fence, dead, that was killed on the 19th of May. I took some things out of his haversack. All of those pictures look just the same as if you were there yourself. Try to get it. Well, I suppose the Ewell Corps is up to Harper's Ferry. If he gets back to Richmond, he will be a smart man. The talk is we are going back to Washington in four or five days. We took 500 prisoners the other night. Well, I will close for this time. There ain't no news of any importance, so good-bye, my love to Em, Mother and Beck. I will write in a few days.

                    Your everloving Son,
                    Charles W. Shepard
                    Saratoga County

I hadn't realized until today that Charles is now a real soldier, his change from our boy to a war-hardened man is complete. His act of taking a dead soldier's contents of his haversack demonstrates not callousness to the deceased but self-preservation in the life of a field soldier whose life might depend on those contents. He seems to have adjusted completely now to being a soldier. I only hope he has hardened enough to enable him to survive.

P24 The dead soldier.

The picture John was instructed to see in Harper's Weekly.

P22 General Hancock in a chair

P23 The page that Charles refers to.

Dear Mother.....I am the Only One Left 113

I had been following Charles Company in Harper's and was quite taken that I could see what Charles had seen and was writing about. The activities of this war became very real.

(written in margin of the letter: This paper is dirty and so am I. I will bet you an arm, you can't read this.)

Petersburg, July 10, 1864

Dear Mother,

It is with pleasure I sit myself on the ground, under a big pine tree to let you all know I am well and in good health and fat as a pig. I hope these few lines will find you well. I am on Picket and its most time to be relieved. I enjoy the picket on Sunday, reading my Bible. I wish I was home to enjoy it instead of on picket. Well Mother, my friend Charly Westover, is very sick and has gone to the hospital. He was very sick. It is awfully hot here. The flies bother me so I can hardly write. I hope you had a good time in New York. Oh dear, how the flies does bother me. They keep my hand a going all the time. Never mind, next winter should bring me out of this thing. I hope. So far, I am tired of it. I have seen enough of war to go home, settle down and be contented, I bet, along with every other man, I reckon. Well Mother, there ain't any news of any importance. Most every morning the Rebels make a charge on our right lines. They think that we are gone, but they get slipped up on it. They think we have gone after Ewell. If the Rebel General ever gets back to Richmond, he's a smart man, if he don't get gobbled up it will be a wonder to me. We are going back to Washington in a few days. We think they *will have to send us back. We thought we would go to City Point last night, but we ain't gone yet. Tell Father I got the paper with the tobacco in it. I must close now for it is time to be relieved. I hope this letter will find you all well and in good spirits. My love to Em, Beck, Father, GrandMother and Grandfather and all the rest of the folks. A kiss to all. Oh, how I would like to see you all, I will before many days. I will close, good-bye and God bless you all.*

Your Son, Charles
The Union Forever

After the letter, when Charles wrote of a rebel bullet going through his hair, Mother returned, once again, to not reading her letters. I would either tell her of the contents or suggest that she read it herself. In either case, as in the past, I would leave the letter upon the table should she decide to read it herself. I never noticed her reading them, nor did we ever discuss them further. It is good to read the continuing theme of returning to Washington soon. This move would add greatly to Charles' safety and help ease our minds. At this time, a quick return to Washington is uppermost in our nightly prayers. Mother is always most pleased to hear of Charles keeping faith in his bible readings.

Chapter 7

THE BABY AND THE MEETING AT THE MORGAN HOUSE

The anticipation at home is great right now; Emma is due to deliver very soon. Harriet suggests I look for a tow today that will keep me busy and away for a bit. She knows I am not much help in these matters. Today is a normal Rock Island Flour Mill tow; maybe I can find something later in the day. Deriving some level of comfort with the idea of Charles perhaps returning to the relative safety of Washington and the impending birth of a grandchild, John realizes that he has not felt so joyful in many a month. Perhaps after completing his first tow. he will have a look in at the Morgan House; maybe some of the Knickerbockers will be about. He also realized it had been a long time since he had allowed himself any frivolous thoughts. He also thought of Mary and Harriet. He hadn't in a while. He had petitioned them to look after their brother. It seemed they had. Lord knows Charles has been in almost constant danger, the men falling around him like hail, bullets passing through his hair, and who knows what else. Charles was being protected thus far. And, with this impending birth, wouldn't one's natural instincts remember the most recent births? John was stopped short in his thoughts at this point. When Charles and Rebecca were born, John was still involved in longer towing, which might keep him away for several days at a time. When Mary and Harriet were born, John was there. Charles and Rebecca were easy births; with Mary and Harriet, there were some difficulties, and John didn't know what it was. Is this the reason that Harriet suggested I stay busy today?

My tow to the West Troy Weigh Lock was without event today. Was it a fast trip? My mind was racing. Usually. my thoughts when working the towpath comes in a relaxed cadence as tempered as the walk itself. Today, my thoughts were jumping all about within my mind, breaking my concentration and not appearing in any organized manner. Before I realized it, the day had turned mid-afternoon, and I was headed back to Waterford with a Rock Island light boat. The day was a blur. I can't remember ever having had such a day. After delivering the Rock Island Boat to Mr. Enos, owner of the mill, we spoke briefly of the day's events. It was about three hours past noon as I made my way north on the towpath back to the village. Mentally and physically, I became relaxed. I realized that I had not experienced feeling relaxed in some time and hadn't noticed my lack of being relaxed until now. It was a beneficial feeling that had taken control of me. I felt pleasant and free. It would be a good time to heed Harriet's advice. Soon I was back to the Waterford Side Cuts. There is always a collection of canal people gathered there. I lingered awhile, which is not my custom; the conversation was pleasant; of course, the length of the current rebellion is always a major topic. After the mules had grazed a bit, the men at the locks became busy, and our talk had run its course; I elected to return the mules to their stable. From the stables, I could glance up towards our home; I could sense it would be best to keep my distance. After securing the mules and seeing to their comfort, I decided a walk up to the new Weigh Lock near home would be in order. This was the second full year of operation of the Weigh Lock, built-in '62 and opened in '63. He had become friends with Abraham Brewster and Henry Van Denburgh, Canal Collector and Weigh Master at the Weigh Lock. John always felt comfortable on the canal and in the company of fellow canallers. They all, Abe, Henry, and John, agreed that the folks whose towing experience was on the Champlain Canal seemed to be a closer community of canallers than those who used the Erie. The thought and conversation were that because the Champlain was only 60 some miles, compared to the Erie's 360 plus. Those on the Champlain just had the opportunity to see each other more often and therefore become more familiar. During the conversation at the Weigh

Lock, John had mentioned the circumstances of the impending arrival of his first grandchild and Harriet's superstitious wishes that he, perhaps, should recuse himself. Abe, already a grandfather, suggested that the two should "Take advantage of the amenities offered nightly at the Morgan House." He continued that a good meal and a few libations should be in order on an evening such as this. John could offer no arguments; he had similar thoughts this morning before those thoughts became too fast to comprehend. He was enjoying his feelings of being relaxed and his freedom of mind; to spend an early evening with a noble canaller would be in order. John noted that the Knickerbockers always referred to The Morgan House as Morgan Hall while most other Waterfordians would call it The Morgan House. Perhaps because the Knickerbockers considered it a meeting place for both business and celebration, the general public leaned toward the more formal terminology of a finer establishment. Among the curiosities of the village, this was certainly one, Hall to firemen and house to the general public. Again, John's thoughts were becoming frivolous, a welcome relief from where his thoughts had been for the last several months.

The Morgan House was not far from the Weigh Lock, a walk of fewer than five minutes. John could not remember the last time he had walked the village streets for such a purpose as enjoying a meal with a fellow canaller. He had walked the streets many a time, but usually to fill a need. Perhaps to attend church service, a visit to the bank, or certainly to post a letter, more so now than ever, with Charles being away. But never to visit the Morgan House just for the pleasure of the visit. The streets were busy; people greeted one another as they passed and met. It seemed that John's good spirits were being shared and reflected by all that he met that day. When they arrived and entered, John was pleased to see that there were many in attendance that he knew, although not a Knickerbocker in the lot. John had always wished that he had accompanied the Knicks to the Morgan House a few years back when he had provided their tow to the fair. That was a happy day; today is a happy day.

As Abe was a frequent visitor to the Morgan House, I followed his advice and chose baked pork chops for our repast. At the same time, I thought to myself, for such an elegant house, this is a traditional canallers meal. A little different, perhaps, than the meals we used to share years ago when I was still doing trip towing. That was when I would tow to Glens Falls, Fort Edward, Whitehall, and other locations on the Champlain and take my meals with the boatman. The standard fare was usually fried pork chops with boiled vegetables, generally potatoes, and carrots. Here we are in the comforts of the Morgan House, and our meat and potatoes are baked, still a canallers meal and a good one at that. The conversation during dinner was pleasant. Abe, as Canal Collector at Waterford, had many stories to tell. Of course, the Weigh Lock was still brand new to the canallers and was not liked by all, and it did add time to the canal trip, especially if traffic was heavy. Prior to 1863, the collection of tolls had been lax here and sometimes avoided altogether. There was talk among the boatman, John had heard it often, that Waterford's scales and weighing system were not in the boatman's favor. It was ironic that our coins now said "In God We Trust" on them; up to 1864, they hadn't borne that inscription. Many boatmen were heard to utter, "In God We Trust, but not the Waterford Scale." Abe liked to talk often of the following story; although I was not there at the time, I felt like I was from hearing the tale told so often.

As reported in the Albany Argus, June, 1863.
> William Cain, aged about ten years, fell into the weigh-lock of the canal at Waterford, New York, Saturday, at the moment it was being exhausted preparatory to weighing a boat. He was drawn in an instant down through the heavy timbers of the scales, and shot out with lightening-like rapidity by the rushing current, passing under the canal bank through a tunnel about one hundred feet long, and then over a fall of ten feet into the open stream. The bystanders had gathered on the bank, ecpecting to see his lifeless body crushed

and floating down towards the Hudson, when he suddenly emerged and crawled up the hill unhurt. When asked what he thought while coming through the tunnel, he replied that he thought he would be in the river in about a minute.

It was common at the Morgan House for the gentlemen to assemble on the porch after a meal to enjoy a pipe or a cigar along with after-dinner cordials and discuss the news and events of the day. John had heard of such assemblies, but he had never been afforded the opportunity to participate. After all, this is the canal season; this is the time to work. He supposed that if Harriet is correct and our grandchild comes into this world on this evening, he would not take any tows tomorrow anyway. He decided to enjoy the conversations no matter how long they lasted. What a distinguished assemblage it was. John Cramer, it is said, is always in attendance, even harking back to the days of the Demarest Hotel, a predecessor of the Morgan House. Mr. Cramer, John remembered, both solicited and contributed much of the funding for the 22nd Regiment back in '61. The first Town Supervisor in 1816 and very active in government affairs. He is the senior and probably the most learned and experienced in this group and was always allowed the courtesy of the floor. A gifted speaker, one would want to be attentive when he spoke. Luke Kavanaugh of the Bishopton Knitting Mills joined the group on the porch. Luke was a man of science and engineering. He had just been awarded another patent for improving the blades and needles on his knitting machines. Some years back, Luke had emigrated from Ireland. He had been dining with James Dodge, his Company of Dodge & Blake had also just been awarded a patent for the machinery which would polish and grind cutlery. Along with Abraham, the canal collector, and John were several of the local village merchants, John Titcomb, a village trustee, and several others with political affiliations or ambitions. John felt somewhat out of place and decided he would listen to the conversations and, in all likelihood, would refrain from active participation.

John observed that Mr. Cramer seemed to be the unchallenged leader of the conversation topics. Whenever there was a lull or break in discussions, and there weren't many, it would be John Cramer who would set the stage for the next discussion. He is an astonishing man when you consider his age and state of abilities; I believe that he is 83 years old at this time. Although no conversations were heated, different sides of topics would be discussed. John was surprised and pleased by the decorum of these men as they voiced their varied opinions on the news of the day. The first topic was merely the pleasantness not only of the evening but of the gentlemen in attendance as well. My new friend Abraham had affected my introduction to these gentlemen, and I wondered how he had endeared himself so quickly to a group such as this. With the Weigh Lock being a relatively new avenue of commerce, he just hadn't been around long enough to make such contacts. Of course, I hadn't realized then how well-connected politically one had to be to be appointed a Canal Collector.

Early subjects that most were in agreement on were the favorable level of business activity in the village and the traffic on the canals. It was satisfying to me and encouraged me to feel less out of place to hear canal activity as a topic on which no one had any negative feelings. Mr. Titcomb stated that one might judge the business climate in the village by watching the traffic and trade on the canals. Mr. Cramer was quick to verify and emphasized that we young folk don't have the appreciation we should for the canal; he feels that everyone takes it for granted. When John was the first Supervisor for the newly formed Town of Waterford in 1816, there was no canal. It pleased me to hear Mr. Cramer say that. I immediately thought back to Old J. C. Rice up in Mechanicville and my recent talk with him. A thought on the canals that I had never heard expressed before was put forth by Abraham when he theorized that the canal would likely influence the outcome of the current rebellion. I can't remember all the details. His theory was that this was a war of attrition, both of war supplies, food for the army, munitions, and the most common denominator for all wars; the soldiers to do the fighting. In Abraham's mind, the North had the most of all three and could move them from place to place more efficiently thanks to the canals. Mr. Cramer quickly offered in agreement with Abraham's theory and offered his update on the activities of the war.

Make no mistake about it; boys said John Cramer; this is not a rebellion; this is a war and a damnable one at that. At first, I was quite taken by his knowledge of the facts of the war up to this time. I was trying to keep current on information as best I could, but my knowledge of the activity paled in comparison to his. I listened intently. I had hoped the war and the fighting would not be a topic, but it was inevitable at a gathering of concerned gentlemen that it would. Luke Kavanaugh chimed in with a request for the recognition of his fellow Irishmen and their contributions to the war effort. Mr. Dodge suggested a toast to the Irishmen and to the success of the Union. It was at this point that I realized that I was so intent on listening to these men speak that I had not yet succumbed to the temptation of my drink. Yes, a toast was in order. I also thought back to the Knickerbockers and their Three Cheers and a Tiger toasting at the Morgan House and how they adjourned as they got drunk weary. I must be careful that that is not my fate tonight.

Either the toasting or the subject of the war had loosened Mr. Dodge's tongue. He began to relate the trials of his nephew Peter. At first, it was something I didn't care to hear, and then I was to become spellbound.

His nephew was not a young man, 40 when he enlisted in 1862 and made a Sergeant very quickly. Peter was from the West Farm, section of Bronx, New York, which was also home to James before his business brought him to Cohoes, and he is now residing in Waterford. He had answered the call in August of 1862 and was a member of the 6th Artillery. As he stated this, I was taking solace in the comfort of the remainder of my drink and was temporarily not paying full attention until he mentioned 6th Artillery, Charles is in the 4th; suddenly, my attention was in order. Mr. Dodge went on to report on their activities;

The Wilderness Campaign, Spotsylvania, North Anna, Totopotomoy, Cold Harbor, Petersburg, and Richmond.

These were all the same places and battles that Charles wrote about in his letters. He claimed to have news stating that the 6th artillery has suffered less than 50 casualties in the last two years, far less than an Infantry Regiment. John had supposed this to be true with Charles Regiment as well. John found some fraternity by spending time with someone whose kin were experiencing like events.

Not to be outdone and further proof of how prepared and knowledgeable Mr. Cramer is, he removes from his ever-present cache of papers a newspaper from Canandaigua, New York, and reads the following resolution.

CAMP 4th N. Y. ARTILLERY,
(Near Petersburg, Va.) July 9, 1864

We, the undersigned, members of Company M: 4th N. Y. Artillery, desire to express our deep sympathy and grief at the death of our late friend and brother soldier, Edwin O. Gates. Sergeant Co. M., who died at Chestnut Hill Hospital, Philadelphia, July 1st, from wounds, received at Cold Harbor, Va., submit the following resolutions:

Resolved, That while we would not question the dealings of that Province which has removed so dear a friend from among us, but would bow at all times in humble submission to the will of our Heavenly Father, yet we can but feel the heaviness of the blow which came upon us by the tidings of his death.

II. That in his early death, we lose the companionship of one whose manly qualities and moral worth as a Christian and patriot soldier endeared him, not only to his near friends and associates in his own company, both officers and men but to all who knew him in the regiment, and that on our course from the Rapidan up to the day he was wounded, on the fatiguing march through depths of mud or clouds of dust, beneath a burning sun or exposed to the enemy's fire, in every duty he bore himself with fortitude and courage worthy the emulation of a veteran,

III. That we extend our heartfelt sorrow and deepest sympathy to those who mourn, and especially would we bare our heads and share his mother's grief in this the hour of her sore affliction, but would submit to Him who "doeth all things well," the duty of Comforter, knowing that God will wipe away all tears. He died as he had lived, true to himself, his country, and his God.

IV. That a copy of these resolutions be sent for publication to each of the Canandaigua papers. Also, a copy is forwarded to the family of the deceased.

*Signed, Sergeant N. CLARK PARSHALL,
and 13 other Officers of CO'S M. AND C.*

Mr. Cramer concluded by stating that men who are able to put pen to words and expressions such as these should not be at war. There must be a greater calling for them than war. With that, he offered a toast to the success and safety of our soldiers. This toast also emptied his glass, as it did mine. I marveled at his timing as he announced that due to the lateness of the hour, the advancement of my age, and the emptiness of my glass, I shall take my leave. With that, he bid us all good evening. Soon all had excused themselves to return to their respective homes. I thanked Abraham for an evening well spent and departed for Sixth St. The time had quickly passed; it was nearly nine in the evening. This has been a very pleasant but very long day. I wonder what excitement there will be at home?

Chapter 8

THE BABY ARRIVES

I strolled up Broad St. towards home at a very casual pace. I had enjoyed this evening; I must find time to participate again. The streets were much quieter now; very few were about. The light was all gone, but the lamplighter had made his rounds. I hope my requested absence from home has run its course and I am free to return. John visited the Grogh St. stable to look in on the mules, not a normal practice, to delay his inevitable return to the house. Soon there, he paused for a moment and assessed his surroundings. Sometimes, when something is wrong, a person can sense that all is not right. I don't think that anyone can explain that; you just can. Maybe, some call it a premonition. In my experience, I seem to have the presence of a bad omen but no forewarning of good events. My pause was favorable; there was no ill will in the air. Things did seem quiet, though. I decided to use my key quietly and not announce my arrival.

    Harriet greeted me with a smile on her face and, at the same time, a finger to her lips, urging me to be quiet. Late this afternoon, Harriet had figured about 4 pm, Emma had delivered a baby girl. She had experienced a difficult delivery and was now resting comfortably. Rebecca is thrilled and in awe; she is sitting with the baby upstairs with Emma. Dr. Heart had been summoned and had left within the last hour. He had reported to Harriet that all was well; Emma would need a few days' rest until she was back on her feet. No one has expressed thoughts about naming the baby; Emma wants to consult with Charles, so she will remain unnamed for a while.

Petersburg, July 18, 1864

Dear Mother,

    It is with pleasure I write to you to let you know that I am well and that this letter finds you the same. It is quite pleasant here this morning. When I first got up, it looked like rain. I was in hopes it would rain for we need it very bad. We ain't had no rain for a long time. In the road it is awful. Well. we had preaching in the camp today by our Chaplain. He preached a good sermon. He gave us all a paper to read. He is a good man. He talks to the soldiers and tries to do them good. We are going to be paid off days, I will send it all home. How does Em get along for money? She wont tell me rather she's got any or not. I hope she has enough until I get paid. What is the name? Tell Em I think of the baby often. Oh Mother, if I ever get in Waterford, I'll know enough to stay there. I bet there will be a great many boys that will know how to appreciate a home once they get there. There was a boy in my Company the other night, the band was playing "Who Will Care For Mother Now?" and he commenced to cry.

    He said , if it wasn't for that tune, I never would have enlisted. Poor boy. In one of our hospitals there was a boy who got wounded, he was dying. He called the chaplain to his side and told him to write to his mother and tell her that all was well, and then he died. Oh. how happy that mother must have been to know that her son died happy. May the Lord have mercy on our soldiers for there are a great many bad ones. Charlie Westover has gone to the hospital, he was very sick. He will go home on *furlough when he gets better. Mother. I wish you would see that Emma gets everything she wants and when I come home, I will make it right. Mother. I will close for now, don't forget me.*

Tell Em I forgot to put my picture in her letter, I will send it next time. Kiss the baby for me. Your Son, Charles.

Charles mentions the band played "Who will care for Mother Now?"

P25 "During one of our late battles, among many other noble fellows that fell, was a young man who had been the only support of an aged and sick mother for years. Hearing the surgeon tell those who were near him that he could not live, he placed his hand across his forehead and, with a trembling voice, said, while burning tears ran down his fevered cheeks: Who will care for Mother now?"

1.
Why am I so weak and weary?
See how faint my heated breath,
All around to me seems darkness.
Tell me, comrades, is this death?
Ah! how well I know your answer;
To my fate, I meekly bow.
If you'll only tell me truly
Who will care for Mother now?

CHORUS [sung after each verse:]
Soon with angels, I'll be marching,
With bright laurels on my brow.
I have, for my country fallen,
Who will care for Mother now?

Dear Mother.....I am the Only One Left

2.
Who will comfort her in sorrow?
Who will dry the falling tear,
Gently smooth her wrinkled forehead?
Who will whisper words of cheer?
Even now, I think I see her
Kneeling, praying for me! How
Can I leave her in her anguish?
Who will care for Mother now?

3.
Let this knapsack be my pillow,
And my mantle be the sky;
Hasten, comrades, to the battle,
I will like a soldier die.
Soon with angels. I'll be marching,
With bright laurels on my brow,
I have, for my country fallen,
Who will care for Mother now? (39)

    This letter confuses me. We have told Charles about the birth of his daughter, and he barely mentions the occasion in his letter. He writes of the weather, the lack of rain, and the Preacher's sermon. He expresses concern for some of his fellow soldier's behavior and payroll, all before any thoughts of Emma or the baby. He is asking us for the baby's name. We have requested him to suggest a name; we are still calling her the Baby. He does show concern for Emma's care and welfare, but his thoughts expressed in his writing sound as tormenting to him as mine often are to me. I found his references to dying happy, his homesickness, and yet his confidence that he would return home very troublesome and conflicting thoughts. I think this war may be wearing on Charles. I had been feeling quite well about the events of the past several days. I believe when your child is at war, there are no good days until that day when they return.

Petersburg, July 21, 1864

Dear Father,

I received a letter from you and I was happy to hear that you are all well. I hope this letter will find you all well. I am well and fat. Well Father, I seen John Halpin of the 115th Regiment, tell his father he is well. I will go see the rest of the Waterford boys. They are in the 18 Corps. They are about one mile from our camp. Night befor last, I was to work on forts. I seen Edward White, he is well. The Vanderwerken boys are well. Jerry Welch has gone to the hospital, he was sick. We have had a nice rain down here. Suppose you had some rain up north this time. I hope so. If you could see your son, you would hardly know me, fat, dirty and tall, I have grown like fun since I left home. A great many of the boys said I would cave in on the first long march but they got slipped up on it. I have led them very ones on marches and tuckered them out on our marches. They don't say any more about marching. Well Father. There ain't much news of any importance that I know of. I got the Waterford paper with the tobacco in it. Well I will close for this time, I got your picture, it is very good. My love to all, good-bye. Your Son,

*   Charles Shepard*
*   Co. H 4th NYV*
*   Heavy Artillery*

This letter starts out very favorable and informative. I will be pleased to tell our Pine St. neighbor Bob Halpin that his son is well and that he and Charles have spoken. The Vanderwerken boys and the others he has met up with from Waterford are all very good to read. I hope his nonsensical talk of marching and growing taller is evidence of Charles's humor. His humor is lacking in our lives as well as in his recent letters. His words concerning the Rebel in their lines, I don't know if he is using army talk about this; I don't know what he means. It does bother me that there is no mention of the baby nor any name suggestion. I hope Charles still has a good hold of himself. I am hoping for Charles' safe return one day. Until now, I had never entertained a thought as to how surviving a war may change a person.

Petersburg, July 25, 1864

Dear Father,

It is with much pleasure that I now take time to write you a few lines, to let you know I am well and I hope this letter will find you all the same, but not so hungry. Sunday morning, about 4 o'clock, we were called up to work on a fort. We did not have no time to get something to eat so we went and worked till noon. Then there was a loaf of bread fed to you. We came into Camp about 7 o'clock and we was so tired we didn't get anything till this morning, so I feel much better, I seen Edward White, William Coones and the two Vanderwerken boys, they are all well. Their Regiment is going to Washington in a day or two. They feel quite good over it, we are building a big fort for our Regiment. I was out in the front lines and I could see the Rebs walking about their works, looking in on our lines once in a while. They will get a lot of them together and then our artillery will let fly on them. They get down quick. I came across Billy Johnson. He belongs to the 44th NY Regiment. He works for Ben Murry. Perhaps you don't remember him and John Timbrooke. They are all well. I came across someone from Waterford almost everyday. I seen John Halpin, tell his father he is well. It rained hard here last night. There ain't much fighting on our front. Along the 9th Corps the Pickets are firing all the time. They are undermining the Rebel Forts. I expect to wake up some fine morning and hear the greatest noise that I ever heard in my life.

My Regiment still lays back in the woods. I should like to stay back until the war is over. Well, I suppose now that Atlanta has been taken by Sherman, I hope he will capture the whole Johnson forces. I was sorry to hear that Uncle Abrams is dead, poor Aunt Rebecca. What will she do? I hope she can get North. Well Father, I will close for this time. My love to all, I will write in a few days. My love to you and all. Good-bye. Your Loving Son,

Charles Shepard

This is more cause for concern, four days have passed, and he writes again some of the very things he related on the 21st. There is still no mention of the baby, let alone a name. He mentions, "I expect to wake up some fine morning and hear the greatest noise that I ever heard in my life." I don't know what that means, maybe a celebration that the war is over? He did demonstrate concern and remorse for his Uncle's death and his Aunt's situation living in the South. He also mentions Sherman taking Atlanta. After John's night of participation with the gentlemen of the Morgan House, he had been paying closer heed to the war activities. Prior to that evening. he was only following those events that Charles had written about. Now he would read all that would become available in print, as well as what became available on the canal. He knew that the campaign for Atlanta was going well but was far from completion.

Sherman was assigned the mission of defeating Johnston's army, capturing Atlanta and striking through Georgia and the Confederate heartland.

> *Grant stood by me when I was crazy, and I stood by him when he was drunk, and now we stand by each other.* (40)

William Tecumseh Sherman (8 February 1820 – 14 February 1891) was a United States Army general during the American Civil War. He succeeded General Ulysses S. Grant as commander of the Western Theater of that war in the spring of 1864. He later served as Commanding General of the U.S. Army from 1869 to 1883. He is best known for his "March to the Sea" through the U.S. state of Georgia, that destroyed a large amount of Confederate infrastructure. He is widely regarded by historians as an early advocate of "Total War" (41)

P26 General William Tecumseh Sherman.

Petersburg, July 28, 1864

Dear Mother,

I received your most kind letter and was happy to hear from home. I am well and I hope this letter will find you the same. It has been very warm for the last 4 or 5 days. My Regiment has been building forts. We go out to work every day and we work ten hours until we get them done. Well Mother, I suppose that you know, my friend Charlie Westover is dead. He died on his way to New York, so Mr. Mayhew said. He got a letter from home that said he was dead. Well Mother, I can say one thing, he was a good boy, he read his Bible and was a good boy, He was liked by all in the Company. The last time I seen Charlie, I went out to the ambulance and helped him in the wagon and bid him good-bye. I told him to take good care of himself and when he got better to write me. He said he would but I never got a letter so I thought he was worse. Poor boy, he died happy. The Lord only knows what will become of us. I trust in the Lord that my life will be spared to return home. Well Mother, I was out to work yesterday on the front and the Rebels threw a mortar shell in the breastworks the 118th Regiment was in and killed one man and wounded three others. Blowed one man 30 feet in the air, and the leg off another. It was awful, it was the worst thing I have seen since I have been out here. There is only a few of my Company in camp today. I got excused from duty today. The boys that I did tent with at Culpepr, I am the only one left. They are sick, in the hospital, killed or wounded. The 2 Army Corp is gone away for parts unknown. They was ordered to take badges off their caps and if any of them were taken prisoner not to tell what Corps they belonged to. Well Mother. I will close for this time. We expect to get 4 months pay any day. I will write to Em and Beck on my next chance.

This letter was a setback to Mother. I believe a new baby in the house is refreshing her thoughts of Mary and little Harriet. It appears that Charles has arrived at the realization that his time could end. *"I trust in the Lord that my life may be spared to return home."* It was sad to learn of Charlie Westover. He and Charles were such good friends. He writes that all his new friends are now gone, sick, wounded, or dead. John could hear that haunting refrain from the letter of Lawrence Vanderweken to the Knickerbockers.

I pray that the time when you shall again be called upon to officiate at so sad a ceremony, maybe far distant.

This time, John gave no thought to the Great Fire, just the Great War.

I felt a need to take a longer tow tomorrow, a good long tow, and be on my own. He had come more and more to seek the sanity and the sanctity of the canal and its towpath. He enjoyed his time on the canal. There, one can be alone with the mules and his thoughts.

Those you did meet were headed in the opposing direction and had no time or desire to engage socially. If someone wanted to interact with their fellow canallers, there was usually ample opportunity at the locks, line barns, or canalside communities. It was a safe and familiar environment for John; he was well-known, respected, and liked. He had earned these accolades by his actions and held most with the same regard shown to him. A good long tow was definitely in order. The next day when I retrieved the mules, I could see several canal boats made fast along the wall at Broad St. This was unusual. I soon learned that there was a problem north of Mechanicville, and a section was being drained for repair. No one knew why we never did until after it was over. We would hear plenty of reports, though. Traffic was still traveling south, but nothing was going north. I was hoping to go north for a good stretch. There was plenty of activity at the Side Cut Locks. It was determined that they would lock down to the river all southbound traffic as it arrived. There were about 30 canal boats at the battery. As time and space allowed, they would be let in to line up for the Waterford Weigh Lock, but there would be no northbound traffic until the existing block to navigation was satisfied. Word was received at the Waterford Side Cuts from one of the late canalers yesterday of a slowdown to navigation. As more canalers arrived from the north, many conflicting stories were related; low water, the integrity of a canal bank, sunken boats. To whom do you listen? What mattered was there would be no towing for John today.

Many of the problems encountered in improving the Champlain Canal stemmed from its original design. Canal boatmen claimed that the canal was built about as crooked as a corkscrew. The canal's original engineers were under the misguided notion that if the canal were made straight, the current would be too strong for the upstream boats to make any headway. As a result, the canal was made as nearly the reverse of straight as possible with sharp bends that collected sediment, reducing the depth and width of the canal prism. This situation made it nearly impossible to maintain consistent depth and width in the canal prism. (42)

GENERAL REMARKS. Champlain Canal. Parish lock has been constructed during the past two years and was brought into use in the past season. It was constructed on the enlarged and improved plan and is a permanent and reliable structure. Fort Edward lock is now under contract for reconstruction, and there still remain nine other locks upon this canal that are yet unenlarged. They are all old and are, in greater or lesser degrees, out of repair, and it is doubtful whether some of them will last another year. All of them should be rebuilt at the earliest possible period. The greatly increasing business of this canal, at the present time, when other canals are falling off in the number of tolls received from them, fully warrants and really demands the expenditure for that purpose. (43)

Author's Note: The above accounts may have been the reason or contributing factors for the holdup and delay on this day.

Although he wanted some solitude today, he found himself at the Weigh Lock with his friend Abraham. He had returned the mules to their stable; he did not want to go home. The Weigh Lock was very close to John's home. *If I can't be alone with my thoughts, I may as well be in the company of canallers.* The Weigh Lock was a natural gathering spot when traffic was tied up. As expected in these situations, the crowd in attendance all had tales to tell and opinions on the news. Too often, though, in these times, the talk seems always to lean toward the conflict between North and South. The discussions always seemed to be most intense when the subject was the length of the war, the number of casualties and was either side winning. John liked to hear all the theories on why the canal was closed. Eventually, he would find out the reason, either through a newspaper or in several days on the towpath, as the real story became common knowledge and spread. John was usually amused by how far astray from the truth of the actual reason for the closing was. John didn't contribute much to the conversation that day; he was happy just to be among his peers and to feel safe and comfortable. He noticed another man there, who also had little to say. William Brewster was the man's name; he was a clerk at the Weigh Lock, and he was Abe's son. He seemed to be about 30 years old. Abe also had an 18-year old son named Daniel. The younger of the two did not appear to be employed or apprenticed and looked to be of sound mind and body. John recalled learning that night at the Morgan House that one needed to have some proper connections to win the appointment as Canal Collector. John and Abraham had become friends due to their mutual activities at the Weigh Lock. John hadn't known his new friend for a long time and really knew little of his background. He has heard from the canal boatmen that those who hold Canal Collectors positions on the canal are often able to take advantage of that post for their personal well-being. Now he discovers that one of Abe's sons is employed there as well. John has heard the complaints of the boatmen in regard to unfair or unjust tolls, but he has always dismissed it as a universal complaint loosely based on fact. One of those things that supposedly everyone knows is happening, yet, no one can prove it. John, as a trip mule driver, did not pay tolls; he had no experience with it. He liked Abe but couldn't get the well-connected theory out of his mind. What about William and Daniel, Abe's sons? Why were they not among the rest of the Waterford Boys off to war? Was Abraham that connected? Had he paid for replacements for them? Maybe they gambled that Waterford would meet her quota, as it did, so they would not be drafted. If Charles had elected to exercise that option, he might have been a civilian yet. Charles didn't even consider it; he did not want others thinking of him, what I am now thinking of the Brewsters. John had heard of some families paying for a substitute but was unaware of any. I have always felt that Charles enlisted, not out of fear of the draft or concern for what others may think, but for the financial incentive to help pay for the empty lot near our home.

While working on the canal, newspapers from around the state would sometimes become available. John had seen several, especially from the Buffalo and Poughkeepsie papers. These accounts demonstrated the money that could be had for enlisting and the ability to provide a substitute.

VOLUNTEERS WANTED!

To New Recruits
$690 00.
TO VETERANS,
$865 00.
$300 Cash paid down!

JNO. C. PUDNEY,
Recruiting Agent, City Hall, Poughkeepsie

> **PREPARE FOR THE DRAFT.**—The undersigned have constantly on hand Aliens for Substitutes at low prices. Principals will save money by calling immediately at No. 158 Main street, Buffalo, up stairs.
> de9t22   LEWIS S. CLAPP & CO.

P28

This day had not developed as planned. John had hoped for a long trip on the canal in relative solitude to come to terms with all that was about his life at this time. Charles, the war, the yet unnamed baby, and all this has brought daughters Mary and Harriet to the forefront of his now very mixed thoughts. Now he had, perhaps jealous or maybe envious, thoughts that his new friend Abraham somehow had the means to exempt or buy out his son's military duty. John found all of this very disturbing. The walk home was very short from the Weigh Lock. I will have to find myself in better spirits before I arrive at 6th St. Suddenly, the name Charlene mysteriously violated John's attempts to lift his spirits. It amused him; he felt better; perhaps I will suggest that tonight, he knew he wouldn't.

Chapter 9

THE DARK DAYS BEGIN

Charles departed from Cohoes on December 29th. It was August 4th when we received the next letter. He had been away from us for more than 220 days now. It feels like he has been gone for an eternity; sometimes, it feels like it was yesterday. The passage of time, like many other normal experiences, no longer occurs in any sense. We have attempted to prepare ourselves and adapt to our new family situation. At home, within our own walls, there exists no method to cope with these issues. We, as well as Charles, have trusted in the Lord to guide us through this. After absorbing this letter into our thoughts, we independently arrived at the realization that Charles was in dark times. No one expressed these thoughts to each other, but we all knew it.

Dear Mother,

I received your most kind letter and was glad to hear that you were all well, but Em. I hope she is not very sick, quite a prize. I am glad it is so pretty as you tell about. I would like to see it myself. Kiss it for me 3 or 4 times. Well Mother, your letter didn't find me very well. I have been in another awful battle. Friday night my outfit was detailed to go up to a fort in the front. The name of the Fort was Fort Tilton. You might see the name of that Fort in the papers for it done great damage. About 5 o'clock Saturday morning we were called up to get ready so while the Captain was waking the rest up I got up on the Fort and was looking down on the Rebel lines. Oh. Mother, I had been up there about a minute before I saw a Rebel Fort going up in the air. Oh. it was an awful fight, I tell you. The Fort hadn't been blown up a second, when the Artillery began to throw solid shot and shell from both sides. It was one of the hottest places I have ever been. It blowed up about 2000 Rebels. Oh, it was awful. Our men made a charge of their works drove them out. Then the Rebels masses their Troops together, drove them back. Well, we made another charge and did the same. There was charge after charge made on both sides. Oh Mother, there will be a many poor mother or wife hear of their sons or husbands got killed. It was one of the awful battles for the times that the Army ever saw. I suppose a good many of the Waterford boys is killed, wounded or taken prisoner. I haven't seen none of them yet, but as soon as I get time I will take a walk up that way to see if any of them, god forbid, any more of such cruel murdering. The dead was piled up in piles on both sides. Well Mother, the Lord has been good to me. He has seen me past a good many dangerous places. Well Mother, I will close for this time. My head aches. So you can name the baby among yourselves, I can't think of anything now. My love to Em, tell her to take care of herself and the baby. I will write to her, Father and Beck. So, good-bye. A good kiss for all and 6 or 7 for the baby.

      Your Truly Son
      Charles Shepard
      Heavy Artillery

In your next letter put a little mustard in it, it goes good.

Author's Note: In this letter, Charles mentions Fort Tilton. My research did not reveal any Fort Tilton in operation near Petersburg during the Civil War era. It was the only time that something was mentioned in one of his letters that could not be documented. It was the Battle of the Crater about which much has been written. To date, I have located no mention of a Fort Tilton, or derivatives thereof, concerning this battle.

Harriet had once again stopped reading Charles's letters. After my first read, I told her that Charles requested some mustard in his next letter, he was maintaining his trust in the Lord, he had a headache, and that we should name the baby as he can not think of anything currently. After the passage of a few hours, I told her with no detail or explanation that I felt the likelihood of Charles being in great danger was very real. I left the letter, in the envelope, on the table. I don't believe that she ever read it. Separately, I told both Emma and Rebecca much the same thing. Poor Emma has looked at me with those sad eyes ever since I have known her. I don't believe I have ever seen her happy. I doubt that I will in the days to come. Rebecca had become withdrawn, which was very unlike her.

What John was able to learn from reading various accounts of this battle was that it soon became known as the Battle of the Crater. As Charles said in his most recent letter, "It was one of the awful battles for the time that the army ever saw." The idea of the Battle was for a Pennsylvania Regiment of coal miners were to dig a tunnel under the rebel fortification, pack it with black powder, blow it all to hell, then charge during the confusion. As far as I could gather, the explosion was tremendous, but half an hour later than expected. It served its purpose, but the Union Soldiers were slow to respond. One of the Black Troops was scheduled to lead the attack. At the last minute, the Generals changed this order and had the troops draw straws to see who would lead. The Black Troop had been trained for this event. The troop that drew the short straw was thought to be a particularly weaker unit. Their commanding officer was drunk at the time and far removed from the scene. It was thought that if the Union had won this battle, the war would soon be over. The initial Union attack for this battle was leaderless and ineffective, leading to many Union casualties and a prolongement of the war.

P29 The entrance to the tunnel they dug as it looks today.

Although I felt closer to Charles reading these accounts, the too-often references to the officers being drunk and mistakes that caused the war to continue would infuriate me to the point of distraction. After learning more details of this assault, I could relate to Charles's inability to suggest a name for his new baby. I would suppose a man who sees death every day is not really in a world that is looking at tomorrow. I believe Charles is in the realm of here and now; he needs to be.

Petersburg, August 4, 1864

Dear Sister,

As I have one more sheet of paper and such good news I thought I would answer your letter today. I have written Father today and to George Steenburgh so I am pretty well wrote out. Well Beck, my Regiment is going to start for Washington in the morning. The boys are kicking up at a great rate. Such a noise you can't hardly write. I have not been well for the last 5 or 6 days, but I think I am well enough now. Going back to Washington is the best news I have had yet. Well Beck, I suppose you get to be Auntie. Well such things will happen. This is a curious world. Well Beck, I must close. My love to all. I will write a good long letter next time, so good-bye. My love to the baby and all of the rest. A kiss from your absent Brother.

C. Shepard

Rebecca was alive with excitement after reading this letter. She ran through the house yelling, Charles is going to Washington, Charles is going to Washington, over and over again. She was waving the letter over her head, and it took several minutes for her to calm down. I had snatched the letter from her hands and now had read it myself. This is potentially good news. Charles has been in the field for 100 days with the 4th Brigade. The usual practice, at this time, is to relieve those units with either new or fresh troops. The 4th's 100 days were up several days ago, so this is welcome news. I thought I detected a hint of color returning to Harriet's complexion; she had looked so pale lately. And Emma? There seemed to be a look of quiet relief about her as she gazed upon the still unnamed baby.

Petersburg, August 5, 1864

Dear Mother,

 I received yours and sisters letter yesterday and I was glad to hear that you was all well. I am well and enjoying myself. How I would like to see you all. I hope and pray that this cruel war will soon end. I sometimes think that the rebels will lick us for just about the time there is going to be a battle fought, you will see our officers all drunk. That was the reason we lost that fight the other day. Lord forbid such if we had good praying men to guide us. We would lick them every time. They will drink so musch they don't know what ginger is and don't know how to give commands. Our soldiers had a soft thing on the 30th of July, if we had sober officers to guide us. Well Mother, I ain't seen none of the waterford boys yet so I don't know if any of them was killed or not. I suppose there was because there was awful hard fighting where they was. The boys of the 115th Regiment, told me that George Cole and James Geddins was wounded and a prisoner. They saw them when they were taken. I was very sorry that C. Westover was dead. Well, he was a good boy, he was liked by all in the Company. I miss him since he left. I hardly know what to write. My thoughts don't come fast today so I will close. We are going to Washington. We expect to go any minute, so I may be in Washington when you hear from me again. So I will close for this time. I will write to Em and Beck the next chance I get. Kiss the baby for me. My love to Em. Beck, Father, Aunt Fanny, Granmother, Father and my friends. You ain't *heard nothing from Aunt Rebecca, poor soul? I hope she will get North, May the Lord bless us all and spare our lives until we can meet again. Your Truly and Loving Son,*

C. Shepard

Send me some mustard in a letter

This letter is so full of bad news. With one hope of redemption, It is our fervent prayer that our next letter will be received from Washington, as Charles says. Damn the drunken commanders in this war; their actions condemn so many of our boys.

Chapter 10

DOES ANYONE KNOW WHERE THE LOVE OF GOD GOES WHEN THE WAIT, TURNS THE MINUTES INTO HOURS?

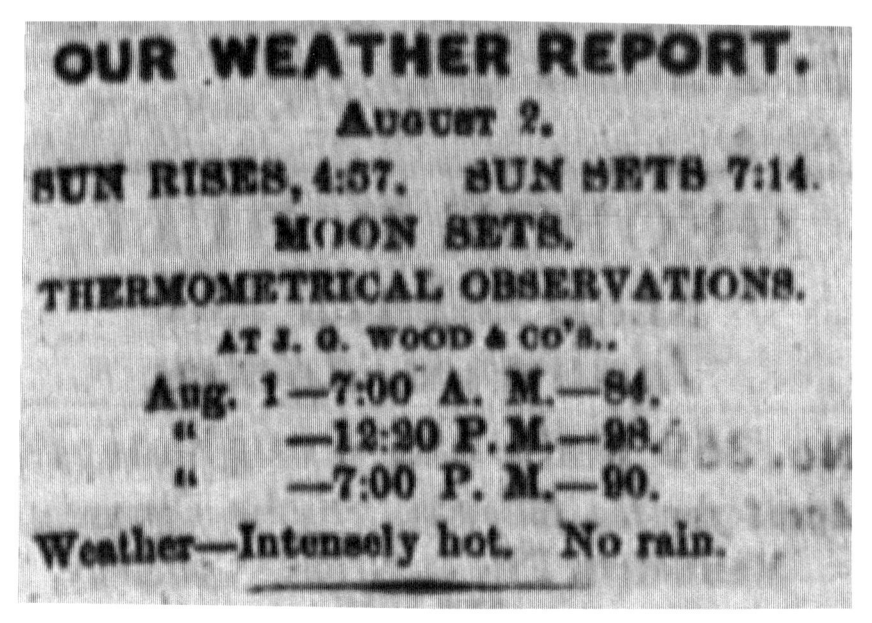

> **OUR WEATHER REPORT.**
> AUGUST 2.
> SUN RISES, 4:57. SUN SETS 7:14.
> MOON SETS.
> THERMOMETRICAL OBSERVATIONS.
> AT J. G. WOOD & CO'S.
> Aug. 1—7:00 A. M.—84.
> " —12:30 P. M.—98.
> " —7:00 P. M.—90.
> Weather—Intensely hot. No rain.

P30

It is generally always hot in July and August on the canal; this year seems worse. As the news reported, it is intensely hot, and it would do well to have some rain.

Smells are something we grow accustomed to, and the right smell at the right time can make a person right within himself. Charles enjoyed the smells of the bakery in Waterford. He could just stand near the business and breathe it in; his eyes would be closed and with a look of contentment on his face. Harriet, on the other hand, was quite pleased when the lilacs were in bloom, and their smell would be carried with each gentle breeze. She would spend as much time as possible in the company of our bushes at home. Rebecca's favorite was the air after a light spring rain. Mine was the canal. It was a mix. Sometimes the mix was just right. The wood fires burning in the cabins of the canal boats, coupled with the coffee and likely bacon that was on the stove, could create a welcome home aroma for those of us who felt at home on the canal. The rope used by the canalers could also have a uniqueness of smell, and the dry rope would smell different than the wet. A person unfamiliar with the canal would probably not smell it at all. The various cargoes on the canal boats would add their aromas of fresh-cut timber, hay, wheat, and other farm products. Even the animals and, to some extent, even the deposits left behind by those animals, when they all blended together in a good and gentle breeze, that was the canaller's smell. It welcomed the canaller and made him feel safe, alive, and content. John lived for that smell and looked forward to it. But not today. John is above the upper 2 Lock (Lock 6 on the Old Champlain Canal). He is waiting with his tow in a line to enter the lock. Below the lock, there are many waiting to enter from the south end. This was to be a long wait. He is committed to staying with this tow until he delivers it to the Waterford Side Cut Locks. He is less than three miles from home. His watch shows ten forty-five in the morning. John knows each lock through, if all goes well, will take about 15 minutes, and there are more than thirty tows ahead of his, maybe fifteen or more on each side of the lock. It will be much later in the day before he can hope to be through this lock.

The smell of the canal is not so inviting when you're sitting and waiting. Charles can enjoy the bakery smell, but eventually, you move on. Even Harriet would grow tired of her lilacs and move to something else. Rebecca's fresh rain smell would eventually go away of its own accord. The canal smell, to hold its allure and attractiveness, needed to be experienced while you were moving ahead. It is not a stationary enjoyment. The intense heat, the stillness of the air, and this damn wait are playing hard on all the canallers. Those who make their living on the canal are not keen to wait.

I had taken a rare overnight trip to Stillwater because I desired to be away for a bit. We have heard nothing from Charles in nearly three weeks. I was eager to pass through the locks; I wasn't sure if I was eager to receive his next letter. Such confusion lately in these letters. In the last two, he mentions going back to Washington. If he is in Washington, why haven't we received a letter? If there, he should have access to paper and the like. Has he been wounded, injured, or taken ill? Is he in the hospital? Why don't we hear something? When will we ever lock through?

I returned home late in the evening, nearly ten-thirty at night. I had seen to the comfort of the mules and was pleased to find Harriet still about and of even composure. I was fearful that she would be on edge due to the lateness of the hour. Harriet told me she had heard talk of a wait at the Upper two lock when she was on Broad St, and later that afternoon, she had called on Mr. Brewster (my friend Abe) at the Weigh Lock to inquire what he might know. He had been kind enough to tell her of a situation at one of the northern locks earlier that had created a wait above Waterford. She warmed me some chicken for dinner and retired for the evening after announcing a letter to me from Charles. I was surprised that she would be off to bed at this point; I hadn't even opened the letter yet. I suppose the wait and the love of God affect each of us differently. I chose to delay the opening a while. Again, the thought that would not go away was if this were a good letter, it would have been here sooner. I did not want to open it with trembling fingers or feelings of anxiety. I was glad that Harriet had the foresight to let me view its contents privately. I was hoping for the very best; while at the same time, prepared for the very worst.

Reams Station, August 25, 1864

Dear Father,

I received your most kind letter and was happy to hear that you are all well. I am well and hope this letter will find you the same. Well Father, I have been on the go since the 12th and I am most played out. The 2 Corps left Deep Bottom Saturday night and marched all night. It rained and it was awfully muddy. We marched about 25 miles. We got to Petersburg Sunday morning about 7 o'clock. I was about done in. Well, we went in camp, I put my tent up and went to sleep. About 11 o'clock we heard the 5 corps had taken the Weldon Railroad. We was ordered to pack up. Well, we went down to the railroad about 4 miles and stayed there all night and had a good rest. In the morning we were ordered to go down to the railroad and tear up the tracks. We tore the tracks up for about 10 miles. I tell you the 2 Corps has seen tough times since the 12th. We are going back to today or tonight, then I will get a chance to write more. At least I hope so, well Father, I will tell you about a scrap that my Company and Company A got into and its a scrap I don't want to get into every day. Company H and A were sent out to support a Brigade of Calvary. When we got there we found them dismounted and in a line of battle. Well, our two Companies formed on their right and made a charge, We charged and drove them back about a mile, till we got in a nest of them. Then they drove us back. Oh, how hot it was. We lost 25 killed and wounded. Half our Company got sunstroke. I got back by the skin of my teeth. Well, I must close because I am afraid we will move. So. good-bye. I will write to Em, next chance I get. A kiss to all, 6 or 7 for the baby. Good-bye and God bless you all. Tell Em, that John Troy is killed or a prisoner. C. Shepard

It was good that I read this alone. I am sure that I would not have been able to masquerade my emotions aroused by this letter. I have a feeling within me that is all too familiar. It is unfortunate that a parent can experience so many painful events that he can now forecast them. The feelings that swept over him were the same that he had felt when his daughter Harriet died. He recognized them again when little Mary met the same fate. Even with the passage of several years and the fact that Charles still lives there, there it is that same feeling. It won't go away. That talk of going to Washington must not have been true. They had served their 100 days in the field; why were they not back in Washington? John had experienced a full range of emotions since Charles's departure. He was at one time proud of what he was doing. He had fear of what he was doing. Worry was almost a constant. Concern was ever-present. But anger, anger had never been a part of it. Tonight, John is angry, and he is angry with God. He wanted Charles back. He did not want to wait. He wanted his boy to come home. He didn't want any more letters.

How will I tell the others of this letter? They must all know that it has been received. Harriet will want to know, but she will not ask. I am surprised that Rebecca hasn't found a reason to come into the parlor, perhaps she is asleep, or Harriet warned her to stay in her room until morning and not bother her father. Of course, I am sure that Rebecca will be full of glee, as she is certain that Charles is in Washington, shaking hands with Mr. Lincoln. Emma will not ask. Emma has been with us now since December, on and off, but she still hasn't taken to me. She is paying close heed to Addie, that is the baby's name. Harriet is very pleased with that. John has decided that he will attempt to show no apprehension. He will report that Charles has not returned to Washington, as all had prayed. He is still in the field and still in Virginia and working on a railroad. He elects not to relate Charles's report concerning John Troy. He is a mutual friend of both Charles and Emma, but I just think that this news is best kept to myself at this point. This letter will not be laid on the table; I shall keep it with me.

The morning arrived with no break in the heat and still no rain. I was to take a tow for Mr. Enos of the Rock Island Mill today. Mr. Enos said to tow to the West Troy Side Cut Locks. This area in West Troy (Watervliet) is not an area I care to be about in. It can be a rough and tumble place. But, I should arrive early, I would think it safer in the daylight hours. I need news of the war activity; West Troy often hears news before others as reports seem to travel up the river and canal; sometimes, in newspapers, we wouldn't often see or just talk of that news. I will linger there as long as I dare. This area was a busy area for local activity on both the Erie and Champlain Canals and the Hudson River. Many who worked the canals had money in their pocket. There are many saloons in the neighborhood, and those houses of lesser reputation were well staffed as well. A careless canaler could soon find himself separated from his money, sometimes voluntarily, sometimes not. John would be careful here. He wants news.

There were many stories from those on the boats. One story was about a large contingent of Rebels in Canada preparing to attack the canal at Lockport, and the 74th was preparing to defend. Another report about the Colored Troops in battle, some of their performances and bravery; still others of their lack thereof. One only had to ask, as the canallers were about their business, "Any news of the war?" Were the stories true? How could the Rebels gather a force in Canada? Then John heard a loud discussion, something about Old Tidball and the Two Corp runnin' a railroad.

Tidball was commander of Charles' Division under General Hancock, and he mentioned the railroad in his last letter. I joined that conversation. "What know you of Tidball and the railroad" I called out. He claimed that General Grant had assigned Colonel Tidball's Two Corp to close down the railroad. Maybe after the war, he'll put the canal (he pronounced it kaynal) out of business. Hungry for more news, I cried out anything more? No, he said Two Corp is a good outfit, one of the best. "Maybe, Old Tidball will close down all them damn railroads, wouldn't bother me a bit."

This information, though pleased to have it, did not answer the question of why Charles was not in Washington. Charles, or at least his regiment, was still in Virginia, now well past their 100 days. A few days later, John did see this news account. He figured if this news he thought couldn't be true appeared in the papers, there must have been something to it. He felt once again, even in these times, the canal was his friend; it even brought him reliable news.

John did not know how out of date this report was. The news gathered that day at the West Troy Side Cuts someone spoke of the Rebels invading Lockport through Canada. They were, but it was old news. As evident by this August 10, 1862 account in the New York Tribune.

> There is commotion in Buffalo in consequence of a story that Rebels and their friends in Canada contemplate a raid upon that city, to burn it and destroy the canal at Lockport. Mayor Fargo therefore protests against the departure of the 74th Regiment, which has just got ready for their hundred days duty. It is stated that General Dix, on being applied to, said he was aware of the plot, but could do nothing in the way of force to resist it. We doubt this part of the story, and have very little faith in any of it.

Chapter 11

THERE ARE NO FACTS, ONLY INTERPRETATIONS

It has been nearly one month since we last heard from Charles. It is very busy on the canal; I am thankful for that. The busier I am, aids the passage of time. I try not to think of Charles. I have settled in my mind that no good can come from whatever he is in right now; he may well already be gone. I have read battle reports from the Weldon Railroad and Ream's Station. I have said nothing to the others. I really only have my interpretation and thoughts about what I have read. I don't know the real story and do not know where to turn. Harriet, Emma, and even Rebecca are very taken with caring for Addie. That and the normal labors of the day are a full day's endeavor. Our garden has done well this year; despite the long dry period, the wells on Crow Hill (Upper Waterford, north and west) remained quite sufficient to water during that dry spell. Harvesting, canning, and caring for Addie will create a lot of distraction for the ladies.

    I find myself starting to take longer trips on the canal again. I have found a few to go to Fort Edward. This will keep my thoughts at bay, and being with people I am not accustomed to has helped ease the not knowing. I have the comfort of the canal community when we stop for the evening. None are aware of Charles. The talk will generally be about the war. I offer nothing to the conversation. There are always other topics. I have started to carry a bible. If there is enough light, I will read some of Charles's favorite passages. It is good to be away. The wait at home for news is unbearable at this time. I fear that our next letter will not be in Charles's handwriting. I am not ready to face that fear. I long for the true news; at the same time, I fear it.

It was early in September when this copy of the Philadelphia Inquirer came into my possession.

The Philadelphia Inquirer.
HEADQUARTERS ARMY OF THE POTOMAC,
Friday, Aug. 26, 1864.

The action at Ream's Station, in which, on our side, the First and Second Divisions, Second Corps, were engaged yesterday, is an event of which I hardly know how to speak. Many look upon it as a disaster, and there are some reasons for regarding it in that light if we were to consider it without regard to the other side of the picture, the punishment inflicted on the enemy. But when we recollect that in three successive charges, the enemy was repulsed with great slaughter and that their losses in killed and wounded greatly outnumbered ours, it is evident that our occasion for regret is on account of the adverse moral effect of a reverse more than the losses actually entailed thereby. Even the guns they captured were nearly paid for in killed and wounded, and we can far better afford to lose guns than they can afford to lose men.

The Second Corps had but just returned from the extreme right on the James River when, on Monday morning, the First and Second Divisions of it were started off on a long, wet, and muddy march to the extreme left on the Weldon Railroad. From that time up to yesterday, they had been hard at work tearing up the railroad, burning the ties, twisting the rails, leveling embankments, destroying bridges and culverts, and, as thoroughly as possible, demolishing everything that could be of any service to the enemy in facilitating the repair of the road in case it should again fall into their hands.

This work had been completely accomplished to a point between three and four miles south of Ream's Station, making in all ten miles of road, or a little over that distance, effectually destroyed.

There can be little doubt that in the engagement, they outnumbered us two to one, for the men of the two divisions we had there were so exhausted by fighting, hard marching, and their laborious work on the railroad that their effective strength had been very materially reduced.

Charles had reported all of these events in his letter of August 25th, and we have not heard from him since. He also mentioned his friend John Troy being killed or taken prisoner; I fear that this may be Charles's fate as well. After reading this account, I feel a closeness with Charles that I have never felt before. I feel that he is reaching out or perhaps calling out to me. I can't hear him or touch him, but I can see him and can't make a connection. It is a strange and somewhat eerie feeling. I am uncomfortable, a bit dizzy, mind you, but, at the same time, at ease.

I have a need for information. There is nowhere to turn for assistance and a lack of reliable news from the battlefields. Some of the Carolina papers are reporting battlefield information from the Northern Side and the Rebel Side; the stories seem to conflict. It bothers me that they count the dead and the missing as some kind of a means of keeping score in a baseball game. Some even claim victory just for receiving fewer casualties than the other team, I mean, side. Are all the young men to perish before a winner can be declared in this now a war of attrition?

As an example to support John's feelings consider these reports in the *The North Carolina Standard* September 1864.

Battle of Ream's Station - Official Report

The following is General A. P. Hill's official report of the battle fought at Ream's station, on the Weldon railroad, on yesterday week:

I have the honor to report the correct list of results in the fight of the 25th at Ream's station. We captured twelve stands of colors, nine pieces of artillery, ten caissons, twenty-one hundred and fifty prisoners, thirty-one hundred stands of small arms and thirty-two horses. My own loss in cavalry, artillery and infantry is seven hundred and twenty men killed, wounded and missing.

Very Respectully,

P. Hill, Lt. Gen. (Confederate Repot - Ream's Station)

Next in the same newspaper is the Union Report - Labeled The Yakee Report, on the same battle.

The Yankee Report

To Major General Dix, New York. On Thursday, the 25th, General Hancock, who was south of the Ream's station on the Weldon railroad, was attacked several times during the day, but he repulsed the enemy in every assault. At half past five P.M. on Thursday a combined attack was made on his center and his left, which, after one of the most desparate battles of the war, resulted in the enemy withdrawing from the field, leaving their dead and wounded on the ground. The details are given in the following brief reports of Generals Grant, Meade, and Hancock.

The Chief of Artillery reports he lost about two hudred and fifty horses. My own loss including Cavalry will probably not exceed twelve or fifteen hundred, but this is a surmise.

The callousness with which these reports were issued weighed heavy on my soul. Comparing the number of enemy colors, horses, rifles, and artillery captured with the lives of soldiers killed or captured and each side somehow claiming to be the victor was a comparison that I could not draw nor appreciate. My son seemed an awfully small part of these overall proceedings, much like everyone else's son. I did not realize that until now. Charles, or Hiram Clute, or the Vanderwerken or Vandecar boys, were no more important than a captured color, banner, rifle, or horse. Just a way to keep score. I was searching for news. I was finding reports.

I was beginning to see that Charles's accounts of battles in his letters were very accurate to the newspaper accounts.

Not knowing if Charles is dead or alive, injured or imprisoned, deserted? I am becoming calloused to the point that I will likely find no sorrow if the news is bad nor the ability to rejoice if our prayers have had merit. I feel that I will be thankful just to have the relief that I know our son's fate. The mystery and the torment will be over; perhaps I desire that for selfish well-being. I do feel some guilt for these feelings. Eventually, we must know. Rebecca knows of her two sisters, Mary and Harriet. She was just a child herself when they left us, but she remembers them. Charles was a doting brother to Rebecca, and now he may be gone. The good Lord has blessed Harriet and I with four children, and now he may have taken a third from us. Poor Emma, Charles's wife, orphaned at four years of age, married at eighteen, a mother that year, and a widow by nineteen? How much sadness can those sad eyes endure? Little Addie, our only grandchild, will she have no father? For our family, the passage of time has lost its reality. One day quickly turned to the next, yet the days really have no beginning, nor did they ever end. Our lives had become enclosed in one neverending day. We just didn't discuss Charles; somehow, it made it easier. So much time has passed that it is nearing time for the canal to close for the season. I have stopped taking the longer tows, at the season's end, the Flour Mill will have extra work, so I will be staying close to home.

It had become my desire to read all that I could find in regard to the war. Over the years of towing on the canal, I had established kinship with many canallers. During this time period, I had quickly become well-known and recognized as one who was in search of newspapers. On the canal boats, newspapers from many areas were available, and some could be months old. I was eager to review them all for a chance at some information that would give some indication of what may have become of Charles. I happened upon this one in mid-September.

The North Carolina Standard, September 3, 1864.
The Troops Engaged

The cavalry engaged on the part of the enemy (Union Forces), were commanded by the noted Colonel Speer, who is believed to have had a brigade. All accounts agree that they were soon routed, and that they moved out of the way as fast as their horses could carry them. The infantry consisted of the famous Second Corp. under General Hancock and all prisoners concur that it numbered ten to twelve thousand men. They fought more valiantly than the cavalry, but were finally compelled to give way before the impetuous dash of the brave North Carolinians, and although the engagement did not become general until about 3 o'clock, before night the entire entire Corp was utterly routed and flying in wild confusion east of the railroad towards Prince George. They left all their killed and wounded, over two thousand prisoners, and nine pieces of cannon in our possession.

I have read this report a number of times; I feel like I was there. We have not heard from Charles since this battle. In his last letter he mentioned much that is in this report. My fear is that he has been killed in this battle or, at the least, taken prisoner. We just don't know.

From what I had learned up to this time, I could sense that this report seemed in order and truthful. Of those in Waterford who had suffered the loss of a family member on the battlefield, and there were several, they had been informed in due time. We have received no announcement. The number of men from Hancock's II Corps who were taken prisoner along with the canon has now caused us to believe that Charles has been captured. He is likely among those 2,000 captured. Charles had reported to us that John Troy was either killed or taken prisoner in his last letter to us back in August.

Chapter 12

PERHAPS A VISIT IS IN ORDER

Lately, John had been haunted by so many thoughts and memories. Especially those dealing with the sorrows that had been visited on the other Cohoes, Waterford, and Troy families. Starting with his friend Lawrence Vanderwerken and the loss of his son John from illness early in the war. The family had received notification and was fortunate enough to be reunited with their son's remains. This, at least, allowed the family the comfort of a Christian burial. Odd, John thought, to use the words fortunate and comfort in this regard, almost being envious of this family's lesser degree of sorrow. The several families who lost their sons and brothers at the first battle of Bull Run, they, too, had received notification in due time. Even my friend William Cole's nephew, who had been captured, was paroled, and the word was received back home. Our sorrow is increased by this nearly unbearable feeling of just not knowing. One must maintain hope. It is difficult.

I decided to pay a visit to the Westover family in Cohoes. Their son Charles was friends with our son. He had passed from disease in July. It is now mid-September. Perhaps I should happen by. John often said that he would do these things; he seldom followed through. This time it would be different. His mind and his life at this juncture were taken up with the pursuit of information about Charles that would unshackle his own life. John thought how ironic that in his own carefree and comfortable life, he had spiritually become a slave to his own desire to know the welfare of his son. His son, who ostensibly was fighting for the freedom of others who were physically enslaved. It was fortunate that at this point in John's life, he was not financially beholden and had scaled back his towing endeavors. He maintained his operation with Mr. Enos at the flour mill, and it's guaranteed two days of work each week. On his next trip for the mill, he told Mr. Enos of his plan to visit Mary Westover in Cohoes, and he might be a bit late to return. If that were the case, he assured him that he would secure the boat and place it for loading and then call on him personally to ensure that all had been completed. Harriet has never accompanied me on any of my trips in now more than twenty-six years of towing. That evening I told her of my intentions and the purpose of my plan to visit Mary Westover. I also welcomed her to join me. I wasn't surprised when she elected not to take part in the journey. There was just too much to look after at home, but to offer Mary her best thoughts and wishes, she told me. Harriet still, outwardly at least, seemed to be much more at comfort with the situation with Charles than I was. We were not discussing Charles at home. What would be, will be, was Harriet's final thoughts on this subject; when the time is right, we will know. It is out of our hands, and there is nothing we can do. I was not pleased to think that she had a better view of our current situation, but I admired her strength in the darkness of our times.

My tow to West Troy was uneventful. I started to think, how many times have I made this tow? Several hundred? Probably one thousand, could that be? Twenty-six years of towing, I guess it could. It was pleasant that September day, as were my fellow canallers. Everyone that I encountered was someone familiar and the kind of people that you were happy to have met. This is why John loved the canal. It has always been kind to him. Provided his comfort of living. Was a friend indeed. The sights, the smells, the friendships, he had to admit, he was happiest on the canal. Quickly, so it seemed, he had completed his tow to West Troy. He had decided to tow the Rock Island canal boat to the lower Cohoes Basin before calling on the Westovers. He was confident that the boat and the mules would be safe there. It was but a short walk to the Westover home, and he had arrived unannounced. He decided that the boldness of the act of just showing up at their home would be better for him. He felt that a chance encounter, as opposed to a planned event, would make the conversation more spontaneous and unrehearsed. John was a man of many thoughts and fewer words, and talking about an unpleasant subject was difficult for him.

John was thinking about how to start this conversation as he approached their house. Much to his surprise and liking, on this fine September day, Mary Westover was hanging laundry; she had seen him before he had noticed her. She called out happily, "Why John, John Shepard, what brings you to our home?" John realized at that point he hadn't heard a woman's happy voice in some time. Yes, Rebecca ran happily through our house, yelling Charles was going to Washington about three months ago. Since that time, even with the baby, there have been no happy voices from Harriet, Emma, or Rebecca anymore. I don't hold them responsible; I am certain that my tone has been less than cheerful as well. She had put me in comfort right away. I expressed my sympathy for her son Charles and mentioned how our Charles had noted in his letter about the last moments that he had shared with his friend. Mary thanked me for Charles's thoughtfulness to her Charles and to be sure to thank Harriet for her letter of condolences. John hadn't known that Harriet had sent such a letter. Her husband John was at work at the mill, and all things considered, they were doing well. John Jr. and Nancy were in school. I told her how Harriet was busy processing our garden's harvest and taking care of Charles's daughter. Our conversation was pleasant; I was surprised by how well she had adapted to the loss of her oldest son. Her gay spirit was lifting my spirits. She inquired about Charles' well being. I was proud of the fact that I could answer her question with greater ease than I had anticipated. I was glad that I hadn't rehearsed it. Mary had made us tea. It was a nice drink on a September day. In a blur, I repeated all that I knew and emphasized that we had no knowledge past the August 25th letter. We were quite sure that he was involved in the Battle at Ream's Station and feared that he was one of the thousands that were captured that day. The purpose of my visit was to learn that maybe her Charles had become friends with John Troy as my Charles had. As Charles had reported to us that John Troy might have been captured the day before, I wanted to contact the Troys to see if they had any news. I was hoping that if she knew John Troy, she might know how to contact his family. After telling what I knew of Charles today, the good spirits that Mary Westover had unleashed had now returned to their new normal. I admired Mary's ability to stay in good spirits. She told me that her son had sacrificed his life so that others may live. Yes, he had died of illness, but, at least to her justifiable thinking, he had contracted this illness after battles, and he died as a result. If, in fact, that was the reason for her Charles to make that sacrifice, don't we all then owe it to him to live our lives as happily as we can in his memory? I could not, nor did I dare, argue with Mary's philosophy on this topic. I hoped I could be as strong and determined to do right by my Charles, if that is to be his fate, as she is doing right by her boy. Mary had taken our teacups away and told me that John Troy and Charles had become friends when John worked in Cohoes. He is from Ireland. His parents remain in Ireland. John lives with the Ganty family in Rensselaer, I believe, in the 9th Ward. Upon leaving, she wished me success in my continued search and left me with this thought. When her son was in battle, she would only hear of it through his letters, and the same with illness. Once he reached the hospital in Maryland, information was more forthcoming away from the battlefield. Soon enough, we were informed of his passing. It must be difficult not to know, but please, there is hope. You have received no notification; Charles is still alive; I just know it. How quickly the time passes when your mind is so busy. I had been away from the boat for several hours; it felt like several minutes. The day was still young; I would be home at a normal hour. I do feel encouraged after my talk with Mary Westover. Tomorrow I will plan my visit to Rensselaer.

    After returning to Waterford, I settled up with Mr. Enos and continued on home on the towpath. I noticed my mind was suddenly clear, my head and my gait unusually light. The mules were tended to and made secure and comfortable for the evening. I will not tow tomorrow. I felt I had a purpose, and I was determined to pursue my desire to learn more, if that is possible, about Charles. Harriet met me at the door; she appeared relaxed and in good spirits. That was good to see. Rebecca was holding Addie, and Emma was resting. For the first time in months, the atmosphere in our home was relaxed; no one spoke of Charles, which had become the norm, but relaxed, just the same. After the rest had retired for the evening, I told Harriet of my visit with Mary Westover. I told her how well she had accepted her son's fate and her philosophy on the same. I think now that it may be her thoughts that have made me feel lighter in step and of mind. Harriet was not surprised at Mary's thoughts; she is a very strong woman. She didn't say if she agreed, and we did not labor the point. I also stated my intent to find John Troy's family tomorrow in Rensselaer. Harriet wished me well in this endeavor and made me pledge to be careful on this journey.

I came to the realization after Harriet retired for the evening that after working on the canal now, for more than a quarter of a century, I don't know the best way to travel somewhere that is not on the canal. Everywhere that I go is either on the canal or just off it. I am a canal man; I'm not a riverman. I have no contacts on the river. The river is the best route to take. I want to go tomorrow. I know if I delay this, I won't do it. I can board the 7:10 am train in Waterford and should be in Albany by 8:00 am. There is a ferry to Rensselaer that leaves with good frequency. I should be there around 9:00; that should be time enough.

I will admit that I was taken with anxiety and great apprehension for this trip. I have never engaged in such a bold venture. My move from Massachusetts to Waterford was not as great and unknown as this trip would be. I had guidance and assistance from an acquaintance in Waterford. That trip was a great adventure, full of anticipation, yet with a favorable outcome expected, the anticipation never turned to anxiety. This was a favorable journey that had a very positive effect on my life. This time I don't know the people I am looking for; they don't know me. I don't know where they live. Yes, it is the 9th Ward; I trust some good soul from the Rensselaer will respond to a request for assistance. There is no anticipation of a favorable outcome to this journey. I have never experienced such anxiety. Perhaps I will call on a local parsonage, maybe, City Hall? That would be better than just asking people on the street. All I really know is the family name of Ganty.

John knew this trip was a shot in the dark, and in that respect, he wasn't disappointed in his unsuccessful findings. He could take comfort in the fact that he had tried. He didn't feel so helpless if he could stay involved and convince himself that he was doing all that he could to learn where Charles was. He did call on City Hall and one of the local churches to no avail. He stopped in two of the city's saloons, inquiring if anyone was familiar with the Ganty family. The answer was the same in each case and at every stop; no one was aware of any such name in the city or of John Troy. As he made his way back to the ferry and while traveling across the Hudson River from Rensselaer to the Capital City of Albany, he remembered his recent visit to that city and to Pease's House of Fantasy. His recent visit, yes, it was only nine months ago. A much happier time. A successful canal season had just ended, and Charles and Emma had just been wed. We received the news of the summertime arrival of our first grandchild. We devised a plan to purchase the lot next to us on Sixth Street (West St.) for Charles and Emma to start their life together. It was a good time for the Shepard Family. Now, here I am in the middle of the Hudson River, on a Ferry boat that will take me to a train and back to Waterford, and all for naught. I have learned nothing; I have accomplished nothing. John was at least amused by his thoughts. He would spend his towpath hours in contemplation of what was and what was to be. He believed that this was a curiosity of the towpath that relieved the boredom and gave a man the time to be right within himself and perhaps with his God. As he was crossing the river for the second time today, he noticed that the tides had changed. In the morning, the river current was flowing south; now, in the late afternoon, it was flowing north, and every day, it did the same thing. John felt a kinship with the river as every day; he would tow a boat on the canal in one direction and then tow it back to his starting point. John wondered did the river accomplish anything, or do I? The river seemingly never changes. It may appear low in times of drought, and during the spring freshets, it may become angry and destructive, but in time it rights itself to its normal back-and-forth motion. John hoped at this point that he, too, would conquer the freshets in his life that had made him angry and were destroying his well-being as well as that of his family. Would he, like the river, find a way to right himself?

The ferryboat was docking now in Albany; John was the last one off the boat. For some reason, he felt secure on the river, but the reason was unclear to him. The train ride back to Waterford was relaxing. John did not know what his next step would be. He had learned a great deal about the last battle that Charles was in and greatly suspected that he was probably a Southern prisoner at this time, but he simply did not know. The newspapers provided by the traveling canallers had given good accounts of the battle.

John had learned that when a soldier was killed in battle or had died of disease, the family could expect a notification from one of the officers if they knew how to contact the family. In Charles's case, Judson Smith, his Sergeant, had been killed in the May 2nd battle, and Captain Augustus Brown had resigned from his position when the Company, formed as Artillery, was assigned to Infantry Duty. Colonel Tidball's Gettysburg wound caused him to leave the 4th Artillery soon after the Battles at Ream's Station. His new officers likely did not know Charles. John had also learned that during the first years of the war, prisoners were allowed to write letters to kinfolk; the mail passed through the lines during formal exchanges or by way of friends though such correspondence was rare. The most common way to notify the family of a captured soldier was a letter from the soldier's company, noncommissioned officer, or his friends who knew the family would be worried. In Charles's case, all of his friends had either been killed in battle, died of disease, or had been taken prisoner. There was no one left to write.

As John was exiting the train, he saw a copy of the Morning Express. It was a paper that John was not familiar with, and he was apprehensive about just taking it. There was no one else in the car, and as he glanced at the date, he saw that it was several weeks old. He picked it up and exited the train. It was a short walk home, he knew that Harriet would be awaiting his arrival, and he was anxious to be home. The family would likely be interested in his adventure on the train and the ferry. It was early evening when he arrived, Emma and Addie had retired for the evening, but Harriet and Rebecca were in good spirits and pining to hear about my trip. They had dinner ready for me, and for the first time in a long while, we talked until late in the evening. The paper that I had brought home with much guilt was lying on a shelf above our cloak rack; I would retrieve it in the morning. There was guilt attached to this paper because the paper that I would receive from the canallers was freely given. I felt like I stole this one off the train. Tomorrow was a Rock Island Flour day, so we adjourned for the night.

Chapter 13

INFORMATION ARRIVES IN A MYSTERIOUS MANNER

The next morning John was late to rise; this was very unusual; a canaller is always up early, especially during the season. He was quick to eat his breakfast, but because they had dined so late the night before, he wasn't as hungry as he normally would have been. He hurried to the Grogh St. Barns; the mules knew that it was time to go as they were braying as to say, where have you been? We quickly made our way to the flour mill to pick up our barge. It was at that time that he realized that he had left behind, at home, the guilty newspaper that he was hoping to read today. It will still be there tonight. Traffic was busy today on the Side Cut extension from the Side Cut Locks to River Lock 4. All that could work against a boatman was in place today. A high river necessitated a lock-through. There were many mills on this one-mile stretch of the canal, and most were either loading or unloading a canal boat, the basin near the swing bridge was filled to capacity, and the worst thing for the boatman was that all the waste weirs on this section were in use powering the industry that bordered the canal. To the canallers, this was the most serious effect. It could draw the level of the canal down to where a loaded boat could be difficult to move. All of these things, combined with the lock's filling and emptying, were going to make for a tedious morning. John wished he had taken his newspaper. It took John most of the morning just to cross the Mohawk River and enter Lock 3 in Cohoes. Once through Lock 3, activity was back to normal. The trip back to the mill was without incident, and John was keen to be home. He was looking forward to some normalcy after the events of the last several days.

The entire family, including Emma and Addie, were at the dinner table; it was cool enough now that we had the fireplace in use, and it was very pleasant at dinnertime. We cleaned up after dinner. Harriet, Emma, and Rebecca all fussed over Addie while I sat down with the weekly Waterford Sentinel. This, of course, brought back thoughts of Charles. It had become our custom to read the paper, place some papers of tobacco in it and send it off to wherever Charles might be. I wish that were the case still, but the paper will be read and some other use made of it. After a while, Addie was put to bed with Emma, and Rebecca was soon to follow. Harriett had had a busy day preserving some of our garden produce and preparing dinner and soon announced her intentions for bed. I explained that I wanted to read that Morning Express newspaper I had discovered on the train. Discovered sounded so much better than taken. I had hoped the guilty feeling would have passed by now, but it hasn't.

The Albany Morning Express newspaper was a daily paper with both a morning and evening edition. The Waterford Sentinel was a weekly paper, usually four to six pages in total. The still guilt-ridden Morning Express this day was fourteen pages in its entirety. It will take some time to read. John's nature was to read the entire paper, and one of such magnitude may take more than one reading. He remembered that evening a while back spent at the Morgan House and how John Cramer would produce a variety of multi-page newspapers from around many states. He would know and be learned of the content of them all and be able to discuss, debate, or dismiss the subject of each in a knowledgeable and convincing manner. John realized then how Mr. Cramer had been such an influence on Waterford, the Capital District, and the State of New York.

John began to read the Express. As most papers were wont to do, a few words on the weather would be listed on page one. This would be followed by news of battles and skirmishes related to the Great War and then move on to foreign news. The next few pages would be filled with news of the State of New York and the City of Albany. This was followed by advertisements and notices; the final pages would be news from correspondents not employed by the Express. There was a lot to read. John read that evening until his eyes and mind became weary. The battle on the front page was, in fact, Ream's Station. John had become quite familiar with various news accounts. The Battle of Ream's Station is the last knowledge we have of Charles. He wrote of it in his last letter. Even with a background of good information on this battle, John read it, searching for any clues he might find about Charles; or just anything, anything new. He read it again. There was no news. He finished the front page of War News and foreign news. At this point, he decided to stop reading for the evening and turn to bed. Tomorrow he would seek one quick tow on the canal and dedicate the remainder of the day to reading the newspaper. A good night's rest and a short workday would work in John's favor to complete his self-imposed reading assignment.

The next morning he prepared the mules early and led them to the Side Cut Locks in hopes of catching a local tow. He said good morning to Fred Bass, a workman on the Side Cuts, and mentioned his hope of a quick local tow. This day would start with good fortune. Fred had been petitioned by Mr. Titcomb of Titcomb Distillery the day before of the need for a tow on this day. The regular driver and team used by Mr. Titcomb's operation had been delayed further north and would not be in Waterford in time to make this towing assignment. Titcomb Distillery was located just east of the railroad bridge over the canal, and their boat would be docked just north of the bridge. Fred said he mentioned that they should finish loading at about nine a. m. The boat only had to be towed to and through the Side Cuts, where a small Steam Tug would pick it up and tow it to the Cornell tow being assembled in the Hudson River.

John hurried his mules north on the towpath and secured them near the Division Street Bridge. There was a path known as the Heel Path that connected Division Street with the Weigh Station, the Weigh Lock Grocery, and the Distillery near the railroad bridge.

P31 The towpath can be seen just above center on the right. The heel path can be seen to the left of the canal boat waiting in line at the Waterford Weigh Lock. It ran from the current Division St. Bridge to the Black Railroad Bridge. Titcomb Distillery was to the left of the bridge. They could ship by wagon, rail, or canal. The closing of the Original Champlain Canal in 1918 and the passage of the 18th Amendment in January 1919 put an end to the Titcomb Distillery.

 John hoped that the earliness of the hour would put him in a position to be granted this perfect local tow. He arrived at the Distillery and introduced himself to Mr. Titcomb, and offered the services that Fred Bass had outlined. The Titcomb family was large and influential in Waterford. One was a local Butcher, another an attorney, still, another was a Village Trustee, and one of the local fire companies had been provided by and named Titcomb Hose Co. #2 in their honor. John didn't know why, but he felt uncomfortable in the Distillery owner's presence. Maybe he was just anxious; he wanted this tow. It would be perfect for his planned day. Mr. Titcomb was as eager as John was anxious, and a deal was soon at hand for the tow to be accomplished for fifteen dollars. John was also instructed not to stop at the weigh station as he and Abe had a mutual agreement. After retrieving his mules, John was soon on his way. It was not quite 10 a.m. With continued good luck, he could have the mules back in the barn and home by noontime. He was. After a quick lunch, he was ready to read the rest of the day and into the evening if necessary. He turned to where he had stopped the night before and read with great interest the goings-on in the City of Albany and of the State Legislature. He had never realized to what lengths its members went to in enacting our laws and regulations. He was fascinated by it and read several more than once to obtain a better understanding of what was taking place in the city. He had just finished those two pages, and Harriet had announced that dinner would soon be ready. She warned everyone to be prepared and ready. John found it curious and perhaps fateful this evening. Dinner was baked pork chops with boiled potatoes and carrots. Not only was this a common canallers meal, but also the same one he enjoyed that evening at the Morgan House with Abe and later the discussions with John Cramer. As these thoughts danced through John's mind, Harriet announced that she had purchased the pork chops from that new butcher, Mr. Titcomb, and what a nice gentleman he was.

After dinner, John returned to his reading. and then suddenly, there it was, a field report from a reporter not on the staff of the Morning Express, but glaringly, there it was.

Morning Express, Albany, New York, August 29, 1864
CAMP 4TH NEW YORK ARTILLERY
Near Petersburg, Va., Aug. 27, 1864

FRIEND KELLY:
The following is a correct list of our losses in the last battle of Reams Station on the afternoon of August 25. We have no way of knowing how many of the missing were killed or wounded, for we suppose they were all taken prisoners:
Lt. Col. Thomas Allcock, wounded through the neck, slight.
Major Wm. B. Arthur, wounded through the cheek, is serious.
Major Frank Williams killed.
Adjt. Henry J. Kopper, wounded through the thigh, slight.

COMPANY H.
Missing:

William B. Syke; Corporals Hobart Dodge, D. A. Hawkins, Chas. Marsh, Henry Mead, Joseph Mott; Privates Owen Eagan, Fredk. Blair, Augustus T. Blodgett, Carlton Barber, James Bannon, John P. Davis, Joseph Gass, Louis Jerome, Ira D. Lyon,

Adam Kennedy, Rudolph Malenka, James McManus, Roger Molanphy, G. W. Mahew, Patrick McDermott, William Pye, Ellestes Rose, Albert Reuss, Harry O'Brien, James Stephens, Levi B. Shennan, Zadock Smith, Jno. A. Schmidt, Charles Sheppard, Hubbard Spring, Peter Turner, Rufus W. Travis, Jno. Thornton, Geo. B. Wiltsie, William S. Wilson, Henry B. Whitman, Casper Wagner, Jno. Troy.

Wounded:

Corporals Jno. O'Connor, Michael Connor, leg; Private Bartholomew Lynch, arm.

Listed as missing. My thoughts were blank. News? Yes. Information? It seemed like the air had escaped from the chamber of my body. In its place in my mind came a flood of uncontrolled thoughts. Does he still live? Is he injured? Taken prisoner? Maybe he is wounded and in a hospital; maybe he lies yet on the battlefield, unclaimed? Maybe in retreating the field, he has been mixed in with a different unit? What does missing mean?

An unknown amount of time had passed, and John's mind went blank. When he reentered reality, he knew from this point on his existence had to have a purpose. That purpose was to do all that he could to help Charles if, in fact, there was anything that anyone could do.

Chapter 14

INTO THIS HOUSE YOU'RE BORN, INTO THIS WORLD, YOU'RE THROWN

John was not accustomed to planning. Yes, his towing business required plans on a daily basis. He was successful. His clients found him dependable, And. to his credit. He had earned the goodwill that his lifestyle had created. He didn't need to plan out each day.

He had provided for his family, he treated his work animals fairly, and he was known and respected in the community. All this came easy to him. None of the activities that brought him success in his life so far had made it necessary for him to enter, so to speak, a new world. As a young man in Massachusetts, he grew up around horses. Moving to New York wasn't entering a new world. He was still going to work with horses but on the canal. Again, changing from horses to mules in his towing operation was an easy transition. Things just seemed to progress nicely, and, naturally, Meeting Harriett, getting married, and raising a family, sure, there were trials and tribulations. The joy of owning their home on 6th street, being blessed with a successful livelihood, and the heartache of losing two children, all of these occurrences were natural in life. They required no planning on John's part. Even if he wasn't, he felt like he was in control of his destiny.

He doesn't know what to do about Charles listed as Missing.

His thoughts turned to all the Waterford boys involved in the current conflict so far. Several have died from disease. Of course, there have been battleground deaths; this is a war. A great number have been wounded. But, Missing? Is he lost, captured, prisoner, killed, and unrecognizable in death? I am no longer in control of my own destiny.

John enjoyed his independence on the canal. He took care of his mules, and his mules responded for him. He tended to the needs of those canallers needing a tow. The canallers provided his monetary needs to support his family. He was reliant on others. He needed to purchase feed for the mules, pay the farrier, buy a new harness from time to time, and other expenses. This was business. In life, he was independent; in business, he was reliant.

Charles is missing.

In life, he is now dependent and reliant. He will need help to satisfy this unknown. Is it better for it to remain unknown? If it remains unknown, there is always hope.

Who could he turn to for help in finding out where Charles is? He thought again of John Troy and the Ganty Family of Rennsellear; he had already searched unsuccessfully for them. He did remember that Charles reported in his, to date, final letter that John Troy had been killed or captured; the day before, Charles was listed as missing. And what did that printed report say about missing?

We have no way of knowing how many of the missing were killed or wounded, for we suppose they were all taken prisoner.

Prison. Of all the categories on my list, is prison a favorable one?

John needed help from someone with influence and possible government contacts who may be able to ask the right people the right questions. Just yesterday, he had the opportunity to tow for the Titcomb Distillery. They were influential in Waterford. He decided he would drop in at their place of business, thank them for the business, and let them know I was keen to do more. In so doing, perhaps they could offer some assistance if he could work his current situation into the conversation. John remembered he had felt some trepidation the first time he dealt with Mr. Titcomb. But, Mr. Titcomb was eager to do business with him, and he soon gained comfort when dealing with him. Harriett had reported that his brother, the butcher was a nice man. The other brother was a lawyer and a Village Trustee. John also remembered his friend Abe Brewster at the Weigh Lock and how well-connected one had to be to acquire the position of Collector. Yet, Mr. Titcomb had an understanding with Abe concerning tolls. In John's world, this was connected.

At this point, John felt a little short of breath and noticed his heartbeat was fast. He felt like he had just done some hard work. His thoughts were coming fast. He was always a quick and thorough thinker, but this was different. Oftentimes in the past, an idea would enter John's thoughts and be well thought out but never put into implementation, much like visiting the Clute Family to pay respects. Today he was taking action. First, he had to gather himself. But, he would take action.

He told Harriett that he had no tows today; he was off to tend to the mules. He said he likely would stop at the Weigh Station and check in with Mr. Enos at the Rock Island Mill. He did not tell her of his actual plans. Harriett doesn't know that Charles is officially missing. She still holds hope, as do I. She need not know; I believe that she is at peace with her thoughts. My breathing had returned to normal, and so too my heartbeat; suddenly, I had a purpose and a mission. I was ready to do whatever needed to be done.

Leaving the house, I went in my usual fashion to the barns on Grogh St. and saw to the mules. Wasting no time, I was a man dedicated to a purpose. I was off to visit Mr. Titcomb. Arriving unannounced at his business, I was received in short order. There was no trepidation this time. I was surprised by the calmness and ease of my presentation.

I thanked him for allowing me the privilege of towing his canal boat and said that I would be eager to do so again if the need or occasion arose. He reported that he had heard of my activity on the canal and would certainly look to me for future tows. Then Mr. Titcomb added, "One never knows, in these trying times, with the war and all that's about."

John hoped his face and demeanor didn't expose his eagerness in his coming response. This is the opportunity he was in search of. To make Charles the topic. There it was; the conversation could now be turned to Charles and the current situation. John went on, and he hoped not at length; he had to get it all out. He wasn't even sure what he said. He thinks he told of the most recent campaign at Ream's Station, how he had hoped, at war's end, that Charles would become a canaller, how we think he's been captured, the influence of the Titcomb Family and Charles; daughter Addie, and he needed assistance to learn where Charles is now. Mr. Titcomb was sympathetic to John's story and mildly amused that John thought that the Titcombs were influential. He did encourage him to visit his brother, who was a lawyer and Village Trustee and relate his story and concerns.

John liked much about Waterford. One of his favorite statements was that Waterford has everything, and nothing is far away. He soon had made his way to Attorney Titcomb's Office on the corner of Third and Broad Sts. He hadn't noticed before, but John Cramer had an office in the same building. John Cramer was in attendance that night at the Morgan House not too long ago. I didn't know Attorney Titcomb, and I don't think he knows me; he acted as he did. I felt at ease as I told of Charles' plight and of Harriett's and my interest to learn more. I'm sure that I related to the tale better and was more relaxed the second time. I think adding in a mother's grief and worry would work in our favor to gain some sympathy and, hopefully, action and answers.

Attorney Titcomb was understanding of John's concern and sympathetic to the plight at hand. He encouraged John to relate this story to Daniel King, President (Mayor) of the Village. Perhaps through an Army Chaplain, some discovery could be forthcoming.

At this point, who should appear at the office? None other than John Cramer. John Shepard's porch discussion mate from that evening at the Morgan House. Mr. Cramer, who for many years was a most devout subscriber, supporter, office holder, and kingpin in the Democratic circles. At the outbreak of the Civil War, he had lent his entire efforts and some of his fortunes to the Republican leadership and the war effort. When the 22nd marched to Pleasantdale for training camp when the war broke out, John, in his 80s, led the march and provided most of the financing. He states loudly for all to hear. Daniel B. King is a Democratic fool. Aren't you that canaller I had the pleasure to meet a few nights past with Mr. Brewster from the Weigh Lock? You and Luke Kavanaugh were comparing notes on two fine members of our Volunteer Artillery.

Yes, sir, replied John Shepard, one of those members was my son Charles.

John Cramer is 86 years old at this time. He will live five more years. He is involved in life until the very end. He was likely the smartest man in town, one of the wealthiest, and known for his sympathy and generosity. He invites John Shepard to accompany him to the Morgan House. John Cramer's good friend Thomas Vanderwerken is the proprietor these days. We all know that the Vanderwerkens have suffered during the Southern Democrats War. John Sheppard is amazed at this turn of events. If there is anyone who could help, it's Mr. Cramer.

Chapter 15

A RETURN TO THE MORGAN HOUSE ..... AND ETHAN ALLAN

Upon leaving the offices at Third and Broad, headed toward the Morgan House, across the street, and down the block. Mr. Cramer cautioned me. Son, I like to walk, and I like to talk, but I don't like to walk and talk at the same time. A man could trip in the street and be thought a fool, especially walking into or out of the Morgan House. A man might trip over his words while walking and talking, being proven a fool. And there is little worse than an old fool. John Cramer was certainly not an old fool. It took us about a quarter of an hour to arrive at the Morgan House. A journey that should take but a minute or two. Not through any infirmary of Mr. Cramer or his advanced years. It was a perfect October late afternoon; the streets were alive with people. John Cramer knows everyone, and everyone knows John. Many were eager to engage this charismatic, old-time Waterfordian in conversation, and he was happy to accommodate them. I have only been in his company twice, each time he has the everpresent sheaf of newspapers and other documents with him.

    Finally, we arrived at the House. I am anxious for our conversation to start in earnest. There is a full realization that Mr. Cramer will set the pace and tone of any conversation. I noted that he controlled, cleverly, not forcibly, the topics, themes, and mood of the previous session on the Morgan House Porch. Veranda, as Mr. Cramer referred to it. One could also take note of a new atmosphere within the confines of the House. Out on the street, it appeared that all were welcome to either engage or attempt to engage him in conversation. Now that we are within the confines of the House and we have taken what I believe is his table, most have acknowledged his presence, but no one has attempted to make a breach of his area. I got the impression one would need to be invited or welcomed to join him there. Later I was proven correct in my thoughts.

Without being ordered or requested, shortly after our arrival, a black pouring container arrived at our table along with a drinking vessel. I know not what its contents were, nor did I ask. The server requested my desire. I asked for tea. Expecting a cup, I was surprised to receive a pot. I hoped this was a good sign. Mr. Cramer's pouring container was of a good size, and I had a pot. It looks like our conversation won't be hurried. I am quite ready for it to start. Of Mr. Cramer's obvious many talents was the ability to put a man at ease. Does that make me more vulnerable to being influenced or cajoled? Or does it create within me a more confident demeanor? We shall soon see. I wondered if it might be in order to sample a product of the Titcomb Distillery. Maybe another time.

At last, John was ready to hear my story. It really wasn't a long passage of time. The oft-delayed walk here and my desire for some action and answers, along with my inner anxiety, which I don't think it shows, has made the passage of time lose its normalcy. I am ready!

After becoming comfortable with his beverage, Mr. Cramer said, "Please, begin; we won't suffer interruptions."

I was put further at ease by his opening statement.

I chose to tell him that Charles was an industrious boy. He had received a Waterford Education and was doing well as a peddler. I made mention of Charles' excitement when together we looked on and cheered as the 22nd marched off led by yourself. I emphasized that he was only 16 at the time.

It was brought to light that Charles had taken a bride last year and has only recently become a father. I told of the anticipation of buying the property next to mine on 6th St. for a post-war home for Charles and his new family. How he had volunteered after the new draft issue had been announced. This would not only provide a means to purchase that property but work towards meeting Waterford's quota to lessen the number drafted. I mentioned the time spent in Washington, D. C. at Fort Ethan Allan. I told him of all the battles, The Wilderness, The Crater, and others. We spoke of the letters, his friend John Troy and the last information that I had from the early September newspaper. (I should have brought that with me. I never thought I would be in discussion with the likes of John Cramer today.)

By the time I got to the end, all I could say was we wanted some news. The unknown was becoming too unbearable. Of course, I wanted a lot more, but some news would be a relief.

I was never interrupted or questioned. I could see that I had his attention the whole time.

He began his reply by stating that both Harriett's and mine situation had the sympathy of the entire community, as well as their appreciation of his willingness to perform on our behalf during this cursed rebellion. We have to realize that the war effort affects us all. All are suffering, the at-home and ill-informed families of those who serve even more so. He reflected on the deaths concerning the Vanderwerken boys, the Vandecar family, the wound to artist Ralph Savage and others. He agreed that the unknown of being listed as missing is a burden on all of those families and is a heavy one to bear. He agreed with my assessment of maintaining hope. He then went into quite a lengthy soliloquy on the benefits of hope both on the mind and the soul. He quoted Aristotle in saying, "Hope is a waking dream!"

At this point, he went silent for a moment and excused himself to his always-present sheaf of documents and papers. Yes, here it is, he stated. And, he continued.

From all that you have exposed about your son and his current situation, I am going to take the liberty to assume he still lives. If he died on the battlefield, even in a gruesome disfiguring fashion, word would have been received by now. Of this, I may be incorrect, but I would invest much credit to that thought. I believe our best pursuit to ease your current and worthy curiosities would be to look into the prisoner lists. Therein may lay both the answer and more causes for concern,

This old man, this ancient and revered Waterfordian, his knowledge and understanding of the world around him is beginning to provide me with great relief. I don't know any more than I did earlier, but I feel better about it. He has given me permission to think that Charles is still alive and perhaps even safe. I didn't need his permission; it was good to know that such a man had the same convictions as me.

Mr. Cramer then refilled his cup from his pouring container; I believe now it was a lager, but I am not certain. I have barely touched my tea.

He went into a rather long and apparently studied explanation of the policy of dealing with prisoners of this war. He started with the First Battle of Harper's Ferry early in the war and involved many of our Waterford boys. I believe Geo. Cole's nephew, from the Christmastime tow, was among them. He continued to explain that at the outset of the hostilities, the prisoner-of-war situation was quite a gentlemanly, honorable, and mutually beneficial operation. Using Harper's Ferry as a model, he explained that thousands of our troops had to surrender. The rebels confiscated all the rifles and cannons. The troops were released but escorted from Maryland to Chicago to sit out for a certain time period. Eventually, they returned to duty. This caused me to revisit the thoughts I had held earlier, where the activities seemed like the scoring of a game.

The scoring was how many flags and banners your side confiscated, how many canons, horses? How many soldiers were killed or captured? It made me angry when I had the original thoughts, and it is renewing my anger now.

John soon continued that the first method of handling prisoners evolved into each side establishing prisoner camps. I remember that Charles' first camp in New York was Camp Elmira. It became a prison camp and was known as Camp Hellmira,

Mr. Cramer explained that, at first, this system worked quite well, with like numbers of prisoners being exchanged at short intervals after capture, some released after a few days. It was known as a parole system. There were rules; the parolees were supposed to sit out for 30 days before their return to duty. Of course, this was unenforceable, but it worked. As the war has dragged on, this system has deteriorated and has broken down. The release time to achieve parole has been greatly extended. The prisoners in both camps, North and South, are not receiving proper rations or care. The prisoner exchange system has stalled. The South was receiving their prisoners back in relatively good condition. The Northern Troops were much worse for the experience. When the slaves were emancipated in 1863, and the United States Colored Troops were coming more into play, the Confederate leaders refused to recognize them as free men and include them in exchange or parole. As a result, at this time, there is no system in place. From the prison camps in the south, what little reports are received are not pleasant in their content. So, I say to you, if he is in a prison camp, he is far from being out of danger but likely still alive. With your permission, I would like to request the owner, Thomas Vanderwerken, to join our conversation. Is he known to you? Yes, I am familiar with many in the family.

Chapter 16

EATHEN ALLEN AND THE VANDERWERKEN FAMILY

I can't imagine why Mr. Cramer would seek my permission to invite Thomas Vanderwerken into our conversation. The Vanderwerken Family is known to all in Waterford. By numbers, it may be the largest family in Waterford. Many are business owners, such as Thomas, and most are well respected. Many are members of the Masonic Lodge. Unfortunately, William T. Vanderwerken was responsible for one of Waterford's darkest days just a few years past. Because the Vanderwerken name was linked to the cause of this event, many now immediately associate it with the family when the event is mentioned.

Just four years ago, in July of 1860, William T. Vanderwerken (the family was so large there were 3 William Vanderwerkens in Waterford at the time) assassinated Village Trustee Harrison Sherman. This event occurred on a pleasant summer's day on the corner of Third and Hudson Streets. The act was performed in broad daylight, in full view of many people. Several members of both the Sherman and Vanderwerken Families were among the many witnesses. (44)

Vanderwerken was immediately arrested and placed in the Waterford Jail. Harrison worked for the railroad. When the railroad men learned of this, a crowd of them assembled there with ropes to hang Vanderweken. Waterford Constable Bonce was able to quell the crowd's fervor for justice, and the crowd dispensed with their activity.

Waterford bore witness to the largest funeral procession anyone had ever seen. There were more than 250 Masons in the procession, 100 firemen, and nearly the entire village. It was a very chaotic and emotional time in our village; many recall it now just by mentioning the name. I feel bad for the family, they don't deserve the notoriety, but it's there. (44)

I am not in a position to wonder why Mr. Cramer would want to introduce Thomas into our conversation and would never express opposition to it. I am very concerned and inquisitive to learn the motive. Through the years, I have been friends with John Vanderwerken. However, I have had no real association with any of the others. I have no doubts about John Cramer's motive, and I am eager to learn.

When Thomas joined us, Mr. Cramer explained my concerns in incredible detail, demonstrating the attention he made to my report. Upon his completion, he inquired of Thomas: "Is your cousin Gilbert still active and about in Virginia and our nation's capital?" This question both surprised me and interested me. I knew that the Vanderwerkens were influential, but I didn't know that they extended to our nation's Capital.

Cramer and Thomas Vanderwerken spoke at length about Thomas' Cousin Gilbert. Through this conversation, I was soon to learn that Gilbert had left Waterford in 1847. He had moved to Washington, D. C. and had become quite successful. He was born in Waterford and, as a young man, moved to New Jersey to apprentice in the manufacturing of carriages. After a time, he opened his own business and went bankrupt due to the economics of the times. The Panic of 1837. He returned to Waterford, working in family businesses. In '47, he moved to Virginia. There he was employed by the Washington Omnibus Line in Washington, D. C. In some manner, he was able to obtain the company and renamed it the Vanderwerken Omnibus Line. He had a very successful operation and a fine estate in Virginia, where he bred the horses that he utilized In his transportation business. Much of that has changed during the current war.

Gilbert's business is still doing well, but the war has greatly altered Gilbert's activities. For the defense of the Capital, the government has taken his Virginia Estate. On his lands, they have constructed both Forts Marcy and Ethan Allen. The very fort that Charles was stationed in before he entered the battlefields. General Tidball is now living, when he is in Virginia, in Gilbert's house. Other buildings there are being used as a hospital. (45)

Mr. Cramer inquires if Thomas maintains contact with Gilbert. Thomas indicates that he does. Mr. Cramer then considers perhaps Gilbert could request intelligence of any further news of the location of the men listed as missing from Ream's Station on August 23 - 25, just past. Thomas expressed a willingness to mail a request to Gilbert. He further stated that he wished he could deliver it in person. Many in the Vanderwerken Family would vacation there and enjoy Gilbert's hospitality and horses. No one has enjoyed this hospitality since 1860. Damn, this war and the rebels! At this point, Thomas and John Cramer have a sip of their drinks. I sample my now cold tea.

John Cramer points out that General Tidball is now operating under General Grant, as is the Division that Charles is assigned to. His actions in this conversation thus far have been unemotional and very matter-of-fact. He suggests to Thomas that when he contacts Gilbert concerning the missing soldiers from the 4th, he show concern for all the missing men and, lastly, single out our hometown boy, Charles Shepard.

Thomas stated he would do so tomorrow.

I was exhausted. This conversation was now three hours old. John Cramer is the most enchanting man that I have ever met. At the same time, I was exhilarated. I really felt like we had done something to learn more about Charles. I no longer feel helpless. I am anxious to report today's activities to Harriet.

Announcing my planned departure and expressing, I hope, not over-expressing, my gratitude. Mr, Cramer interrupted me. Please, John, we would like to obtain some satisfaction in this endeavor. There is no guarantee that we will acquire the intelligence we seek or that it will be favorable. As I mentioned earlier, wherever he is, he is likely still in real danger.

After I made my leave, I got thinking back to the Knickerbocker's celebration at the Morgan House many years past; I'm glad that I did not sample any of Mr. Titcomb's wares. If I had, I'd likely be hosting a Chorus of "Three Cheers and a Tiger for John Cramer!" "Three Cheers and a Tiger for Thomas Vanderwerken!"

Chapter 17

A STORY POORLY TOLD?

John left the Morgan House intending to hurry straight home to Sixth St. and Harriett. His head was spinning. His thoughts were good but unconnected. He wasn't accustomed to being in the company of such worldly men as Messrs Cramer and Thomas Vanderwerken. As a canaller, I am accustomed to the language and the environment of my fellow canallers. He took comfort in the thought that if they entered his world on the canals and the situation was reversed, it would be their heads that were spinning at his knowledge and contacts on the canals.

He realized that he had been absent from home much longer than he had anticipated. To gather my thoughts, I will check on the mules and prepare myself to report to Harriett on the events of the day. Also at the barns was young canaller John Walker. John Shepard had taken a liking to this mule driver. He was everything he wished Charles was right now, home and working on the canals. Their mules were boarded in the same shedrow, and young Walker was helpful and eager to learn. His industrious ways and helpful nature are what have endeared me to him for the many months now that we have shared quarters. We talked pleasantly. Walker and I cross paths often. Almost daily during the canal season at the barns. Twice a week, I tow for Mr. Enos of the Rock Island Flour Mill to the West Troy Side Cuts. Walker makes the same trip often for Mr. Chandler of Whitehall. A line driver would make the tow from Whitehall to Waterford, and John Walker would complete the tow from Waterford to the West Troy Locks. John Walker is known to frequent the temptations at the West Troy Side Cuts. They can be dangerous.

Suddenly, I'm wondering why is this young man not in service to our country. My thoughts suddenly become very suspicious of my young friend. I have never entertained these thoughts before; why now?

I quickly excused myself. With now too many thoughts in my head, it was time that I hurried home.

John had left home at about nine this morning. It is about six now. I know Harriett will be concerned.

I need not use my key; Harriett has left the door for me. This is a good indication. After expressing my apologies for being absent so long on this day, I realize my hunger is quite strong. I haven't looked forward to meals lately and have eaten from necessity rather than dining for satisfaction. I tell Harriet, I have had an exciting day, there is a lot of news, and I am very hungry. She appeared to take both pleasure and interest in my statement.

Tonight marks the first time in a while that we all sat for dinner together. Since the letters from Charles ceased in August, the family activities have relaxed, and we have been withdrawn from each other. Conversations have been lax of late. We are all concerned about Charles. No one wants to talk about it, and it may be best unsaid. Dinner passed with the saying of grace, which hadn't occurred in some time, and a silent prayer for Charles' safety and well-being.

After dinner, Emma, Rebecca, and Harriett saw to the kitchen. Soon Emma and Rebecca had gone to tend to Addie and prepare for bed.

When all were settled, I elected to tell Harriett of the excitement of my day. As I reflect, perhaps excitement was the wrong word to use. I also mentioned that I may have news of Charles' situation. This, too, was a poor choice. Harriett wanted that news. I saw a need to relate all of the day's events.

I began with my visit to the Titcomb Distillery and a follow-up with his brother, the attorney. Harriett thought that this was a curious place to start. What about Charles? She asked. Let me explain, I patiently retorted. I mentioned how during my conversation with Attorney Titcomb, John Cramer happened on the scene. That curious old man? Harriett shot back. (She does not look upon Mr. Cramer with the same reverence as I do) What would he know of Charles?

I continued to report on our walk to the Morgan House. Harriett wanted to know what type of business is conducted in the Morgan House so early in the day. She always says nothing good ever goes into or out of the Morgan House. Were any of those Knickerbockers there? Harriett has never been to the Morgan House; perhaps one day, when all is well, we should go.

I explained to her how Mr. Cramer had overheard my conversation with Mr. Titcomb and had taken an interest in my story about Charles, and he recalled me mentioning him in our previous encounter at the Morgan House. At least the mention of Charles had piqued her interest again. It was because of Mr. Cramer's invitation to join him there that I willingly accompanied him.

I told her how I had related all we knew about Charles' activies since he had left Fort Ethan Allen, all of his battlefield reports, the arrival of his daughter, all the events leading up to the Battle of Ream's Station, and the discovery of the report of him being listed as missing. At this point, she was listening with clearer attention. I mentioned how Mr. Cramer had paid attention throughout and allowed me to speak without interruption.

Harriett had been sitting at the edge of her chair; she now assumed a more relaxed posture, sitting fully in her chair. I think that she has resigned herself to hearing the whole story.

It was a good feeling to see her a bit more relaxed. Since we made the discovery of Charles being listed as missing, Harriett's overall decorum has been sullen and disinterested. My story was putting some color or emotion on her face. Some signs of emotion were good to see. Of late, she had become quite removed from life. Her involvement and response in this exchange were, at the same time, bothersome but a welcome change from her sedated ways.

Now I had to report on the response of Mr. Cramer. I felt it necessary to explain how at age 86, he had sat through my lengthy story, again without interruption, and had full comprehension. His report to me was longer than mine to him. I had no reason to suspect the validity

Dear Mother.....I am the Only One Left

of what he told me or the accuracy of his sources. Mr. Cramer believes that from what I had told him that Charles is likely still living. He may very well be in a prison camp. He further stated that he is still in very real danger, but we should still have hope. I could see by the look on her face she wanted to have hope, but I could see that she didn't share my likely misplaced optimism.

I paused for a moment; I had been talking nonstop. Harriett questioned, is that it? I don't see that changing anything except for what that old man thinks.

I couldn't defend my optimistic feelings. I begged that the story is not complete. There is more to relate.

I explained how Thomas Vanderwerken, the owner of the Morgan House, had been requested by Mr. Cramer to join our conversation.

Again, Harriett interrupted the flow of my talk with a welcome display of emotion. Those Vanderwerkens, assassins, murderers, and saloon owners! (I had forgotten that William T., the assassin, did own a Waterford Saloon.) What would they know of Charles? I always think that is important for Harriett to demonstrate her emotions rather than suppress them. It makes me think that she is involved in life rather than hiding from it.

I told the story of Gilbert Vanderwerken's success in Washington D. C., his business dealings, and access to General Tidball. Of how John Cramer had suggested that Thomas should contact his cousin and beg the favor of further information concerning the missing men of the 4th Artillery after the August Battle at Ream's Station. Thomas said he would act on that request.

I was done. Harriett sat quietly for a spell. Finally, she replied; yes, John, that was an exciting day; forgive me, if I don't share your excitement, but I believe what you did today was a worthy attempt. Maybe some good will come of it, but we don't know any more today than we did yesterday.

Maybe I should have approached the story differently.

Chapter 18

A DAY IN THE LIFE

Morning came, as it always does. John thought what such a simple and standard event a new morning is. The morning is not dependent on the evening before it, nor does it owe anything to the morning that will follow. Yet, as long as a man does live, another morning will come. He, and perhaps no one else, had control over that. He was amused by this simple thought. He couldn't come to an agreement within himself if this were a profound thought or so simple that it was silly. He didn't like being silly; certainly, the business of yesterday was profound. Today is a new day. I am satisfied that yesterday's experience has strengthened my ability to feel that I am doing something that could be to Charles' benefit. I did what I could; I did something. Life goes on; time goes on. The war goes on. Charles is missing. Time to look for a tow.

John had been busy with personal affairs. The canal season was entering its final months now in October, with November and some of December still to go. It was time to earn enough to carry us through our winter needs. I can do no more for Charles at this time. I have done what I can.

He reports to the barn and meets up with John Walker again. Walker is most pleasant this morning, which is his usual state if he hasn't tarried too long in West Troy. He inquired where I was towing today. I was quick to admit that I was in search of a tow. Young Walker stated that he had two. One was an overnighter to Fort Edward and another to Mechanicville. The Mechanicville tow was for a regular client, and he felt an obligation to tow that one, but the other was more money. Would I be willing to take the local tow?

John Shepard thought something was on his side these days, the meeting with John Cramer yesterday and now this good fortune with young Walker. It was good to be back on the canal among my people; it just felt right.

The next day was a scheduled Rock Island Flour Mill day. The day after that and many subsequent days went by as they always do at the season's end. There would be a flurry of activity as the boat owners would try to get as many trips in as possible before the winter freeze. As the days get shorter and the weather turns cold, the canal is not as pleasant a place as it is in other months. All the smells that I enjoy that make the canal seem like a friendly and familiar place disappear when a heavy chill exists. All you smell is burning wood. You don't hear the chatter among the boatman or the teamsters on the path. There can be sheets of ice in the canal, and the towpath is less firm and reliable. Canallers are uncomfortable. Tempers can be short. The canal is still familiar, but it just isn't as friendly at this time of year.

Considering how our lives and attitudes have changed since Charles has been in the war and is now listed as missing, the season's closing is being kind to us. That kindness was about to end.

In Mid-November, on a particularly cold day, John arrived home. He was happy to see that Harriett had a good fire in the hearth. A warm home with a hot meal felt good this time of year. I reflected on how Charles was happy to take over the chore of keeping the fire. It made him feel proud. Harriett spoke on the news that President Lincoln had encouraged everyone to honor Thanksgiving this year in honor of our soldiers. She thought we should honor our grandchild's arrival on this special day in November. Addie has been with us for nearly three months. This cold day reminded him of waiting in the cold one February day with Charles to catch a glimpse of soon-to-be President Lincoln. On February 10th, just 4 years ago. Charles and I braved the cold on that early morning. Mr. Lincoln had visited Albany and was staying at the Delavan House in that city. It became known that he would board a train at the Albany Station, and it would proceed slowly through Green Island, Cohoes, and Waterford before traveling to Troy's new train station and then continuing its journey. It had been announced that the train would only stop briefly in Troy but would proceed quite slowly in the selected towns and cities named, giving many at least a chance to view Mr. Lincoln and wave. Charles and I were eager to attend. Harriett and Rebecca did not share our enthusiasm. Rebecca had the desire but was not partial to the cold. Several hundred Waterford souls braved the elements that day. We were to learn later that there were thousands in Cohoes and nearly fifteen thousand in Troy. Charles and I were happy to have had the opportunity to view the president-elect as we did. One has to realize the significance of seeing the man elected to that office is truly a once-in-a-lifetime experience for most people. Charles was thrilled; I was pleased that we were there. I think back now that Charles had written in one of his letters from Fort Ethan Allen that the only time he had leave was that he was going to visit Washington D. C. and shake hands with President Lincoln.

BROOKLYN DAILY EAGLE
February 11, 1862
MOVEMENTS OF MR. LINCOLN

Mr. Lincoln and suite left Albany at 8 o'clock this morning.

The Burgess corps turned out as an escort and made a splendid appearance. A large number of citizens surrounded the Delavan House and lined the depot of the Northern road, sending up enthusiastic cheers as Mr. Lincoln proceeded to the cars. Mayor Thacher, Alderman James J. Johnson, chairman of the Council Committee, and other officials conducted the party to the depot. The departure of the train was the signal for prolonged and hearty cheers. In consequence of difficulty in crossing the river, the special train was taken up to Waterford Junction. Not many persons were out on the line of the road except in Cohoes and Waterford, in consequence of the early hour at which the train started. At Green Island quite a number of persons assembled and at Cohoes the people turned out en masse, thousands of factory employees, including a large number of females, welcoming the train with hearty cheers. At Waterford there was also a large and enthusiastic assembledge. No stoppages were made at these villages, but the train passed slowly through, giving the crowds ample opportunity to gratify their curiosity and vent their patriotic feelings.

Looking back now, perhaps Charles and I should have gone to Troy. Although in Waterford, we were two of several hundred and were able to see Mr. Lincoln well and wave, in Troy, we would have been in a party with fifteen thousand. We likely made the right decision. It even felt like Lincoln waved back to us; Charles was sure that he had. In Troy, we may not have actually seen him as close up as we were. We were only about twelve feet away. It was a good experience despite the low temperature.

It was good to be lost in my memories with pleasant thoughts of Charles. Simple thoughts of him coming of age to take care of our home fires. His light-hearted letter about his intention to shake hands with President Lincoln. Our vigil in the cold to witness the president's slow ride through Waterford. All pleasant and long-held, dear memories.

My rare moments of relaxation and restful, pleasant thoughts were interrupted once more by Harriett as she announced that dinnertime was upon us. Another welcomed time on such a cold but, thus far, satisfying day.

After dinner and the completion of nightly chores, Harriett joined me near the fireplace. I had replaced the wood supply, Which was one of Charles' jobs that I now had to resume. She remarked that I seemed at peace this evening and more relaxed than I have been of late. I agreed and mentioned my good fortune of helping John Walker yet again, with that same tow today. She knows Walker's habits well and stated she hoped it didn't involve the West Troy area; I soothed her concerns by stating that Walker had gone ahead to Fort Edward and I had journeyed to Mechanicville. I also mentioned how I had become accustomed to Charles taking care of our hearths and of the time we saw Lincoln on the train. Other talk involved the daily activity about the house, the comings and goings of Rebecca and Emma, how close they are becoming, and how Addie is growing. Now, in the calm of the evening, she announces that a messenger came around this afternoon from John Cramer's Office and left an envelope for you.

I fell silent. It had been a good day; because of the war and our concerns about Charles, there were so few really good days. What could be in this envelope? The choices are endless. Good News? Bad news? No news; maybe there is nothing to report. This has ended my relaxed time. I wanted to chastise Harriett for her delayed reporting of this visit and receipt of the envelope. I chose not to. My desire was to receive news of Charles' situation. The contents of the envelope may have some bearing. I requested her to supply me with the envelope.

She quickly returned with the envelope and set it on the table next to me. I did not reach out for it. Inwardly, I was very apprehensive concerning its contents. Outwardly, I'd like to think that my demeanor was steadfast. Aren't you going to open it she asked. I have been home now for several hours, and there was no presentation or announcement of the receipt of this envelope earlier. She has elected to wait until now. Now that we are alone? When I told her a few weeks back of my discussion with Cramer and Vanderwerken, she felt little would come of it. Now there is interest.

I had gathered myself enough to ensure that I could learn the contents of it without opening it with trembling fingers; Harriett's outward appearance was one of interest yet braced with fear. I opened it with an accompanying release of a deep breath. Paused and announced its contents.

Mr. Shepard.
 Our efforts with General Tidball, through Gilbert Vanderwerken, have been fruitful. At a time convenient to you, please repair to my office to further our discussion.
  You're Servant John Cramer

Dear Mother.....I am the Only One Left

We spent the rest of the evening in a mutual state of not discussing the obvious matter at hand. The thoughts of what it could mean were unending. We felt it better to maintain our hopes and not bolster our fears. We both gazed into the comforting fire for much of the remainder of the evening. I kept seeing Charles. Harriett seemed at peace once again. I won't see John tomorrow. It is so near the end of the season I can't delay any of Mr. Enos' deliveries. I must execute his tow. Other than to ease our curiosity, my urgency to speak with Mr. Cramer will have no bearing on Charles' situation, good or bad.

Chapter 19

.....HURRY UP & WAIT

Almost every canaller lives their life to these words. Many people believe that the canaller's life is slow-paced. The mules and the drivers are advancing at a relaxed pace along the towpath. The canal boats are being towed two or three miles an hour. To the non-canal observer, it looks rather idyllic. Beneath the surface, it can be hectic and frenetic, well hidden to the noninitiated.

The canal is business. The canal, the rivers, and the railroads account for a large part of the economy of our divided nation and the war effort itself. The canallers are always in a hurry to complete their current delivery, to load and deliver their next cargo, to get through the next lock, and to keep on schedule. It just doesn't look like it, and most canallers would chuckle at the word schedule. They are a breed of people who must accomplish assignments as quickly as possible and move on to the next job. That is their economy, to take the opportunity to earn as much as possible in a canal season, which no one ever knows for sure when it will end. The quicker or earlier a good freeze comes often, will put an end to the canal economy. One can risk the possibility of being frozen in place if they stay too late in the season. How often will there be breaks in the canal, sunken boats, low water, or other stoppages of canal traffic? The sooner a canaller can earn enough to carry him over to the spring opening, the sooner he can plan to get off the canal before the freeze and the close-down becomes a reality. The greater age a canaller attains and the more experienced in the ways of the canal he becomes, the more he understands; hurry up and wait.

John finds himself in the embodiment of hurry up and wait as he begins his day today. He never likes to trap himself in the hurry-up-and-wait game, but today he's in it,

This morning he arrived at the barns early; neither his usual barn companion John Walker nor any of the others were in attendance as yet this cold morning. John Shepard was not keen on conversation or company today. He was in a hurry. He prepped his team, hitched up, and was on his way. He experienced a slight delay on the towpath at the head of the Side Cuts. Fred Bass was locking one down from the Champlain Canal to the river, so the portable bridge had been set aside to affect the lock through. John assisted with the bridge replacement and exchanged necessary pleasantries with Fred. "On your way to the flour mill today, John?" "Yes indeed," was the reply, "a right day for it." He hurried off.

Thankfully there was no wait at the mill. Mr. Enos and his hands, as is their custom, had the boat loaded, staffed, and ready to go. To John's dismay, though he noted, looking down towards lock 4 and the Mohawk River, going into Cohoes, there were many lined to go. Mr. Himes from his mill had three boats ready, and there appeared to be two from Massoitt Mills. This mill was started by one of the Whites. John had forgotten if it was Hugh or Canvas; it may have been both. John had learned that the canal may never have become the success that it is today without the cement perfected by White that would hold underwater, making the locks and aqueducts workable. John felt if you have to wait, may as well be a result of a man who made the whole thing possible. Here I am, hurrying up and waiting.

Oftentimes during a wait, conversations will develop between the boaters and the drivers. Sometimes the drivers would gather on the towpath and discuss what could be done to speed things up. John was not in a sociable mood. He had a lot on his mind concerning the upcoming meeting with Mr. Cramer. In an effort to avoid the anticipated talks among the canallers, he expressed a need to them to stand by his team to make the passage of any opposing traffic easier, should something come this way.

Thinking back now of the envelope of last night, John felt it best not to appear too eager to learn the content of what he had discovered.

As much as he wanted to know, he began to realize that on the canal, the hurry-up-and-wait doctrine had become his way of life. He has been fortunate for many years on the canal. Let the hurry up and wait continue. John had already asked his Crow Hill neighbor Robert Halpin to stop in at John Cramer's office and announce that he would appear at his office the next day as he had obligations today. He had considered asking Harriett to complete this task. He had decided against it for fear that Mr. Cramer might tell Harriett what he had uncovered. I don't think she was up to the task of being the first to know. She had stopped reading the letters some time ago. Also, she didn't share my high regard for Mr. Cramer. Tomorrow will be the day.

John was relieved by his thoughts. When he comes to this relief, he feels as though he is in command of a situation, and it's not just fate. He recognizes that he just thinks this; it's not reality, yet creates within him peace of mind.

Hopefully, within the passage of another hour, we'll be through Lock 4 and into Cohoes. We normally only tow to the West Troy Weigh Station. Today we must drop at the West Troy Side Cuts.

Unlike his friend John Walker, John Shepard is not keen on the atmosphere that surrounds the environment of West Troy Side Cuts. Fortunately, the Rock Island light boat (empty) is ready to tow back to the Waterford Mill. He need not tarry there and is soon on his way back to Waterford. The boat preceding him on the return trip is his friend William Cole. John had towed his boat on this trip the last Christmas season when Charles was still at home. William's Nephew George had been captured early in the war. Perhaps I may get the opportunity to explore that incident with William sometime this evening. All day long, he had been avoiding conversation; now, he was looking to instigate one.

At the Juncta in Cohoes. the break-off of the Champlain Canal from the Erie, there was much traffic. The Champlain boats were being held in the Cohoes Basin, the very spot that John had previously laid over when he had visited Mrs. Westover, Charles Westover's mother, seeking information on John Troy's family. This would gain him the opportunity to engage his friend William.

John and William hadn't crossed paths on the canal since that tow in December two years back. They did see each other on several occasions when they would be leading teams in opposite directions. This would lead to an acknowledgment of each other but no time to converse. At that time, they had discussed his nephew's activities on the battlefield. Charles was still at Fort Ethan Allen then. William had reported on George's capture in August of '62 at the first Battle of Bull Run. John had listened the first time but didn't really follow or understand the story. Now with Charles possibly being captured, he would like to learn more about George's experience. John was pleased when William opened the conversation by inquiring about Charles' activities.

He quickly informed William of the several battles that Charles had been in leading up to Ream's Station, his subsequent possible capture, listed as missing, the unknown element that followed, and his discussion with John Cramer.

William agreed, without knowing the full content of that discussion, i.e., the Vanderwerken influence, that if anyone in Waterford could learn that information, it would be Mr. Cramer. William went on to mention how although George was captured, he was one of several thousand that were captured that day. This was early in the war. They were taken off the battlefield, relieved of the weaponry, rifles and artillery, and paroled to a fort in Chicago. The parole was effective the day after the battle. It took several weeks for that many prisoners to travel to Chicago. Because this was early in the war, both sides were operating on a gentlemen's agreement on the handling of prisoners. Each side actually honored the terms of parole. Effectively, this put George and the rest out of the war until spring. By the time parole was up, winter had set in. This gave these soldiers a good amount of much-needed training during this parole period. That first Battle of Bull Run was their initial battle, and they were untrained. As far as we have learned, his unit is now in the Southern Campaign, but we are not sure where.

Author's note: William went on to fight in the Battle of Olustee, Florida. There he was wounded in action and captured. He was released from prison on October 18, 1864, and mustered out from the Foster Hospital in North Carolina on May 2, 1865. William passed in 1912. James Gettings of Waterford was wounded and captured in the battle. He later perished in the Andersonville prison in Georgia.

Henry Drummer and Ezra Stone, both of Waterford, were wounded in this battle but survived the war. They were both mustered out in June of 1865. (46)

His conversation with John Cramer, a few days passed, had given John the ability to better understand the content of George's story.

The first time he had heard William relate this story, it was Christmastime. He empathized with William on George's situation but could not comprehend the brevity of it then as he can now.

The activity stirred up in the Cohoes Basin. The Erie traffic had cleared, we were soon to move. I thanked William for his information and bid him good evening. We were moving again.

Chapter 20

.....THE WAITING IS THE HARDEST PART

After the Erie traffic cleared, William and I were the lead tows to Waterford. After we locked through Locks 1 and 2 in Cohoes, we learned the river was at a proper level, and we could lock straight through Lock 3 in Cohoes and Lock 4 in Waterford. This enabled me to drop the light boat at the flour mill and return to the barns just as dusk changed to dark. On the final part of that journey, I was thinking of the tale that William had told of his nephew's plight and how it had related to my prior conversation with Mr. Cramer. I must visit John Cramer tomorrow.

    I began the day with an abbreviated conversation with John Bass at the Waterford Side Cuts by my own design. I wanted no further conversation tonight; there was too much on my mind to feign being congenial. I had hoped things would be quiet at the locks or John would be off duty. I was happy to discover that one of his new assistants was on duty, and the moveable bridge was in place. This allowed me free movement to the barns with just a courteous wave of acknowledgment to the locktender. I was happy to be headed to the barn. Once there, I was surprised to make note of my neighbor Robert Halpin. I had requested him to visit Mr. Cramer and tell him of my plan to meet with him tomorrow. I hadn't requested Robert to make a report to me. His appearance at the barn gave me cause for concern. We live on different streets. Me on Sixth St. and Robert on Pine Street, but our properties border each other, so we often meet as a matter of course. It is strange that he is here waiting for me.

    "Hello, Bob." I called out, "You startled me with your appearance here." He stated that he was out for his evening walk, thought he recognized me on the towpath and came to the barn. I have known him for many years. I can not ever remember seeing Bob on an evening walk; perhaps I just never paid attention.

"Were you able to drop in on Mr. Cramer," I asked. Yes was his reply, and he is very keen to see you. Bob stated that he promised Mr. Cramer that he would deliver that message to me. By making that promise, he felt indebted to Mr. Cramer to make good on his pledge. He did not want to relay that message through Harriett, as I had requested him to make the visit to Mr. Cramer to avoid exposing her to what it might contain. I thanked him for his efforts and concern on our behalf. He went on to say that Mr. Cramer did not tell him any of the details of his conversation with me. He did, however, question him concerning his son John's time after he was captured. I explained to him that he was captured at the First Battle of Harper's Ferry. After hearing that, Mr. Cramer stated, say no more; I am aware of that battle's outcome. He then went into a lengthy review of the current captured prisoner policies as only Mr. Cramer could. After Cramer had completed his remarks and requested that I encourage you to report to him soon, I felt the need to make that report regardless of the hour or the wait.

I thanked Robert for his attention and his service. I had been attending to the mules as he made his report to me. We walked together back to our homes. As we did, we reminisced about the letter we had received not too long ago from Charles when he wrote how he had met up with some Waterford boys in Virginia and that one of them was John. John and Charles were the same age and were friends. John had joined the army earlier than Charles, and they were in different regiments. How ironic that John Shepard and Robert Halpin should be talking about their sons Charles and John. The two fathers were in Waterford, and the sons in Virginia. They had arrived at their homes. For John Shepard, the wait had begun.

Author's note: John Halpin enlisted August 11, 1862, mustered in as a private, captured in action September 16, 1862, at Harper's Ferry, Virginia, and mustered out June 23, 1865, at Smithville, North Carolina. (47)

He had made the decision to tell Harriett that today was a day like any other on the canal. He would not mention the conversations with either William Cole or Robert Halpin. He mentioned it was a trying and long day. He was tired. Dinner was enjoyed in relative silence. John thought, we now wait for the new day.

The new day came early for John; though tired, he had too many thoughts in his mind for any meaningful sleep. In years past, when he was still involved in overnight towing on a regular basis, John could be away from home for three or four days at a time. In those days, many canallers would retire at nightfall after dinner and awaken before sunrise. All would be tired after ten or twelve hours of towing. Sleep would come easy. Generally, not too much thought had to be put into the activities of the following day. It was routine. There were surprises, but experienced canallers were accustomed to dealing with surprises. With those thoughts and remembrances, John could relax, ease his mind, and set a course for this new day. Eventually drifting off to sleep, he did arise quite rested and ready for what John Cramer had uncovered.

Harriett has been coping with Charles' absence from our home and life since we received the letter concerning the bullet hole in his cap. She does this with silent prayer and thought. She still has not read another letter since that time. I still place them on the table by my chair. She may read them while I am away. If she does, she does not make mention of them. Other than all of us missing Charles and harboring our own concerns for his safety and welfare, there has been very little recent conversation in our home concerning Charles. I would like to have more conversations with Harriett on this matter. I believe that she is coping so well with Rebecca, Emma, and the new baby, Addie, that they are all caught up and busy with household activities and do not have the time for a lot of thought. One of the things that I have always enjoyed on the canal is my time alone to think. If all goes right, towing on the canal can create long periods of time where a man is alone, with only his thoughts to keep him company. In the past, John could always think things through and usually resolve any issue. He had become, over the years, accustomed to sharing many of those thoughts with Harriett. Her opinions on these thoughts were welcomed. Now, in deference to her removal from involvement in thoughts about Charles, I am discovering that I miss her insight.

John elected to have a proper breakfast this morning. He would make his first order of business to address the mules. Not knowing what to anticipate from Mr. Cramer, he just wanted to arrive at his office with a clear mind and a relaxed demeanor. He set no timetable. Upon his arrival at the shedrow that he shares with John Walker, he notices that Walker has done all the work in the barn. The mules have been seen to; John Walker's and his own. He thanked him for doing so but, at the same time, wished he hadn't. He would review his thoughts from the night before while taking care of the mules. Walker soon left to pick up his tow. Again, I was left with my thoughts. I find I can think better when I am doing some work at the same time. Young Walker, while committing an act of kindness, has actually committed a disservice. He meant well.

The wait continues.

As the 1864 season was nearing its end, John decided he would call on Mr. Enos of the Rock Island Mill and establish how many tows would be necessary to West Troy in the coming weeks. Ne needed to fill some time before he felt it right to stop by Mr. Cramer's office. This would be a productive and necessary act, as well as use up some time. If he still wasn't in a mind to meet with Cramer, he might visit with the Reverend Bush Family and make the winter's accommodations for the mules.

He spoke at length with Mr. Enos. It was decided at least two more tows would be effective before the season's end, with a possibility of a third. Mr. Enos wanted to stop production about the second week in December. It had been a favorable season on the canal for John this year; a few more tows should put him in good stead for the winter.

It was nearing ten in the morning; John felt that the time was right, and now he will make his appointment with John Cramer. As he made his way from the mill on the towpath, he crossed the side cut locks and past the blacksmith on Fifth Street; he was soon on Broad Street. The day was cold. There were a good many about their business on Broad St. John had but one purpose, that was to attend to Mr. Cramer. He saw several acquaintances on his walk down Broad to the Barnfather Building that housed Mr. Cramer's and Mr. Titcomb's offices. He nodded hello to several; he didn't want to engage in conversation. He may have mentioned the coldness of the day to those he nodded to as an excuse to continue walking. He hoped that none felt dismissed by his actions. He had a single purpose. He was ready to hear Cramer's report. He could wait no longer.

He was at the Barnfather Building at the corner of Third and Broad Streets. He entered, gave a wave to Mr. Titcomb, then went straight to the stairs for Mr. Cramer's second-floor office. As he climbed the stairs, he quietly wondered why the younger Mr. Titcomb, a relative newcomer to Waterford, occupied the first floor while the octogenarian Cramer was relegated to the second. Mr. Cramer greeted him through his open door as he arrived at the landing.

"Come in, John; come in; I've been expecting you."

He made me feel as though I was on time, though I had no appointed time to be there. I sensed, somehow, that he knew I would arrive at this time. Trying not to show my central interest in the news on Charles, I apologized for sending Robert Halpin as my messenger the other day. Then I mentioned my curiosity about him occupying the second floor.

He walked to the window and asked me to join him. He went on to tell me how he has occupied this corner on the second floor for more years than I have been on this earth. He explained how he had lost this corner in the great fire of '41. How much he felt at home here. When he represented Waterford in the National Congress, he felt most comfortable when he returned home and could observe the activities from his perch above the street. When he could observe the people on the streets and be aware of the commerce on the river and the canal, he knew things were right. Back in 1816, when he was the first Supervisor for the Town of Waterford, he thought where better to look over and shepherd the town's business, but from this site. On the first floor, you are part of the crowd. One can get lost in a crowd. A good shepherd needs to not be above the crowd but needs to see them and be aware of their needs. No first floor for me. I like to think that I have been a good shepherd.

I am always in awe of John Cramer. I made a pledge to myself not to distract him again with my weak attempts at conversation. I did note to myself that, indeed, John Cramer was as at home on his second-floor perch as I was on the canal. This made sense to me.

He had a large desk in his office, at which he had been seated when I arrived. After we had finished at the window, he directed me to take a chair at his table. He then retrieved his ever-present sheaf of papers, closed the office door, and joined me there.

He opened his report by thanking me for coming to him and seeking assistance in this matter. It was wise of us to enlist Thomas Vanderwerken in our conversation. His cousin Gilbert was very influential in obtaining the necessary intelligence to uncover the leads that had been discovered.

From my prior experiences with Mr. Cramer, it begins to appear that if he is addressing a crowd or an individual, he attempts first to put the listener at ease. Not knowing what the content of this report will contain, I don't think I can be put at ease. Am I demonstrating my anxiety too greatly? I must just listen with attention and comprehend what I hear.

Mr. Cramer then harkens back to July of this year and that awful battle that Charles wrote about. It became known as the Battle of the Crater.

He continued, John, there was a great battle fought on the closing days of July this year. It was a battle prepared for and planned over a long period of time. If successful, its design was such that it would have been the impetus to end this rebellion. Several Regiments of men from the Commonwealth of Pennsylvania, many of them coal miners, worked for many days digging a tunnel from under the battlefield to the rebel stronghold. The intention was to stuff it with explosives, and just before the Union charge, in General Burnside's words, "Blow it all to Hell!" It was further designed to unleash a managed and unrelenting attack with fresh troops to take advantage of the confusion and fear brought upon by the explosion. Two major things went wrong. The hour of the planned attack did not occur on schedule. The fuse to ignite the charge had to be repaired at great peril. This altered the timing for the rest of the operation. Perhaps more importantly, the day before the attack, several generals had some second thoughts. The U. S. C. T. (United States Colored Troop) was to be the first to launch an attack. They were inexperienced but eager and well-trained. Some generals thought the first in unit would be massacred. Others thought the first in would have an easy time of it. After much debate, they replaced the U.S.C.T. unit with a regular army unit that was not trained for this special operation. As a matter of fact, they were replaced by a unit drawn by lot rather than ability or experience. This new assignment was borne to General James Ledlie, said by some to be a drunk and a coward. As a result, the wave of charge after charge moving forward turned into the Union forces, all entering the crater left behind by the explosion and staying there. This gave the rebels time to recover from the shock and a position on higher ground. It also gave the rebel forces an advantage. The cost of lives and men wounded in the Union cause has been one of the largest of the current efforts. Had it been successful, the way to Richmond and the ending of this conflict would have been opened. (48)

It appeared that Mr. Cramer had completed his thought. I mentioned how Charles had written to us about this battle. He made mention of many of these points, stated it was the worst he had seen yet, and thought that the Waterford Boys were fortunate to come out of it in good order. He had petitioned us to pray that this war and murder, he called it, would end soon.

Mr. Cramer replied that he offered similar prayers each evening. He then continued his report.

At this time, John, General Grant is readying the army for a siege on Petersburgh to weaken Richmond's defenses. His plans call for the destruction of the railroad lines that supply the Confederate army. It is thought that when the South loses its railroads, it will lose its ability to engage in a war. General Hancock's II Corp has been assigned to destroy the railroad. There have occurred several pitched battles there, with much track being destroyed, many lives lost, and men wounded and captured. Although the Union destroyed some effectiveness of the railroad, they did not shut it down, nor did they win the battle.

I restrained myself from interrupting. I was becoming excited by the fact that Charles had related much of this information in his letters and how clear now it was becoming. Finally, I said, "Yes, yes, Charles told us of this!" I hoped that I had said it excitingly, not in agitation. I was so keen to learn something new. So far, I am hearing more detail about things that I already knew.

Perhaps Mr. Cramer could sense my growing anticipation to hear some real news. More likely, he was just building up to it. I was beginning, I believe, to understand his way. First, he puts you at ease and gains your trust and confidence. Then he releases information on a subject that he feels will draw you into his flow of thought. Once he believes he has your proper interest or believes that you are becoming impatient, he will release the desired information.

He reported. Through the intelligence acquired by Gilbert Vanderwerken, we have determined that Charles and many others are still listed as missing. As best as can be determined, the Ream's Station and surrounding battle areas have been cleared of wounded and casualties, which have been recovered or laid to rest. Anyone who is still listed as missing is now thought to be a prisoner. If a person is still missing and yet unwounded and able, they would have made their way back to a Union Camp by now. I think it best to surmise that he is alive and taken prisoner. There is no guarantee that our summary is correct. Gilbert was able to uncover and report the intelligence from some southern journalists that Union prisoners were being taken to Libby Prison in Richmond, Virginia. There they are processed. The officers usually remain there. The others are then moved to a prison camp on Belle

Isle, also in Richmond. At present, both of these camps are way over overcapacity. Conditions and management are seriously lacking at both locations. There exists information that the Prison Camp at Salisbury in North Carolina will soon be taking transfers from Belle Isle. If all of this is correct, and we have no way of knowing, it is suspected that Charles is somewhere between the Belle Isle Prison to the Salisbury Prison. Under current conditions, it is doubtful if proper paperwork or accounting of new prisoners will ever be forthcoming.

I was silent. John was silent. I could sense that he had not completed his report. As I took in all that he had said, I felt like a lifetime had gone by. Was it my lifetime? Was it Charles? Have I really learned anything? What's next? Are we still waiting? I was lost in my thoughts. I don't know how long I was silent. I did not express any of my questions out loud.

At last, Mr. Cramer, looking comfortable in his chair, arose and went to his window. He gazed out onto a now-darkening Broad Street. He turned to me and said:

John, I have just glanced out from my cherished position on Broad Street. I see a street where it's neither day nor is it night. Our country right now is in the same position. Thomas Fuller, an English Theologer some 200 years ago, stated, "It is always the darkest before the day dawneth." We can only hope that your Charles is in a position of a new day dawning. In my many years of observing the world from this window, I have seen the sunset on many a day, some good, some bad. I have seen the sunrise on both good days and bad.

I know the day will come when I will see the sunrise no more. That day will come for us all. I am prepared; I have had a lot of time to prepare. You, in your life, have witnessed this. I am aware of the loss of your two daughters.

To finalize my report to you, if Gilbert's intelligence is factual, and I believe it is, the future for those incarcerated in southern prisons is bleak. The siege continues. It is a waiting game. The northern forces can outwait the south. Rebel soldiers are surrendering; many are starving.

There are reports of flocks of pigeons that are disappearing throughout the South because the population and the soldiers are eating them. If the rebels can't feed their own troops, this will hasten the war's end. However, if they can't feed their troops, how can we anticipate that they can feed their overcrowded prisons? I don't want to send you away with no hope. Not every prisoner will die in prison, but many will. All we can do now is hope and pray for a timely end to this rebellion and that the good Lord will look over those yet contained by it.

As he finished, I couldn't help but think how Charles's last few letters had stated how the Lord had been looking over him and how he hoped he would continue to do so. He also mentioned in his last letter that he hoped to return from the battle in which he was captured.

I quietly thanked Mr. Cramer for his efforts. I had the feeling that he took no satisfaction in delivering such a message. Somehow I felt better as a result. Relieved is not the correct way to state my feeling, but neither was worried. Perhaps numb with no sense of direction? The wait continues.

Chapter 21

.....HOW DOES IT FEEL?
TO HAVE NO DIRECTION KNOWN

Leaving Mr. Cramer's Office, I felt lost. I felt frozen, not from the cold December day, but more like the canaller who allows himself to become frozen in at the end of a too-long season. The canaller is trapped where he is and has nowhere to go and nowhere to turn. I'm out on the street, alone. The street is busy, but I am alone. I don't want to go home, but I must. At least, unlike the frozen canaller, I can go home. John had amused himself with that thought and now found he was able to go home. He finally took the first few tentative steps on Broad Street; I'm not frozen; I can move. He decided to reverse direction and go down Broad Street to Second Street. Mr. Cramer's advice was coming back to him now. Of hope, even though it may look bleak. Always darkest before the dawn, his pace started to quicken. Yes, we can have hope; we must have hope; Charles would want us to have hope. He would probably joke about it. He had turned off Second Street now and was on Division Street, going up Slades Hill. He was headed home. I will arrive with hope. The Christmas season is upon us, a time for all mankind to have hope.

John thought back to that Christmas not too long ago. Charles had announced that he had enlisted in the 4th Artillery; Emma was expecting; Charles wanted to purchase the lot next to us on Sixth and Division Street; it was a Christmas of good news. Maybe, hopefully, this Christmas will bring good news. If nothing else, we will have hope.

The brisk walk up Division Street instead of Broad Street had given me the time and clear head that I needed to report to Harriett. The cold air and quick pace had invigorated me to the point of now being happy that I was headed home.

I didn't realize that I had been with Mr. Cramer for so long. It was very near dinner time. Rebecca and Emma are not aware of my business with Mr. Cramer, so it will be later in the evening before I will have the opportunity to address the issue with Harriett. I think the best approach will be to offer only necessary information, be as brief as possible, and emphasize the idea of maintaining hope.

After my brisk walk in the cold early evening air, it was comforting to feel the warmth of the house. Rebecca and Harriett were doing some decorating around the house; I was happy to see that. It was minor and restrained, not like the Christmas just past or previous ones from when Rebecca and Charles would excitedly wait in anticipation of St. Nick's arrival. I was happy to see the fine lithograph that I had purchased at Pease's House of Fancy last year was back on display on the mantle. It does signify mankind's hope for salvation by way of the birth of a child. Addie is with us for her first Christmas; there will be hope in the Shepard house this season. Emma is feeding Addie near the warmth of the hearth. It is a pleasant sight, and strangely enough, I see her eyes show some contentment. I usually avoid her eyes; to me, they always reflect sadness. With all of us being resigned to our lack of knowledge or contact with Charles and now armed with the intelligence that I have gained from Mr. Cramer, there is a hopeful atmosphere in our home on this evening.

Emma had finished feeding Addie. Rebecca and Harriett proceeded to serve our dinner. Rebecca has had become her habit some time ago, would say grace at our nightly meal. At the completion, she would quietly petition the Lord to continue to protect Charles. All of us appreciated this and even looked forward to it being said. For the last two months, this is the only mention of Charles. It was not an announced or mutual decision not to discuss Charles; we were all just more comfortable not talking about it. Harriett had mentioned that we all hold Charles in our thoughts, hopes, and prayers; there is nothing else we can do; sometimes, the less said, the better. Everyone has been considerate of Harriett's announcement.

After dinner, everyone attended to their nightly chores. Rebecca was very busy; she had grown up fast during this trying period. She helped her mother with all the household chores very willingly. She enjoyed helping Emma with Addie. They are becoming close, and I believe that may account for the contentment that I now note in Emma's eyes. Rebecca is even making sure that we have enough firewood in the house. In looking for hope, it is in our household. Perhaps hope will benefit our situation.

I was sitting by the fire, just enjoying the atmosphere of warmth and contentment in our home this evening. Harriett was soon to join me. I had a book on my lap; I wasn't reading. Harriett had brought her knitting bag with her and was quietly beginning to knit. It was a contest now; she knew of my plan to meet with Mr. Cramer. Was she going to inquire, or did I need to announce it? Because the evening was one of contentment, and we have been respecting her desire not to discuss Charles and the war, I didn't want to change the mood of this evening by making an announcement. I picked up the book and pretended to begin reading. Shortly thereafter, she broke her silence. "Well, what did that old man have to say?" I don't know why she thinks so little of Mr. Cramer. I'm not going to ask; I'm just pleased that she wants to hear.

Taking my cue from Harriett's terse questioning, I began my relaxed, although unrehearsed reply, in a thought-out manner. My response was planned to be as simplistic as possible and address the realistic potential outcome of the current situation. I explained how through the efforts and contacts of Mr. Vanderwerken, Mr. Cramer had not determined the following, but he believes it has come to pass. Since the day he became listed as missing, it is likely that he was captured on the very day of his last letter to us. This is not known, but it is a strong and credible belief. Other prisoners from that battle are known to be being held at prisons in North Carolina and Virginia. Mr. Cramer reported that intelligence had been received that, coupled with the current siege of Petersburg and food shortages being suffered in the south, this is a most inopportune time to find oneself in a Southern Prison Camp. Mr. Cramer advises that we maintain hope for Charles' well-being. Hope, prayer, the success of the siege, and a quick end to the current conflict would all be our allies in seeing Charles returned to our lives.

I had no more to say. Harriett sat silently. She picked up her knitting, stared into the comforting glow of the fire, and remained still, silent, and staring for an extended time.

I chose not to interrupt or question her. She would come to terms and respond. Eventually, she returned to her knitting but remained silent. After a while, she quietly and, to my surprise, requested to see the last letter we had received from Charles. Honoring her request, I removed the letter from the envelope and passed it to her. To my surprise, she didn't immediately read it; she just held it for some time. I went back to my reading, although I merely had the book on my lap to appear that I was so engaged. Once more, I waited. What would be her reaction? She has not shared many thoughts and has engaged in limited conversation concerning Charles or the war for three months now.

Finally, she reads.

Reams Station, August 25, 1864

Dear Father,

I received your most kind letter and was happy to hear that you are all well. I am well and hope this letter will find you the same. Well Father, I have been on the go since the 12th and I am most played out. The 2 Corps left Deep Bottom Saturday night and marched all night. It rained and it was awfully muddy. We marched about 25 miles. We got to Petersburg Sunday morning about 7 o'clock. I was about done in. Well, we went in camp, I put my tent up and went to sleep. About 11 o'clock we heard the 5 corps had taken the Weldon Railroad. We was ordered to pack up. Well, we went down to the railroad about 4 miles and stayed there all night and had a good rest. In the morning we were ordered to go down to the railroad and tear up the tracks. We tore the tracks up for about 10 miles. I tell you the 2 Corps has seen tough times since the 12th. We are going back to today or tonight, then I will get a chance to write more. At least I hope so, well Father, I will tell you about a scrap that my Company and Company A got into and its a scrap I don't want to get into every day. Company H and A were sent out to support a Brigade of Calvary. When we got there we found them dismounted and in a line of battle. Well, our two Companies formed on their right and made a charge, We charged and drove them back about a mile, till we got in a nest of them. Then they drove us back. Oh, how hot it was. We lost 25 killed and wounded. Half our Company got sunstroke. I got back by the skin of my teeth. Well, I must close because I am afraid we will move. So, good-bye. I will write to Em, next chance I get. A kiss to all, 6 or 7 for the baby. Good-bye and God bless you all. Tell Em, that John Troy is killed or a prisoner. C. Shepard

    The silence continued after the reading was complete. It then appeared she reread it. She seemed collected. She sighed, held the letter to her breast, and asked; we have heard no more?

    Only what I learned through the efforts of John Cramer and Mr. Vanderwerken was my reply. Their summation of Charles being in a war prison is reasonable. If his life had been lost in battle, accident, or disease, we would have learned by now. If he had been wounded, we would have been informed. If he were able, he would have written. It only makes sense that after being listed as missing, he is now a prisoner, like his friend John Troy.

Harriett's response was short and hopeful. Let's hope that he is with his friend John, and together they may help each other safely through this.

She looked more receptive to this news than I had anticipated. She looked more alive. She had been quiet, reserved, and matter-of-fact these past several months; it was good to hear her express her thoughts.

Again the wait continues.

Chapter 22

.....AND IN THE END, THE LOVE YOU TAKE

Having made the last trip for Mr. Enos of the mill, I decided to stop towing for the season. I had called on Mrs. Bush at the farm and informed her of my intent to once again board the mules with her. She was pleased with my intentions and said she would look forward to my visit. My friend Walker was absent from the barns today. I was hoping to wish him well until we meet again in the spring. I realized there is much I really don't know about young Mr. Walker. I know not where he lives. I don't know his family. He has always been helpful and kind to me. I don't know his thoughts on the war; he never speaks of it. Did he serve? Was he exempt? Was he able to pay for a replacement? It bothered John to have these end-of-the-season, Christmastime thoughts. What did it matter what Walker's views on the war or his part in it were? He was a good and honest canaller, a good barn mate, and a friend. None of this had any bearing on Charles.

The end of the season is always a time of mixed emotions. After a good season financially and the onslaught of the cold weather and unavoidable freeze, it can be a welcome and needed relief from daily obligations and activities. It provides time in one's life to enjoy time with family and friends or even just to enjoy the slower pace of life for the next three months. A benefit possibly only appreciated by the local farmers and canallers, but you had to work hard for it.

These were the thoughts on his mind as he led his mules from the Grogh Street Stables to the Bush Farm. It wasn't a long walk for the last of the season. A few minutes at best, a short visit with Mrs. Bush, and the season would be over. After wishing Mrs. Bush and her family well for the upcoming holiday and receiving reassurance from her that both she and Reverend Bush were keeping Charles in their prayers, he took his leave. Now the 1864 season was over.

But, no, it wasn't. John thought of how his connection to John Cramer had helped him gain some knowledge about Charles' present situation. Without Abe Brewster, this intelligence may have gone undiscovered. Abe had welcomed John to join him for dinner at the Morgan House the night of Addie's birth. The subsequent after-dinner conversation was his first personal exposure to John Cramer. I will stop at the Weigh Lock and offer Abe my best wishes for the new year and the 1865 towing season. He suddenly felt enlightened. It must be a mixture of the holidays, the end of a successful towing season, and Harriett's reentry to the current days, all of these things made him feel content and happy. It has been some time since thoughts and feelings like this had entered his mind. It was good to feel this way.

One of John's favorite books and Charles' favorite stories was A Christmas Carol by Charles Dickens. By the time John had walked from the Bush Farm to the heel path to the Weigh Lock, he felt like Fred, Ebenezer Scrooge's Nephew from that story. Upon arrival, he burst open the door to the Weigh Lock Building and yelled out Merry Christmas, Uncle Scrooge! Being the end of the season, few canallers were about, and there was little activity. To John's satisfaction, his try at levity was successful and well-received. Abe and his sons returned John's surprise entrance with delight. Abe mentioned how convenient my arrival was at this time. Mr. Titcomb from the distillery had stopped by and had asked me to make a request to you to visit him. I was just about to dispatch one of the boys to your home.

The Titcomb operation was just up the heel path near the bridge.

After biding everyone wishes for a happy new year, he was off. He was a bit apprehensive when, during his short walk, he thought, what if Mr. Titcomb wants another tow? I've already closed down.

Mr. Brewster probably would have mentioned it if that were the cause for my requested visit. My fears were soon put to rest, and the visit revealed its purpose. Mr. Titcomb was prepared to offer me the opportunity for more tows for next season. This was great news. John was eager and happy to accept. They would discuss terms in the spring. As an expression of good faith and in honor of the season, Mr. Titcomb presented John with a gift sample of his wares, stating that perhaps an occasion would soon present itself when a man might be in need of a celebratory drink. John thanked him for his offer of more business and the bottle of his whiskey. He thought to himself, I would like my first sample of this gift to be when good news is received about Charles.

Suddenly the good mood he had found himself in started to wane. It was a surprising mood that had overtaken him to begin with. He was exchanging and experiencing pleasant thoughts with those about him. Mr. Titcomb's news was certainly welcome and good. The inevitable and uncontrolled thought back to Charles was good, but it brought back the sobering reality. Once the good mood is achieved naturally, then lost, it is most difficult to retrieve it by design. Much like trying to return to the dream once awakened.

He returned home, ready for the holidays and a carrier of good hope. He also hoped the family was prepared for what lay ahead, regardless of the future.

Christmas passed, more of a somber and reserved time. Emma had decided it would not be proper to have Addie in church. She was teething and crying often and sometimes very loudly. We all felt it best that she not disturb the service and draw attention away from the celebration.

Many of the congregants attending the service were Waterford families with family members involved in this conflict. We weren't the only family there with a son listed as missing. Several of the worshipers had already lost family members, and others had been wounded. So many families still had loved ones in the field and some as prisoners. It was not a joyous time, but it was a time for hope. The minister addressed many areas and issues. Some rang very true to us and added to everyone's thoughts that this is a time for great hope but limited joy.

He read from a letter.

"This is Christmas, and my mind wanders back to that home made lonesome by my absence while far away from the peace and quietude of civil life to undergo the hardships of the camp and the battlefield. I think of the many lives that are endangered and hope that the time will soon come when peace, with its innumerable blessings, shall once more restore our country to happiness and prosperity." How often in his letters did Charles express these same sentiments to us? I felt an unwelcome sadness come over me, but at the same time could feel a familiar closeness to Charles that had been missing and not realized until now. I heard the rest of the service. I could not actively participate. Rebecca and Harriett loved to sing; they joined in enthusiastically. I stood and mouthed the words. My thoughts were elsewhere, and they were unclear. I don't believe that anyone noticed that I had withdrawn from the proceeding of the mass. Suddenly, I was somewhere else, though I didn't know where that was. Just as suddenly, the mass was over. I felt relieved. My thoughts cleared, and I was part of the mass again. At dismissal, I listened closely to the minister's words.

"It is Christmas morning, and I hope a happy and merry one for you all, though it looks so stormy for our poor country, one can hardly be in merry humor." (49)

"...Christmas Day! A day which was made for smiles, not sighs - for laughter, not tears - for the hearth, not prison." (50)

A Merry Christmas and a Better New Year for us all! Go forward now as persons of faith and good hope! Share your love in these desperate times.

As we left the service for our short walk home, we mingled with the other families expressing our best wishes and good intentions. On the walk, few words were exchanged, but a temporary feeling of peace was about us. No one spoke of it until much later, but it was there.

Christmas dinner was pleasant; Emma had done a splendid job following Harriett's instruction, Rebecca was happy to help with the serving, and we were all grateful for our hope and each other. I did see some happiness in Emma's eyes. Yes, there is hope.

We chose not to bring in a tree this year. Charles always took great pride in searching Crow Hill with John Halpin in search of the right trees for our families. They would find them, cut them down, and drag them home. We had decided no more trees until Charles was home to retrieve them. All gifts had been secretly stowed near our hearth. Rebecca was gaily distributing them when Harriett announced that she had a special dessert before the opening of gifts. She had purchased some apricots and brown sugar. Along with some of Mr. Titcomb's whiskey, she had made what she hoped would be a very fine apricot, whiskey, fruit cake.

Chapter 23

.....MY FRIENDS IN THE PRISONS ASK UNTO ME, HOW GOOD, DOES IT FEEL TO BE FREE?

At peace? Yes, the minister, the season, coming to terms with the possibility that Charles was now in a Southern Prison Camp, did allow us some measure of peace. The possibility exists that if he is imprisoned that he is with his friend John Troy. I wish I could have been more fortunate in locating John's family in Rensselaer. Ironic how some sense of satisfaction can be gained when one fears your son has met death on the battlefield and one realizes hope exists because he is only imprisoned. And, that comfort or satisfaction is increased by the unknown knowledge that although still in danger, he is not alone. Mr. Cramer had advised me that a Southern Prison Camp was not a safe place to be. What little I was able to read in various newspapers since my meeting with him supported what he had told me.

John had become accustomed to a free flow of news during the canal season and the availability of an assortment of newspapers to review. During the winter, the local paper, The Waterford Sentinel, would only be produced weekly, and they were dependent on outside service for their news of the war. The other local papers from Cohoes, Albany, Lansingburgh, and Troy were sometimes unavailable in the winter. News was neither forthcoming nor available. As he processed these thoughts, he came to the conclusion that perhaps it is best that the news is unavailable. This off-season, perhaps just the feeling of still having hope will be his saving grace.

Harriett, Emma, and Rebecca have Addie to care for and keep them all quite busy and active in their day-to-day lives. This is a blessing of sorts for them. Harriett, of course, had demonstrated several months back of blocking out the thoughts of Charles and his well-being. How she accomplished this, I do not know. I do see the effects it has had on her. She has changed. We all have. Rebecca has youth on her side and misses her brother endlessly but does not brood on it. Her hope for Charles's return is rather an uplifting experience.

Emma, on the other hand, is still a mystery to me. There does seem to be harmony among the three; she and Rebecca have bonded and maintained closeness with Harriett. Having gained knowledge of her early life, I can't help but sense that she believes that nothing is permanent. Losing her parents so early in life, she never really knew them. Living for a short time with relatives before moving to Schaghticoke to live with other relatives she hadn't known. Then, meeting and marrying Charles, only to see him off to war a short time later. Now, the mother of a child who may never know their father. Is she to become a widow in her first year of marriage? It is no wonder that she must feel that nothing is permanent; there is no guarantee of tomorrow.

John realized he was in a house full of people, but he was all alone.

He had no real friends who weren't canal related. Save for Bob Halpin, his neighbor. We will see his family during the holiday season. In wintertime, most folks keep to the tasks necessary to provide for comfort within their homes, required walks to a local market, and a weekly visit to church. All of these activities could be altered by the whims of the winter.

He gave some thought to a visit to the Morgan House. Was it even open in the wintertime? He knew he would never go alone. Again, He wished that long ago day of the fair when the Knickerbockers extended an invitation to join them in celebration at the Morgan House, that he accepted. Maybe if he had been there when the Knicks were giving their accolades of "three cheers and a tiger," John would have been a recipient for his towing services. He would have the confidence now to confidently enter the house. He thought so many things, looking back, could be done differently. It is time now to look to the future. We know what has happened in the past. It is the future that holds both our hopes and our fears.

He thought of John Cramer. He could envision him standing guard over Broad and Third Streets, no matter the conditions. Perched in his upper floor window, observing and somehow, seemingly in control of all he was witnessing. He was a little envious of Cramer's abilities. Few men have his vision, contacts, and yet, compassion for the plight of others.

The off-season on the canal was a period that, after all these years, we had grown accustomed to the welcome, extended period of the slow passage of time. Winter would arrive, Christmas would be observed and celebrated, and the new year would arrive. One of the benefits of being a canaller was the comfort and solitude of the warmth of the hearth. The restrictive company of the family members made our weekly visits to church a welcome break from our wintertime isolation. This annual respite from social activity and interaction was not a period of sadness or boredom; neither was it a time of great joy. After the passage of a few months, spring would be in the offing, and thoughts and plans for the new season would evolve. Next season I will have the Rock Island Flour towing, as well as the Titcomb Distillery. Both are short tows and with good frequency.

This season it is different. Charles is in prison, and so too are we.

There is no word of Charles, and there is no talk of Charles. He is in our nightly prayers, and his name is mentioned on Sunday when Rebecca leads us in Grace at dinner.

Other than the minor excitement created by Addie, our time is spent with necessary chores and reading. I do feel like I am in prison.

Over the winter, John would relive times in his mind that gave him pleasure or times of great interest. On this day, he was thinking about the Great Fire in Waterford almost 25 years ago. He was a younger man then; Charles wasn't even born. Of course, the towing of the Knickerbockers to the County Fair in Mechanicville was one of his favorite events. About 10 years after the Great Fire, John joined the Eagle Fire Company in Waterford. It soon changed its name to the Hudson Engine Company. John had risen to the position of 2nd Assistant Foreman. The Company was only in existence for a short time. When it disbanded, he did not sign on with any others. He was still doing long-distance and overnight towing then and wasn't able to respond to many calls. If a fireman missed a call, he was fined for non-attendance. His membership was a short-term event, but still, he had favorable memories.

Troy Daily Times 1859

At Waterford - Engine Co. No. 2 of Waterford, has been re-organized, the name changed from: "Eagle" to "Hudson," and the following officers elected for the ensuing year:

Foreman - Daniel G. Smith
1st Assistant - James D. Lambert
2nd Assistant - John B. Shepard
Treasurer - Daniel B. King
Engineer - William Peer
Steward - George Van Norden

The Winter of 1865 passed like most of the others. Excepting, of course, our newfound ability not to discuss our anxiety over Charles. I believe we all felt that as time elapsed, it would diminish chances and hopes for his safe return.

It was March now. Soon I would be released from my prison of sorts with the opening of the canal season. By April, one needs to be ready. When weather permits, it will be time to resume transportation. Once the river is declared navigable, the canal boats will arrive. Waterford will be back to an active canal town. Each season is like a rebirth. Fresh, new, and alive, the canallers return. Old friends, new contracts, the mules, the people; I am refreshed, invigorated, and ready to go. It will be good to be productive again. I will go see Mrs. Bush and Mr. Enos soon.

John was aware of General Sherman's actions in Georgia. By mid-February, there was mention of the South being ready to capitulate. News travels so slowly when the canal is not open. John is tempted to check in with John Cramer. Somehow he will have the newest intelligence. John realizes this is the quickest his thoughts have been all winter. It is indeed spring and a new season. His pleasant thoughts are soon interrupted by a knock on the door. He can't recall the last time someone was at his door. Perhaps it is Bob Halpin from across the way. It would not be unlike him to be about, out of the house, and to pay a visit.

The rest of the house is alerted by the knock on the door. It is not uncommon for a neighbor or friend to visit, but in the wintertime, not unexpectedly, save for a holiday visit. Harriet, and all the rest, are anxious for me to answer. I'm certainly curious as to who it might be, certain it's likely Bob, but apprehensive it could be someone with news. The knock on the door was polite. Just a double knock to announce that someone was present. It was not a knock of emergency or urgency.

We have been awaiting news all winter long. Hoping for news. Fearing what it might be. Whatever it was, it would come in its own good time.

The door was opened to a man we did not know. He identified himself as William S. Life, a Presbyterian Minister. It was March 23, 1865. He informed us that he had news to share on Charles and did I wish to gather the family for all to hear or be informed and report to the family.

Fortunately, my mind was active and alert. Had I been in the doldrums of our winter solitude, I may have said, just tell me. I was anxious for news, regardless of the outcome. My mind being active, I begged of him to allow me to give the family the opportunity to make a choice.

I escorted Mr. Life to the warmth of our parlor and joined the others in our kitchen. As they had overheard, this man had news of Charles. I felt if the news were favorable, he likely would have informed us right off. I suspected but did not know that his report would not be to our liking or comfort. Everyone was in favor of me sitting with Mr.

Life to hear his report. Harriet announced she would prepare tea and that she knows what news this man brings.

I then joined our guest. I still held hope for a favorable report, but I, too, shared Harriet's unspoken knowledge that the news would be dark.

The minister went on to explain that sometime during the Battle at Ream's Station, Charles and many others had been captured and made prisoners. Intelligence appears that they were first taken to the Libby Prison in Richmond, Virginia. At some point, confined at the island prison of Belle Isle in the James River. Eventually, he was sent to the Salisbury Prison in North Carolina. There, after approximately 150 days, perhaps more, on or about January 25th, just passed; Charles succumbed to either the diseases of the camp or starvation. There is a graveyard there, and Charles had been interred at that location. (51)

I had no questions. I had no response. The minister sat silent, as did I. Our conversation had been quiet; I don't believe the others knew if our conversation was completed. They are silent in the kitchen. They must be informed.

In my silence, I didn't know how long it was; I decided it best to inform the others with no detail. There really wasn't any known detail other than the truth that Charles did not survive. In our hearts and minds, I believe we had resigned ourselves to the possibility of becoming a reality some time ago.

Ending my silence, I excused myself from the minister to make my report. In the kitchen, I simply stated; our worst fears had been realized. Charles was taken prisoner during that battle at that railroad station. Late in January, he died from disease.

There was an inaudible gasp but no outcry. The result was not unexpected. We had never spoken of this anticipated news. Each of us had anticipated it. Emma's eyes, always sad, somehow looked at ease. Holding Addie, she returned to her room. Becky wiped tears from her eyes and adjourned to her room. Harriet was brave and prepared for this news. We rejoined the minister by the fireplace.

The minister explained to us that his ministry was assisting families in New York and Pennsylvania in seeing to the affairs and final rites of those who perished far from home and loved ones and were interred on foreign ground.

We held a service at church the following Sunday. Not having a traditional service or burial, it was comforting to see so many there to honor and remember Charles. Charles Westover's mother was in attendance. Our Charles and her Charles were such good friends. Many of the Vanderwerkens offered their sympathies. They, too, had suffered losses. My friend, Walker, was there, and Abe Brewster from the Weigh Lock, Bob Halpin, and so many others.

Minister Life concluded the service with the following passage.

To those parents who have so long watched and waited for his return, to that wife, left so young to deplore the loss of one dearest on earth; to that sister deprived of the love of an onley brother, to that young babe who will never know a father's caress; I would say be comforted in the assurance that your loved and lost has exchanged his earthly prison house, where his sufferings were very great, for the blissful shores of eternal peace. His last letter home manifested a perfect acquiescence in the will of Devine Providence. Whatever his fate might be. He offered up freely his young life, as a sacrifice upon the altar of his country. I repeat again, be comforted. "In my Father's house are many mansions. I go now to prepare a place for you. If it were not so, I would have told you." W. S. L. (52)

Strangely, we felt at ease. Charles' journey through life had been completed; ours will continue.

EPILOGUE

As outlined in the prologue, the story just read is true. The names of all people are real, and the stories concerning the canals and the Civil War all occurred during the time of both Charles and John Shepard. Some liberties were taken. Most notably, the conversations with Abe Brewster, the Weigh Lock Superintendant, John Cramer, Johnny Walker, Bob Halpin, the Vanderwerkens, and others. The conversations were utilized to give cohesiveness to the story, holding it together and, hopefully, creating an entertaining flow.

In the epilogue, an attempt will be made to bring the reader up to date and create a happier ending to our tale.

The legacy of Charles Shepard does not end in the graveyard of a Confederate Prison Camp in North Carolina. Although his life ended there, his legacy had only just begun. His only offspring, his daughter Addie was born in August of 1864, just five months prior to Charles' passing. The last communication with Charles was also in late August. I am hesitant to assign a number to his legacy, but I remain pretty comfortable in stating there are likely 100 people living today who wouldn't have been here without Charles' and Addie's influence. I find it remarkable that a young man who did not live to see the completion of his 21st year could have had such an ancestral influence on so many families. Of course, none of these families carry the Shepard name, but Shepard is in their lineage.

I have been researching the Charles Shepard story for a significant number of years. For the past quarter century, I have researched many historical events and reported on them in writing, personal presentation, or both. When I presented my early research on Charles Shepard, on behalf of the Waterford Museum and Cultural Center's Lecture Series, there were many of Charles' family in the audience. I received a wonderful and satisfying compliment that night when several said, "It's like you knew him!"

Keeping that compliment in mind. In the writing of this book, I have tried to tell Charles' story through the content of his letters and the mind of his father. I hope it worked. John Shepard and I are both fathers with a son. Had we lived at the same time, we would have been neighbors. Our families both had the same occupation of transporting on the mule-era Champlain Canal. The greatest part of my research has been on the people who worked on the New York State Canals. If I was successful in expressing John Shepard's feelings and thoughts during this trying time, only the reader could judge.

John Shepard continued working on the canal for the next several years. He died on June 23, 1879, at the age of 59. Harriet survives and resides on 6th Street until her death. Harriet last appears in the 1880 New York State Census. She is listed as the widowed head of the household, which includes a sister and a sister-in-law. Harriet is also noted as sick with consumption. She did not appear in any other Census Report. A person diagnosed with consumption in that era rarely survived. It was the leading cause of death between 1870 - 1910. (53)

Emma Thompson, Charles' wife, remarries and moves to North Carolina. Married again in 1870 to a man named Rettis and moved to Virginia. Eventually, she returns to Waterford and, according to family lore, has an interesting lifestyle. Likely deeply rooted in her turbulent family situation in her young life, nothing ever seemed permanent throughout her life.

Addie continued to live on and off with the Shepards on 6th Street in Waterford. As an adult, she was married to John Buskey and William Rebman. These marriages resulted in three children. John, Chris, and George. It is through their productive marriages that the legacy of Charles Shepard continues. One of Charles' great-grandsons, John (Jack) G. Walther, made the transcription of the letters we just read.

By 1890 Addie had permanently returned to 6th Street.

She and Rebecca (Becky/Becks) remain close for the remainder of their lives. Rebecca and Charles were also close; seven of the thirty-eight letters were to her.

Mention was made in the prologue about the wealth of information that exists concerning Civil War Era Veterans. The following is a prime example.

During the course of the research, Helen Anderson would, from time to time, relate to other family members on discovered reports. This started some more senior family members thinking about stories they had heard about the Shepard, who never returned from the war. This story was an oral report told from a long time ago and a nearly forgotten memory. The story, once told, was written down and received by me.

P32 Addie and her Aunt Rebecca in 1920

> *There was a man who fought with Charlie who came to the house on Sixth Street asking John Shepard, Charlie's father, to forgive him. He had not shared food with Charlie when they were in the POW camp, and he felt responsible for Charlie dying. Ruth told me that John forgave him as it was the war that killed him and to go and live his life.* Source: From the John and Helen Anderson Collection

Certainly an interesting account, but strictly an undocumented account. Was it real? Was it correct? If real, who was this man? What did he do that would prompt this request for forgiveness?

It can be stated with a high degree of confidence that this man was John Troy. There was more to be discovered. The family discussion of Charles prompted another family member to consult a family diary;

Dear Mother.....I am the Only One Left   241

she knew she had heard this story before. It was nearly a year later when the diary entry was found. The diary entry was as follows.

One day this OLD *(OLD is emphasized this way in the diary)* man came to the door at the house on 6th St. He had come to see John *Rebman*. He had to get something off his chest. He had been in the prison camp with Charlie. He said. The prisoners had been made the offer that if they did extra work, they would receive extra rations.

He *(the friend)* declined and advised Charlie not to do it as he was already in a weakened state. Charlie did it anyway, and before long, he was not able to do the extra work and went back to a lower ration as agreed. Before long, he grew very hungry and asked his friend if he could share his portion. After much soul-searching, he said no. After a while, Charlie died. The friend had lived with this decision over the food for all these years. He confessed to Charlie's grandson, John Rebman. John told him, you were not responsible for Charles' death. It was the war that killed him.

This story is very revealing. In the oral report story that had been handed down through repetition, he had related this tale to Charles' father, John Shepard. In the written story from the diary, he is in conversation with John Rebman, Charles' grandson! We are considering that it is possibly 1910 or later. John Shepard died in 1879. The confession occurring thirty years later emphasizes the degree of guilt that John Troy has carried all these years. Why does he feel this need? What did he do? And, most importantly, why is he lying? His story simply is not true. Why is he telling it?

After being exposed to the intelligence of the first oral report and satisfied through a process of elimination of Charles' war contacts, John Troy had to be the man who visited seeking forgiveness. The elimination process was tedious and not worthy of inclusion here. Suffice it to say, it had to be someone he was in prison with; John Troy. It had to be someone he was familiar with to know exactly where he lived. Especially about 50 years after the fact. In my mind's eye, it could only be John Troy.

How do we know his story is not true? If it is not true, what is the source of this guilt that he has burdened himself with all these years?

The last we hear from Charles is the August letter that mentions the battle and destruction at the railroad. He also states that his friend, John Troy, is missing or dead. We never hear from Charles again.

Through research, it is learned that Charles was taken prisoner the very next day. The Shepard family did not learn of that right away. This event also marked the end of communication with Charles. We knew nothing of his prison existence.

My next area of research was to learn all I could about the prison experience. From Charles' Military Records, I could trace his movement from the Ream's Battle Area to Libby Prison, then to Belle Isle, and lastly to Salisbury. He was a prisoner from August 25, 1864, until approximately January 24, 1865. The approximate reference will be cleared up later in the report. I then searched diaries, letters, prisoner's testimony, and other sources of prisoner's stories covering that time period from the prison at Salisbury. A caution to anyone wishing to research these stories, they aren't pleasant. During this time period, nearing the end of the war, conditions were horrendous. The North was no better than the South in terms of prison conditions. The South was out of food; they couldn't feed their troops, let alone their prisoners. It is a strange part of Civil War events to realize that Charles began his training at the Fort in Elmira, New York. Later that same fort became a prison for captured Confederate Soldiers. Charles' military experience and life would end in the Salisbury Prison for the Northern captured soldiers.

When I read the written diary account of the OLD man's visit and read the comment for extra food for extra work. I knew this was not true at this time. So what was the cause of John Troy's torment? The reason listed here was found in several different diary entries and testimonies. These prisons had multiple thousands of inmates that they could not house. They were essentially fenced in with a guarded Kill Line. If you passed that Kill Line, you would be shot. The unhoused prisoners would make do by digging holes in the ground or constructing something to protect them from the elements. When and if the grub wagon came through, the inhabitants would get their meager ration by a head count. This was, quite literally, a head count; no one made certain that the head still had life.

As I learned from several accounts, when a fellow prisoner died, they would keep his body for as long as they could in order to keep getting his ration. I'm quite certain that this was the torment that John Troy carried with him for the remainder of his long life. If, indeed, they were confined in some self-made shelter at the prison, John Troy must have received Charles' ration after he had died. John must not have notified the guards for several days. He truly must have been burdened by this. I believe this was also the cause for Charles to have three different listings for the day of death. John Troy's guilt must have been from keeping his friend's body as long as possible to continue receiving his food. He couldn't bring himself to confess the actual story to John Rebman, so he offered up a more innocent version.

I felt the response of John Rebman, Charles' grandson, was a manifestation of John Shepard's reasoning. I attempted to use his understanding and forgiving comments when I was "thinking" for John Shepard in the preparation of the storyline for our true but fictionalized account of Charles Shepard, his life, and his aftermath.

I hope it worked.

My greatest disappointment in preparing this report was my lack of success in locating a picture of Charles. He claims to have had his likeness taken. It was a new and novel occurrence that many soldiers sought that opportunity. It's probably out there somewhere; I spent many hours searching for it.

Lacking a picture, I will offer this.

The Average Soldier According to historian Bell I. Wiley

The average Union soldier was:

White, native-born, a farmer, protestant, single, between 18 and 29
5 feet 8 inches tall, weighed about 143 pounds. (54)

His military record shows that he is not a farmer or single, but he meets all the other requirements. It also details that he had black eyes, dark hair, and a fair complexion.

An interesting observation. The effort to write the final passages of this book occurred on April 8, 2023. The next morning, Easter Sunday, I opened my email account. There was my daily history report from The History Channel; April 9, 1865, General Robert E. Lee surrendered at Appomattox. This was not a planned event. I was quite taken by it.

P33 This is not Charles; it is Private John E. Perry from the same Company as Charles and served at the same time. John Perry also fits the description of the average Civil War Soldier. He died of wounds received on July 14, 1864, about five weeks before Charles was captured. Until I locate Charles' picture, I visualize him like this.

Dear Mother.....I am the Only One Left

Letters & Battle Summary

CHARLES SHEPARD

NEW YORK 4TH REGIMENT, HEAVY ARTILLERY

Charles departed from the Cohoes Train Depot on December 28, 1863. His destination is the Elmira Training Camp in Elmira, New York. He was at the training camp until January 11, 1864. Two weeks of training. He is 18 years of age. He will live another 377 days.

On the 13th of January, the first letter home was written. (received dates are unknown. Some were delivered long after they were written.)

Washington, Wednesday, January 13, 1864

Dear Mother,

I left Elmira Monday morning at about 3 o'clock in the morning and I couldn't send my money home. I had to wait till I got to Washington. I got 125 dollars and I sent 110 dollars home by Adams Express Company. I ain't go tno time to tell you what I have seen. I am well and fat as a hog. Give my love to all and don't write 'till I write again. I will write as soon as I get to my regiment, so goodbye.

Your truly son,
Charly W. Shepard

On January 20, 1864, one week later, he wrote to his wife, Emma. He is now at Fort Marcy.

Fort Marcy, January 20, 1864

Dear Wife, I received your kind letter and was glad to hear from you. It did my heart good. I am well and enjoying myself. You don't know how good I felt when I received yours and mother's and father's and sister's letters. I threw up my hat. I bet I have the itch back. I am all over it. No one knew it except the doctor and myself. I told the doctor that I would try to make it alright with him if he would try his best to cure me and he took more pains with me than he did the sick, so I gave him two dollars and he would take ten if I gave it to him but I gave him two. Too many! When Mother told me to read the Bible I could not keep from crying but I feel happy as a lark. I will be home in the summer for the war will be over. The Rebels are coming in our lines by hundreds every day. When you see your Mother give her my love. I get paid every two months and maybe longer. I can't write you much this time. Give my love to all. So good-bye.

Your truly husband

It becomes apparent that Emma is splitting her time, living mostly in the Shepard household in Waterford and other times with her own family in Schagticoke. We only have access to three letters written to his wife. One can assume that there were more. They were either not saved or, perhaps, lost to time. She is, however, mentioned in letters to the rest of the family.

He does curiously mention that he is enjoying himself and that he expects the war will end before summer.

His Military service time is distributed as follows. Fourteen days in Elmira, thirty-five at Fort Marcy, part of the Ethen Allen Fort Complex, to defend Washington, D. C. He spends one hundred and sixty-two days in the field, sixty-one of them engaged in battle.

He then is placed in three different prison camps for one hundred and fifty-three days.

The next letter to Mother was written on January 20, 1864.

> Dear Mother,
> I received your kind letter and was happy to hear from you. I am well and in good spirits. I have a good bed to sleep on and a good house to sleep in and good food to eat and dry clothes to wear and I am good and fat and hearty as ever. Dear Mother, I try to keep rid of bad company. The room that I am in they are all good men. We have Church every Sunday here and we have a piano in the church and we have tracts sent to us to read. We have good times. Mother, pray for me that I may be a good boy. So good-by. Give my love to all.
> Your truly son,
> Charly Shepard

Charles mentions roommates. It was determined the three others were Charles Westover, Asa Smith, and Charles Abbey. It must have been confusing with three of the four named Charles.

One has to wonder if perhaps Charly is experiencing some temptations being away from home. Actually petitioning for prayers in order to remain a good boy.

I found evidence that Some soldiers wrote home, with disgust, about the lack of morals that could run amok in the camp. Prostitution was a huge problem. In Washington, D.C., for example, there were said to be over 7,000 prostitutes in 1863! Many soldiers complained about swearing, gambling, and other vices. Evidently, for some soldiers, too much free time was a very bad thing.

The "Red Light" District in Washington D. C. during the Civil War Era.

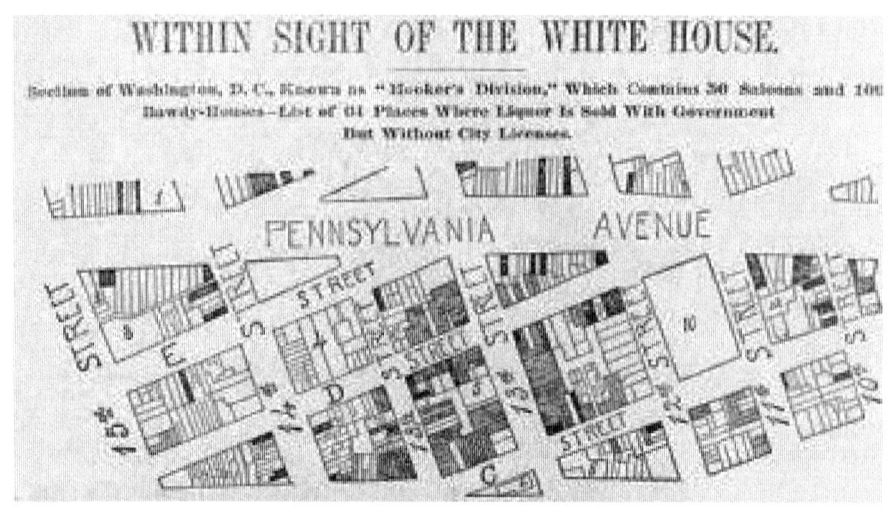

WITHIN SIGHT OF THE WHITE HOUSE.

Section of Washington, D. C., Known as "Hooker's Division," Which Contains 50 Saloons and 109 Bawdy-Houses—List of 64 Places Where Liquor Is Sold With Government But Without City Licenses.

P34

That same day he wrote to his sister.

> Dear Sister,
> I received your letter and was glad to hear from you. I am well and hope these few lines will find you well. It is a nice place here. The sun is hot here and the grass is green and the birds sing and it is a pleasant place here on the hills of Georgetown. I want a pair of boots. Go to Mires and he will know what I want and put a box of blackon and a brush in it. I will write some more the next time. Tell him to make it larger in the instep. So good bye.

It is January in Waterford, New York. There is no green grass, the sun is not hot, the birds are not singing, and it's not very pleasant in a typical northeast January. At the present time, all was quite well in his world.

250   Russ Vandervoort

February 4, 1864, he wrote to Father.

Dear Father,

I received your kind and most welcome letter and was happy to hear from you. I have just come from breakfast and we had a cup of coffee a nice piece of meat and bread and butter. You would hardly know me. I am getting so fat my cheeks are as big as a cow's bag. I am going to Washington the 10th of the month and I will shake hands with the President. I bet. I wish you were here in my room and could see some of the men. Some are writing, some are playing cards and some are reading the Bible and some are blackening their boots and some are getting ready to go on guard. I was glad to hear you got that lot. Now we can all live alone, I bet. It was a blustery day here Wednesday. Today is a pleasant day here. We think we will go down to Bull Run in a Fort in a few months. Bull's Run is about 17 miles from here. This Fort is in Fairfax County, Georgetown Heights Georgetown is about three miles from here. The Chain Bridge is about a half mile from here. There have been 50 cases of smallpox taken from headquarters. There has been one taken from our Company. How are you? 50,000 men drated! You say that Waterford has filled their number. I am glad Waterford has. I will be home in less than 9 months. I bet. The soldiers are in good spirits. Mosby is about 5 miles from here. The Picketts have a brush with him every night. You will hear fun when the Spring opens, I bet. I saw the house that the Rebel General Lee lived in. It is a splendid place, I tell you. They use it for the headquarters of this regiment. Oh we have everything needful in this regiment. Dear Father, it is a hard looking place in the country. I ain't see a fence since I left home. I must close my letter. It is almost for it is time to drill. Good day and good luck to you.

From your son
Charles W. Shepard
Company H 4, Reg. H
Washington D.C

Charles makes note of the Chain Bridge. The Chain Bridge is over the Potomac and was heavily used by the Union forces.

P35 The Chain bridge.

A letter to Mother on the same day.

Dear Mother,

The first one I think of is home when I wake up in the morning thinking how I would like to see all of your faces. Dear Mother, I am sorry that I don't know where that old man is. There ain't no old men in my Company and if I did know where he was I would go see him. Mother, you know how I hurt my finger in the shop the nail is coming off. I have got a very sore finger but it will get well in a few days. Oh Mother, I wish blackberries were as plenty there as they are here. We can go out in the Spring and pick our hats full in a little while. About my boots, I got 5 dollars and another pair for them. I am going to have my gun in a few days. I ain't got all of my other suit yet. Don't send me the New York paper for we get them every day. Send me the Waterford paper. I wish you could see our room. How nice and clean we keep it. They don't allow spitting on the floor. Dear Mother, tell Emma to take a squint at the lot everyday. Oh I don't know hardly what to write. I see the same everyday. I must now close my letter. Tell Becks not to sit up late nights and wipe her nose and don't play on the cupboard Pray for me, your son. Pleasant dreams, good day. Give my love to all.

Your son, I am well,
Charles Shepard

Charles used many colloquialisms in his letter writing. Some were curious to Waterford Canallers, and some were able to be researched. Others remain undetermined. "Play on the cupboard" may have been a Shepard Family private phrase, or it may have some undiscovered meaning.

Dear Mother.....I am the Only One Left

Charles seems to indicate a little homesickness in this letter. The reader should know that in civilian life, according to the census, Charles was a peddler. From the exchanges in the letters, he is continuing his peddler occupation by selling shirts and boots that he has sent to him by family members and then selling them to other soldiers. He also makes mention of the property that Charles and Emma will live on upon his return. His military record shows him to be a machinist. It is either in error or perhaps his military designation. If he were performing the duties of a machinist, he certainly would have written about it.

A single letter jointly addressed to Becks, his sister, and Emma, his wife, was also written on February 4, 1864.

It starts with a joke and ends with a request for ten shirts. Peddling Business must be good.

> For Beck and Emma
>
> One of the canons of St. Paul's being in company with some ladies let fall a handkerchief and in stooping to pick it up again he happened to break wind backwards. Bless me ladies he cried out, I believe it is His Majesty's Birthday for I think I hear one of the canons at St. James. "No Madam" answered another lady then present. "I am sure it is not so far off as St. James as I can smell the gunpowder."

(On the back of the joke card was this note)

> About those shirts, the men want then to wear. Send ten pair. You send them and the men will pay the expense on them and will pay me for what they cost and a little more. They make them at Smith and Gregory factory. I believe that's the one.

Again Charles' interest, time, and energy seem to be on restocking his wares to sell. Other than mentioning to his mother expectations of being assigned his gun soon, there is no mention of soldiering.

Fort Marcy, February 6, 1864

Dear Mother,

I received your most kind and welcome letter and was glad to hear from you. Send me lots of tobacco so I can sell it, I can get six cents a paper for it. The regiment was paid off today and the last of this month we will be mustered for pay. I will get, I suppose, 70 or 80 dollars. I will get 3 months pay and 40 dollars of my bounty. Every six months, I get 40 dollars of my bounty. I will send my money home the same way I did before. I am well and enjoying myself. Mother, when you send me everything, send me a memorandum book. That is what a soldier needs. You want to know how we get our washing done. There is a woman who washes for us. We give her 5 cents to wash a shirt and iron it. The green backs flies around here like paper. I received a paper tonight and 3 letters, one from Lib and one from Bob Shepard. Mother, I give up chewing tobacco for ten days. I could give it up for three years, but I felt lonesome and did not know what to do but go chewing again. I am well and fat as ever. I must now close my letter. So good night and pleasant dreams and a long kiss. Your Son

C. Shepard.

It looks like Charles' greatest area of concern is keeping his inventory up so he can latch on to some of those greenbacks that are flying around.

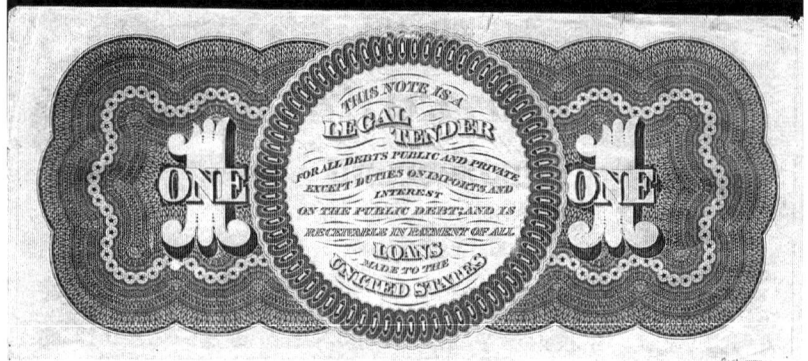

P36 He also mentions bonus money. A bonus was paid to those who volunteered. Some would receive money on enlistment and then periodic payments throughout their service. Many would perish before the entire bonus was realized. Soldiers who became prisoners of war, in some cases, were not paid for their days in prison.

This letter mentions Bob Shepard, assumed to be a relative. In a future letter, he mentions a possible visit with Bob Shepard. He mentions a letter from Lib; I could never determine who Lib was.

The next day, February 7, 1864, Charles wrote.

> *Dear and loving Mother,*
>
> *I received your kind and loving letter and was happy to hear that you were well. I received the box and everything alright. My boots fit me to a Tee. I can get them on with a paper of tobacco in one side and a bottle in the other. I guess they are large*

enough. Mother, that old man you spoke of, I don't know how he is. If I did I would go abd give him some of my cake, but there were some sick men in my room and I gave them some of my cake and they thanked me for it. It pleased me to do a favor for a sick man. The folks in Georgetown try to poison our soldiers. One of the Company soldiers came from Georgetown the other day and he stopped in Georgetown to eat some dinner and they tried to poison him. The soldiers threaten to burn it down if they ever do it again. Georgetown will be burnt in the dust. The Rebels, they need hanging every one of them. Mother, I try to do what's right. I must close my letter for tonight. I want to read a Chapter in the Bible tonight before I go to bed. Then, good night. I guess I won't go to church this morning. I will finish my letter. Before I went to bed last night I read two Chapters of Romans and this morning I read 10 of Romans. Mother you read those two Chapters. I suppose Emma has gone to Scaghticoke. Mother, I will close my letter for I want to write some to Father and Becks.

This letter appears to demonstrate a change in Charles' attitude and demeanor. The letter starts out with Dear and Loving; Mother metamorphosizes into hanging rebels and burning down Georgetown. Then returns to reading passages from the bible but not attending mass. Perhaps the reality of his new world has been awakened. He may have come to realize, the birds aren't always singing, the sun doesn't always shine, and it's not always so pleasant here; people want to kill us.

A gentleman, southern sympathizer, John W. "Bull" Frizzell, was one of the suspects in the poisoning of which Charles writes. Especially for the purposes of this story, we should know that before the injury. Bull was a canaller on the Chesapeake & Ohio Canal.

Washington Post
October 7, 1902

Fisherman Bull Frizzell.--A Georgetown Hercules Whom Many Veterans Will Remember.--Many of the veterans visiting Washington during the encampment will remember a famous character that at one time lived in Georgetown by the name of "Bull Frizzell." He was a man of herculean stature. It is said that at one time, a section of the Chain Bridge fell upon him, pinning him down under the water. The workmen managed to get the weight off him. And he was removed from the water unconscious but soon recovered. Such an accident would have killed an ordinary man.

He was a fisherman and an all-around trusty citizen. When the war broke out, he became a Southern sympathizer and busied himself, it was claimed, poisoning wells on the opposite side of the Potomac where the soldiers were camped just after the battle of Bull Run. He was arrested time and time again, but no proof could be obtained of his guilt, and he always managed to get free. Past Department Commander A.F. Dinsmore, who was then an officer in the Third Michigan Infantry, arrested him just after the return from Bull Run on the charge of poisoning wells and held him for several days, but failing to secure proof of his guilt, was obliged to release him. He died during the latter part of the war.

On February 8, 1864, he wrote to his father.

Dear Father,

I now take the pleasure to write to you. I am well and enjoying myself and I hope this letter will find you the same. I was out in the country Sunday and I had a good dinner and I went out to Falls Church and its a hard looking country old trees cut down in the road to block the Rebels. The Rebel Mosby is about ten miles from here. This regiment is on the Georgetown Heights about 6 miles from Washington. It is a nice place, The Fort I am in is a big one. There are about 18 canons, 5 20 pounders, 8 30 pounders and 2 100 pounders. That is a peacemaker. I tell you it would make things hop. All the soldiers are enlisting over because they think the war will be over in the summer and I think so myself because the Rebs are about starved out and licked out. I have just been out to drill and I am all sweat. It is a hot day here. I ain't had hardtack yet. The boys tell me that I am as fat as a hog and I think so myself. When I wake up in the morning I can hardly get out of bed. We have to keep our clothes clean and our boots blacked up our hair combed up and our necks clean and our guns so bright that you can see your face in them. I thought I would be put into another Company but I was a lucky man. It was a lot of Cohoes Boys. My Company is in the Fort the others are all outside the Fort. The Fort is made up of large logs and there are 4 rooms and they are numbered 1 2 3 4. I am in room 1 and they are all nice men. We have Church in the morning and at night. I think by the talk that we will go to Tennessee in about two months but we can't tell everything about it. I would like to stay here all the time for it is a nice place. We have to drill twice a day but we don't have to do any duty yet. Send me the Waterford paper every week. If you send me a pair of boots, put a brush and some blackon with it. I don't think I will get paid for two months. I must now close my letter. Give my love to all.

Your truly Son
Charles W. Shepard
Co. H, 4th Reg Heavy
Artillery, Washington

One day has passed since his last letter to Mother. The attitude is different in this letter to Father. He has been a soldier for two months now; this is the first real mention of any training. They are an artillery regiment, and he does sound well-informed about the canon. He is living inside the Fort. This is actual comfort. They are not in the field in tents.

When Charles mentions the fort, he says, "I would like to stay here all of the time, for it is a nice place." (February 8th)

On March 26th, Captain Brown writes a similar sentiment. *"The Ethan Allen Fort, where I had fondly hoped to spend the remainder of my military career in comfort and security."*

Having read Charles' description of the Fort, I researched the Civil War information from the National Parks Service to see how accurate his description was. It was very accurate, as were his forthcoming battle reports.

From the National Park Service - Fort Marcy

Fort Marcy and nearby Fort Ethan Allen, among other batteries on the northern bank of the Potomac River, were built to protect Leesburg Pike and Chain Bridge. Construction began in 1861. When Fort Marcy was completed, it had a perimeter of 338 feet and mounted 18 guns, a 10-inch mortar, and two 24-pounder Coehorn mortars.

The fort was not entirely completed until the fall of 1862. It is a relatively undisturbed fort and was named in honor of a native of Massachusetts, the Honorable Randolph B. Marcy, a distinguished soldier, father-in-law, and Chief of Staff to Gen. George B. McClellan. Detachments of the 4th New York Heavy Artillery, 3rd Pennsylvania Heavy Artillery, and the 130th Pennsylvania Infantry were among the troops that performed garrison duty here during the war. After the Civil War ended, Fort Marcy was returned to its original owners, the Vanderwerken family.* The land remained in the Vanderwerken family until after World War II.

*The Vanderwerken Family was from Waterford, New York. The next letter to Mother.

Dear Mother,

I received your kind and welcome letter on the 27th and was glad to hear from you. I was on guard for the first time and I caught a cold. I got a sore throat, but I will be over it in a few days. There are a lot of men going home on furloughs tomorrow. It snowed here yesterday about all day. Today is a pleasant day here. There have been about 50 new men come into this Company since I have been here. Mother, it doesn't make any difference to me what color just as you think best. Make it so it will button all the way up. I just had 2 good crullers a man gave them to me. They were fresh, just came out of the spider. You asked whether I wanted some meat. I would care for a little dried beef. Well Mother I will now close. I don't want anything else now, I will write a few lines to Father. I hope this letter will find you well. So good-bye a long kiss.

Your Son, Charles Shepard

Charles makes mention of some men going home on furloughs. Charles receives an eight-hour pass to leave camp. That was his only leave. His letters eventually mention what appears to be a walk in the country and a dinner outside of Fort Marcy.

Tuesday, February 15, 1864

Dear Sister,

I received your most kind loving letter and was glad to hear that you are well. It snowed here yesterday. it is all melted off today and it makes it muddy. There have been 2 or 3 deserters in my Company and if they catch them they will shoot them. I feel sorry for a farm boy, he saw tough times. Judson A. Smith that is that fellows name. He is a sergeant. He is a nice fellow. I saw a letter you sent him. Dear Sister, you must send me your likeness. I will send you mine as quick as I can. The wind blows hard, we had beans for dinner. I have been quite sick but I am well now and enjoying myself. My pen ain't good for anything. I must now close. Good-bye and a kiss,

Your Brother C. Shepard

Judson Smith is Charles' Sergeant. It is believed that Charles is attempting to gain favoritism with his Sergeant through Becky. The first hint of Charles' likeness being taken is contained in this letter.

A letter to Father, late February 22, 1864.

Dear Father,

I received your letter and was glad to hear from you and hear you are well. I am well and enjoying myself. I just came from supper and had boiled beans, good coffee and good fried bread. We have good times here. I ain't been on guard since I been here. Today is Washington's birthday. I think you write a good long letter. I think Mother will be on the lookout next time. I just bet. I had a good piece of pork for dinner. We soldiers have good times here. We have lots of fun and lots of grub and lots of rebels to look after about 4 miles in the country. It was a wonder that I did not get taken when I went out in the country. I think the war will be over this summer and then I will come home. I ain't in the regular army. I

am in a Volunteer Regiment. They will be discharged when the war is over. I received a Waterford paper last week. I must close. We drill on the canon once in a while. We have to learn with our guns first. I will close. So good-bye. Your Truly and Loving Son.
           Charles Shepard

This letter contains a great deal of thought. It appears to be a young, optimistic man planning not only for today but for his future.
Father also receives another late February letter.

Dear Father,
   I received your letter Wednesday the 24th and was glad to hear from you. I am well and fat, only weigh 150 that ain't so much, so I am going to weigh 160 pounds in side of 3 months. There ain't much new. Mosby made a raid on a small body of troops and took them all prisoner but 5. That is bad. It is only three miles from here. He is a bold man but he will get jerked up one of these times and if they do ever catch him around here I will send you a piece of him. Father, I am a bold soldier, so the first battle i go in I'll make my way to the rear rank upon order march, boy, that is the way to fight. I write enough foolishness. So I will now close my letter, so good-bye, Your Son,
           C. Shepard

It is a short letter, but sadly prophetic. In a few words, he states:

"Mosby made a raid on a small body of troops and took them all prisoner but five. That is bad." Little did Charles know that six months after this letter, he would suffer the same fate.

Dear Mother.....I am the Only One Left

A letter to Mother.

Dear Mother,

I received your most welcomed letter and was happy to hear from you. I am well and as hearty as ever and full of fun. You said in your letter what I want. Well, I want a vest and a pair of gloves. My vest is good yet but I thought I would want another. I want a couple of shirts. We won't go away from here I don't think. I ain't chewed tobacco in ten days. I took a chew today but I won't take anymore. You can send me 100 papers of tobacco. I can sell them for 6 cents a paper and they will go like hot cakes. I will let you have all the money I will sell them for. I got a new straw bed today and went out in the country and got some straw to fill it. Mother, if you send me a box, send me some butter. I want some butter. You know I never went back on butter. Mother, I am getting fat as pork. I weigh about 155 pounds, I think. I would make a good fight on the Rebels. Mother, if the war stops in the summer this Regiment will be disbanded. You ask me what's our Captain's name. His name is Captain Augustus Brown. He is a nice man. He makes everything comfortable for his men. Mother, how is Em when she is home? Does she work good or is she slack in her work? I hope she is a good girl, takes hold and helps you. I can't write any to beck at this time. Give her my love. She writes me good letters. I think a great deal of her. I must close my letter, so good-bye, my love to all, Charles

P37 Captain Augustus C. Brown, Co. H, 4th NY Heavy Artillery

Charles responds to his mother's request to know who his Captain is in this letter dated February 22, 1864. I have access to the Captain's Diary, but it does not begin until March 26th. We will attempt to compare the information contained in his letters to the entries in the Captain's diary as we proceed. It is interesting to note that the day that Charles is captured is the same day Captain Brown reports to the field hospital. Although Charles was taken prisoner and Augustus was hospitalized, both ended their military career on the same day.

His Diary was published after the war. It was an immeasurable asset in comparing Charles' letters to home with entries in the Captain's Diary. Their accounts would support each other. (55)

Fort Marcy, Sunday, March 5, 1864

Dear Sister,

I received your letter and was glad to hear from you. I am very well. I have been out in the country today and got my dinner. I had ham and eggs and two cups of tea, cabbage, cake and pie. We have everything that is good down her by paying a good price for it. That is cheap. Becks when you write to that fellow again, direct it Judson A. Smith. That is his right name. Where I had dinner today, I had an introduction to a young lady. Her name was Rebecca Mark. She took quite a shine to me but it will do her no good. She was pretty good looking but she can't come in. When I was on guard duty the other night I came across two boys by the name of Shepard. I ain't had no tobacco for eight days. I stopped once before for 12 or 14 days. When I get homesick I take a chaw to pass away the time. I don't chew a paper a month. I can't chew much in this part of the country. It makes me sick. Kiss Mother and Father for me. Give them my love. My love to all. I will now close my letter, so good-bye, a long kiss.

Your Brother, Char Shepard

This is the letter that caused Emma to disappear for a while.

As an example of facts that are researchable through Civil War Era Records, I offer the names of the two Shepard boys Charles met on guard duty.

Although Charles has not been on the battlefield yet, he will soon be engaged in the Wilderness Campaign. We also know that Charles is taken prisoner at the Battle at Ream's Station. I was able to find a listing of all Regiments in the affected areas and research the alphabetized reports to create a list of Shepards. I am unable to state with absolute confidence that the two listed here are indeed the Shepards mentioned in the letter, but I have a high degree of confidence that the likelihood is great.

SHEPHARD, WILLIAM.—Age, 21 years. Enlisted, January 24, 1862, at Port Richmond; mustered in as private, Co. A, to serve three years; re-enlisted, February 9, 1864; reported missing in action since August 25, 1864, at Reams Station, Va., and at muster-out.

William is in all the same battles as Charles and is captured on the same day, at the same place.

SHEPHERD, GEORGE H.—Age, 21 years. Enlisted, December 26, 1863, at Granger; mustered in as private, Co F, December 26, 1863, to serve three years; captured, May 6, 1864, at the Wilderness, Va, no further record.

Charles was in this same field of operations. He and George were both in the Wilderness on May 6th.

Perhaps the two Shepard boys from guard duty. Guard Duty usually consisted of a few men from different Companies and Regiments throughout the encampment to stand guard overnight.

The next letter is to Mother

Fort Marcy, March 11, 1864

Dear Mother,

I received your most kind and welcome letter on the 10th and was glad to hear from home. I am well and hope this letter will find you the same. If you send me a box send me a pipe and some smoking tobacco. I have stopped chewing tobacco. Smoking is the best thing a person can do. It keeps away sickness. I ain't chewed no tobacco in two weeks, it makes me sick to chew in this part of the country. We have just raised a flag pole in the Fort. It is a nice one. It is about 60 feet high. We have got a nice flag to put on it. Mother, send me two dollars. We will get paid in a month or so. Mother, I must close my letter. So Good-bye, a long kiss.

The references to tobacco usage are interesting in modern times. It makes him sick to chew tobacco. Smoking is better; it keeps sickness away.

March 15, 1864

Dear Mother,

I received your letter and was glad to hear that you are well. I am well at present and enjoying myself. Where is Emma? Is she to Schagticoke, or is she home? I sent to her in Schagticoke and one to home. Mother, I have often thought since I left home what good parents to advise me and tell me what's right and wrong. I have looked back and see now what a bad boy I have been to my Father and Mother. Now it makes me feel bad. I will try and be a better boy. Don't forget me in your prayers. I want to write to Father. You must excuse these few lines. I don't know whether Emma is at home or not. If she is give her my love. So good-bye.

       Your Son, C. Shepard

The results of Charles' letter of March 5th. When he had an introduction to the pretty girl while out for dinner. He certainly appears wrapped in guilt in this letter, likely promulgated by his thoughts after his last letter to Emma. He must be reliving in his mind any questionable past behavior in his young life.

      Fort Marcy, Thursday, March 22, 1864

Dear Sister,

 I haven't nothing else to do this afternoon and I thought I would write to you. Well, there is nothing exciting to say. Bob is in Washington. His Regiment is in Washington and I am going to try to get a pass to go to the city to see him. I wrote a letter to Ira Welch and George Steemburgh. I am as fat as a pig. We had beans for dinner and I made them suffer, I bet. They are firing the big guns around Washington. It sounds like a big battle. They are going to transfer this Regiment to a Light Artillery Regiment, I guess, that is the talk. There has got to be one and they think we will be the one. Well, who cares? For who cares, let them. I think the war will close by the Fourth of July. That is the feeling among the soldiers and I feel so myself.

You know I was always a good gauge. The rebs are trying to bother us, but they can't come in. They are trying to make a raid on us, but Mosby ain't got no bottom. You know what that means, they ain't smart enough. We have got three lines of picketts out. I stood picket guard for the first time. I stood out in a big pine grove and it did look spookish. I tell you, but I kept my big eyes on guard. The first one I saw I would have given him a bullett that would make him hop, I think. Then look out for a run. Well. I think you could not see my heels for the dust. Well Beck. I don;t know what else to write so I will close. My love to Emma, Mother and Father and the rest.

Your Truly Brother

Charly Shepard

Co. H 4th Regiment

Heavy Artillery

Here he writes about Bob. Quite sure that this is Bob Shepard. He hopes to visit him when he gets his one and only pass.

Charles makes light of the potential of the 4th Heavy Artillery being redesignated as Light Artillery. It doesn't happen now, but it does prior to the Ream's Station Battle time. The change from Heavy to Light prompts some of the officers in the 4th Brigade to resign their positions. It causes Charles to be involved in front-line battle charges instead of firing from the rear. Did this cause his capture and ultimate demise? Perhaps. It is certainly debatable. At the very least, a contributing factor.

The redesignation, as recorded in the Captain's Diary, actually takes place on May 5th. When he notes, "I shall never cease to condemn in the strongest terms the action of the Government in enlisting us for one branch of the service and then, without our consent, transferring us to another."

Also, on Thursday, March 22, 1864.

Dear Sister,

I will now finish this paper, Beck, I received 3 letters tonight, one from home, and one from Cohoes and one from Lib. I had got papers from home. The man came up with the letters and he kept calling Shepard, bully for Shepard he has got friends enough. Beck, I don't know what to write. I wrote to Bill Hardy today and my head is all gone. Beck, you must excuse these few lines this time. I received some stamps. So good night from your brother, C. Shepard, a long kiss, good night all.

In several of the above letters, he mentions Bob Shepard, likely a relative, Ira Welch, George Steenburg, and Bill Hardy. I attempted to ascertain who these people were in relation to Charles' life. Starting with Bob Shepard and having no information with which to work, I located many by that name from this era from New York State. I could not uncover a link between any of the Roberts to John Shepard.

Because he is mentioned in letters to the family, it increases the probability of being a relative.

Ira Welch. It was discovered that Ira was born in Stillwater, New York, in 1846. The family moved to Waterford in 1855. Ira was involved in the Civil War, enlisting in May of 1861. He returned to Waterford in 1865. He eventually opens an undertaker's business at 72 Broad St. His son Ira C. joins him in that business and later opens another in Saratoga Springs. One must assume that if Charles was writing to Ira that they must have been friends prewar.

George Steenburg. Again Charles has stated he wrote a letter to George. George's family resided at number four, Fourth St., not far from Charles. It is likely that Charles, George, and Bob Halpin were all boyhood friends. By 1865, twenty-two-year-old George is back living in Waterford.

He suffered some injuries in the war. After the war, he became a carpenter. He lived in Waterford until 1927, passing at age ninety-seven. It appears that he didn't start collecting his Civil War Pension until he was 82.

Bill Hardy is also a friend who is engaged in the war. He, too, returns to Waterford and resides on Third St. He becomes a machinist following the war and lives until February 18, 1905. He is buried in the Waterford Rural Cemetery.

Late March

Dear Father,

I received your letter last night and was happy to hear from you. The Army is all a moving now. We were inspected yesterday by General Barney. We were inspected to go away in a month or so. Send me a pipe and tobacco when you send my box. The men are all crazy to move. There ain't nothing new in camp. How did you like the paper? Send me two dollars. I will now close these few lines, so good-bye.

Your Son Charles Shepard
Fort Marcy

The following is a field correspondent's report to the *Cohoes Republican*. Much of what he reports supports the information that Charles has written in his letters. Charles mentions. "We were inspected to go away in a month or so in mid-March. This report comes to us on the 30th.

Letter from Alexandria, Va.
HEAD-QUARTERS. RENDEVOUS OF DISTRIBUTION,
VIRGINIA, March 30, 1864

MR. EDITOR:—We want our friends to hear from us occasionally, but we have written without hearing from them until we are both tired and ashamed. Now we must write to someone, and if you say so, we will choose the Republican (The Republican is a Cohoes Newspaper). During this month, we have enjoyed the most pleasant weather with but one interruption—quite unbecoming the "Old Dominion"—a fall of about eight inches of snow on the night of the 22d, but the next day however, came so warm that it soon disappeared, greatly swelling the streams and making the historic Potomac almost the color of a road puddle.

Lieut. Col. McKelroy yet remains in command of the Rendezvous. He was relieved for a time per Brigadier Gen. Abercrombie, and we believe he was ordered to report at a court-martial, but he was soon reinstated and has shown that he can "keep a hotel." A neat little sheet is printed here every Wednesday morning entitled the "Soldier's Journal." Seven numbers have been issued, and the paper has a tolerable circulation.

Hon. Mr. Morrill, U. S. Senator from the State of Maine, addressed the Soldier's Temperance Society on Wednesday evening last, and we never saw a more attentive and appreciative audience convened on any occasion in the army. After briefly alluding to the political condition of the country, he proceeded to the discussion of the matter in hand—Temperance among the soldiers—and was frequently interrupted by the applause of the audience.

The 4th N.Y. Heavy Artillery, which has been doing garrison duty for a considerable length of time in this Department, passed through this camp on its way to the front on Sunday last. It has recently re-enlisted almost en masse and received large accessions in recruits. We understand that its present strength is over two thousand. The artillery practice at the various forts in this vicinity has become very brisk lately, and the roar of guns and whir of shots greets us daily on all sides.

Much of what appears in this field report was covered in Charles' letters during the period mentioned.

All letters from Jan. 20, 1864, through April, have been sent from Fort Marcy. This is the first from Camp near Culpeper.

At this point, in late March, we know that Charles has been at Fort Marcy since his arrival on approximately January 20, 1864. He has taken up residence with three others. They have comfortable quarters inside the fort and, from all accounts, plenty to eat. They have been issued their guns and have trained on their artillery equipment. Other than guard duty, they have seen no action.

Captain Brown's Diary on March 26, 1864 (excerpted). Shows the following.

Fort Marcy, Va., Saturday, March 26, 1864
I was suddenly awakened at 5 o'clock this morning by Capt. McKeel of Company A, who rushed frantically into my quarters with the intelligence that the regiment had received "marching orders" and was immediately to join the Army of the Potomac. McKeel appeared to be in great glee; he declared that he had long been "spoiling for a fight"; that now the grand object of his military existence was to be attained.

I did not myself receive the news as enthusiastically as he did, perhaps, becoming an officer so far away from the front. Indeed I may frankly say that just at that moment, no order could have been more unexpected or undesirable to myself. I had just completed for the officers of my company a residence within the fort, where I had fondly hoped to spend the remainder of my military life in comfort and security. The fort itself was a model of architectural beauty, considering the purposes for which it was erected.

Summoning Sergeant Theben, I directed that the company pack up and send off all superfluous baggage and effects and be ready to march at daylight the next morning.

There was a decided apprehension that it meant Infantry instead of Artillery field service. A deputation to Headquarters at Fort Ethan

Allen gained but little information, except that it was rumored there that we were to report to the Chief of Artillery of The Army of the Potomac, that Col. Tidball, our Colonel, was to take command of the Artillery Brigade of the Second Corps, and that the regiment was to have a Siege Train. This thought was very unsatisfactory.

At 7 A.M. on Sunday, March 27th, the companies of Fort Marcy by the Third Pennsylvania Artillery, and as soon as the companies at Fort Marcy could join the main body at Fort Ethan Allen.

On March 31st, the regiment was called out on dress parade for the first time since leaving Fort Marcy.

The Diary of Captain Augustus C. Brown, March 26, 1864 (excerpted)

All of this fits with the information that Charles has reported in his letters.

> Camp near Culpeper, April 3rd
>
> Dear Father,
>
> I now take pleasure to inform you where I am. This regiment is in the 2nd Corps. We are a Brigade today, but I don't know what Brigade, nor what Division but i will know in a few days. We are within 3 miles of the Rebs. We can climb up on Pinney Mountain and look into the rebel camp. We moved from general Meade's Headquarters, Friday April the 1st, and marched about 5 miles, mud up to our knees.
>
> Our Siege Guns have come to the regiment. Our camp is right by the Blue Ridge. I will tell you they are big mountains. It is awfully muddy here at present. This is a hard looking country, You can bet the rebels comes into our camp in flocks, coming in every day. They say them that wants to fight can stay, but they

say that they ain't many who wants to fight. They are hard looking men. They look at our soldiers and say, "A right smart lot of men." I reckon they're going to pay off in a few days. You must try to read this. I ain't got any ink, so I had to write with lead, I must close, I ain;t got any good place to write. My love to Em, Mother and Sister, so good-bye.

Charles, I am hardy.

Charles reports to his father that they are now part of the II Corps. A Corp is anywhere from 9,000 to 12,000 in number. His regiment numbered 1,000, and his company 100. In early April, they are preparing for battle, but as yet, they have not been engaged.

Note that this letter is the first that mentions Culpepper. This is a County in Virginia. Many letters will originate from somewhere in Culpepper. The Virginia Encyclopedia offers the following. Culpeper would be a focal point for military action. Geographically, it sat midway between and slightly to the west of Richmond and Washington, D.C., and railroads linked it to both national capitals. The Orange and Alexandria Railroad ran northward from the county seat of Culpeper Court House to Alexandria; the Virginia Central connected the county to Richmond via Gordonsville. In addition, the Rappahannock River formed the county's northern boundary, and Culpeper marked the first point on the river where an invading Union force could ford the Rappahannock during most of the year. Outside of the Shenandoah Valley, it was one of the best invasion routes in the state.

Consequently, armies from one side or the other occupied the county for most of the war. (56)

April 3rd

Dear Sister,
I received your most kind and welcome letter. I hardly know

what to write to you. Well, I said I didn't know and then a nice young fellow told me to send his best respects to you and he is a gay young fellow. I wish I had your face to look at once in a while, Beck. I don't hear Mother to call me up in the morning, but, I have a good bed to sleep in, good grub to eat and lots to eat. I see more niggers every day than you can shake a stick at and the poor bucks, their lips stick out a foot. I suppose I have seen more than three thousand niggers since I left home. I am down on the buggers. One big buck nigger comes to me and said you are a nice sort of fellow. I reckon you don't see no white women here. Once in a while you will see one but they are almost as black as a nigger. Well how did the black mare do? Did she win? I bet. I wish you would send me your likeness in the next letter. You would laugh to see the men jump up and take their hats off. When an officer comes into the room we have to jump up and take our caps off. Well, Sister, I ain't got nothing more to say at present, so good-bye.

My love to all

I see this as a typical mid-19th-century exchange between a brother and sister. I don't think that Charles is purposely degrading the black men he is encountering. I believe he is just using the vernacular of the times and was likely influenced by the environment that he was in. Charles was certainly an aware young man growing up in Waterford. He must have known of the aid provided and given to our Southern Friends. A gathering place and a loading location for the Southern Friends was the area of the Grogh St. barns. This is where John kept his mules, a very short distance from where Charles lived.

April 5, 1864, Emma (wife) This is the last letter we see for Emma.

Dear Wife,

I got paid yesterday and I sent $25 to you. I got paid $40 and they took out $8 for clothes and that I overdrew and paid the Sutler $4 for eatables that I got since we came out to the front. We don't get enough to eat sometimes and I kept 6 for myself. Em. I don't spend no more than I can help. You be close. When I return home we will want all the money we can get. Well, Em dear, I ain't got any more time to write at present. I am well and hope that these few lines will find you the same. Some of these poor soldiers didn't have no money to send home to their wives who have children. I will get paid next month again. Kiss Mother and Father for me. We marched 6 miles today. We are in Culpeper now and will stay there. We are going to do Provost Duty in Culpeper. Well, Em dear, good night. My love to all. As soon as I get settled again I will write.

Kiss Your Husband Chas. Shepard

In this letter, he writes of the Sutler. He is a person who follows a military unit and sells the soldiers needed items. Charles doesn't like the Sutler.* The Sutler is competition for Charles' peddling. He also mentions Provost Duty. I found no evidence of this occurring. Provost Duty would be a peacekeeping force in a defeated area. There is not much else to consider here. A typical husband-to-wife letter concerning finances, the future, and feelings. It is generally thought that there was more communication between the couple. we just don't have access so many years later. Although, I have often wondered how well they really knew each other.

*Excerpt from the History of the NYS 4th Brigade of Heavy Artillery. There are two sutlers at this post, and to show you what enormous prices they put upon their goods, I will give you a list of

Dear Mother.....I am the Only One Left   277

the rates at which some of these articles are sold. It is an awful price--butter (half lard) is 45 cents per pound; cheese 20 cents; apples from three to five cents a piece; pies 25 cents each; candles 5 cents each; tobacco 10 cents per paper; boots $7 to $10 per pair; besides hundreds of other articles sold at extravagant prices. Army sutlers are a humbug, and the soldiers ought to hoot out every one that comes into camp or garrison, for they are daily making their fortune out of the soldiers' hard-earned money. (57)

At 7 A.M. on Sunday, March 27th, the companies of Fort Marcy by the Third Pennsylvania Artillery, and as soon as the companies at Fort Marcy could join the main body at Fort Ethan Allen.

On March 31st, the regiment was called out on dress parade for the first time since leaving Fort Marcy.

April 1st, we received orders to report to the Artillery Brigade of the Second Corps, and striking tents marched nearly over to a place called Stevensburg. Here we camped on a side hill, and a worse spot could not have been found in the whole vicinity. It began to rain when we were about halfway from Brandy Station and continued the rest of the day. We pitched our tents as best we could. The morning of April 2nd found the ground covered with four inches of snow. The men suffered greatly from cold and exposure. The boys looked homesick and dispirited. The weather continued very disagreeable for a whole week, but the sky brightened a little on the 12th when the paymaster arrived, and things were much pleasanter on the 13th when we were paid off, the sutler looking positively happy. (58)

> *HEADQUARTERS ARTILLERY BRIGADE,*
> *SECOND ARMY CORPS, April 9, 1864.*
> *SPECIAL ORDERS, No. 23. (Extract.}*
> *By order of JOHN C. TIDBALL, Commanding Brigade.*
>
> *After being paid off, the First Battalion, under Major Sears, consisting of Companies C, D, L, and M, broke camp and marched over to the Sixth Corps Artillery Brigade, commanded by Colo-*

nel Charles H. Tompkins, pitching tents near Brandy Station. The camping ground was a grassy plain, the soil of which was quite sandy. This brigade included the following:

On the 15th, the Second Battalion, made up of Companies D, H, K, and E, under Major Arthur, left regimental headquarters and reported to Colonel C. S. Wainwright, commanding Artillery Brigade Fifth Corps, near Culpeper. The tents were pitched in an orchard near an old house occupied by an elderly lady and her daughter, also by the Brigade Commissary. The brigade included: Fourth New York Heavy Artillery, Second Battalion, and Major William Arthur. *

Considerable drilling was done by each of them in infantry movements, and the suspicion was rife that our heavy guns would be carried on our shoulders during the coming campaign.

The reason for this drilling was the following.

*See the next letter concerning the orchard.

The entire regiment served as a part of the Second Corps Artillery Brigade until June 25, providing manpower for understrength batteries, working as laborers, and in some cases performing as infantry. Five companies charged as infantry at the Second Battle of Petersburg in mid-June 1864. (59)

April 16th

Dear Father,

I received your most kind letter and was happy to hear from you. I am well as ever, thank God. I am down here where you can look into the Reb's camp. We had a heavy skirmish at Robson's Ford the other day. Some part of the Army has been ordered to pack their knapsacks with hardtack to be ready to march at a minutes warning. Culpeper is a hard looking place. Some of the buildings are all to slivers. There is hardly a home in Culpeper that window left in them all knocked out by our soldiers. It looks like war down here. I tell you. There is more soldiers around Culpeper than you can shake a stick at. Well, there won't be quite as many by next winter, I think. You will see them walk right through the Rebels. Culpeper Court House is full of Rebels and they send them away every day. You must try and read this letter because I have no place to write. We are in camp at an orchard. It is a nice place. I received them postage stamps and the Waterford paper. Well, Father, there ain't any extra news today so I will close for this time. I must read some in the Bible. So goodbye, pray for me. My love to all. Good morning.

Your loving son, Charles W. Shepard

*Note that Charles writes of the orchard mentioned in the previous report.

A comparison of Charles' April 16th letter to Captain Brown's April 15th diary entry.

Friday, April 15th

The Second Battalion, under Major Arthur, composed of Companies D, K, H, and E, took up its line of march for the Fifth Corps this morning, passing through a pleasant, open country stretching away from the foot of "Pony Mountain," and after a march of about six or eight miles reached its destination near the village of Culpepper. Here, in an old orchard near a large but dilapidated brick house about a mile from Culpepper, we located our camp and pitched our tents. We found the town almost wholly deserted by the inhabitants; the fences and buildings destroyed or badly damaged, and the streets full of army wagons and straggling soldiers. Gen. Grant, and Gen. Warren of our Corps, have established their Headquarters here, though there are but three or four houses in the town that are not riddled with shot and shell or have windows and doors left in them. The churches are being utilized as hospitals. (60)

As mentioned earlier, Charles is now in a Corp of 7,000 - 12,000 men, and they have joined with the VI Corp of equal numbers. Thus, his reference to more soldiers than you can shake a stick at. Charles writes It looks like war down here. Robson's Ford is mentioned in this letter. They are on the Rappahannock River; I find no evidence of a Ford by that name.

From a Civil War article by Clark B. Hall, titled, *The River's Role in the War*, we learn the following.

More pitched battles have been fought on the Rappahannock's banks than any other river in this country. The Rappahannock immortally marked the river as the bloody vortex of eastern military operations. The Rappahannock meanders eighty miles to Fredericksburg. It provides the eastern boundary of Culpeper County. The first Culpeper Ford is Richard's Ford, and almost forty miles north, just above Waterloo, is Dulin's Ford. Sandwiched between these two flank crossings are crowded more than twenty Colonial era and Civil War fords; almost all of them were abandoned and forgotten.

With this information, we can make several assumptions. The first would be that Charles misheard Robson for Richard, or perhaps his great-grandson mistranscribed Richard to Robson. Charles' information in his letters is seldom in error, but at this point, he is writing with whatever is available on whatever he had. Some letters were written on the backs of old envelopes. It is also a possibility that, as Mr. Hall states, some were abandoned and forgotten.

Culpeper, April 17, 1864

Dear Sister,

I received your kind letter and was happy to hear from you. You must forgive me for not writing before. You know when I write a letter home I mean it for all. You say your friend Smith don't write anymore. Well Beck, he ain't much anyway. How did you like Westover's letter? It was a good one, I got it. I had a letter from Julia Thayer the other day and she is well. Well I am on my way down in Old Virginia, far away from home and I would really like to have your likeness, Mother's and Father's, and Em also. I wish you could look in my tent and see how we live. Charlie Westover is asleep and another boy with the mumps is very sick. Poor boy, no one to take care of him but

us and we do the best we can. I have got to be quite a cook. I cooked dinner today and I will tell you what it was. It was bread fried in grease. That's all. That was bully for us. Well Beck, the soldiers have to take it hard sometimes. You write to Westover he's a good fellow. He writes a good letter. Well, Beck. I will close for this time. Westover sends his respects to you and says he would like to hear from you. So, good-bye kiss.

Your Brother Charly Shepard

The connection that Charles was trying to create between his sister and Sergeant Smith is not taking hold. He is now encouraging a letter-writing exchange with his friend Charles Westover. He states to Becks that he, Judson Smith, "ain't much anyway." There must have been a falling out or some sort of disagreement between Charles and Judson.

From April 17 until May 22nd, there are no letters from Charles.

Augustus makes entries every day; in this time period, there is nothing of any consequence. On May 2nd, he writes.

> *Still in camp near Culpepper. Nothing of interest has occurred since the 23rd of April beyond the daily routine of camp life, except that large bodies of troops have been moving up and camping near us or passing by towards the Rapidan.*

During this time period, he is in the Overland Campaign in the Wilderness, a battle that lasts for an extended period.

The most personal account of Charles' first battle experience is from Captain Augustus Brown's Diary. An excerpt from May 20, 1864.

Friday, May 20th

At daylight this morning, I was informed that Sergt. Lock "got" his sharpshooter last night, but that the man was of no use to himself or anybody else after the Sergeant's attention. Getting my little squad in line, we moved by the flank in rather "open order" through the woods and across the fields to the camp which we had left the day before, where I found that many of my men had preceded me during the night. Lynch was most demonstrative in his welcome, announcing in stentorian tones that the Captain was not "kilted after all." Upon mustering the Company for roll-call, I found that we had suffered severely, Sergt. Judson A. Smith, Artificer Gould R. Benedict and privates Joseph Housel, Jr. and William R. Mead having been killed, and First Sergt. Theben, Corp. Harned and privates Abbey, Adams, Brockelbank, Butler, Bullock, Cole, Phelps, Allen R.

Smith, Sanford, and Lyke, wounded, while Sergt. David B. Jones and privates Asa Smith and Charles M. Struble were missing. The day was spent caring for the wounded, burying the dead, our own as well as those of the enemy, and throwing up a line of rifle pits where we were engaged the day before. (61)

Several issues for the reader to consider. This is not Heavy Artillery regiment duty. This is Charles' first experience. His Sergeant, Judson A. Smith, who had written to Rebecca, has been killed. Charles, in future letters, never tells Rebecca of Judson's fate. In fact, he tells Rebecca, "He wasn't that much anyway." It is believed he didn't want her to know his true fate so as not to scare or worry her. Privates Abbey and Smith were two of Charles' roommates back at the fort. Abbey is wounded, and Smith is missing. For Charles, the war has become very real.

In the opening of this letter, Charles writes of receiving a letter from Julia Thayer. I could not determine who she may have been with a high degree of confidence. Two thoughts came to mind. She may be a friend from Waterford. Performing a census search, I discovered no Thayers in Waterford. Could she be a relative? Again, unable to determine. An old girlfriend, perhaps? After the alienation of Emma following Charles' introduction to the pretty girl back in late February, I would hope that Charles would not repeat a similar mistake. It is beyond my belief that Julia would have fit that category, and then Charles wrote home about it. I did discover the following, which makes sense, but I can not confirm its accuracy or authenticity. I did locate a Julia Thayer, who lived in Rensselaer. She is the same age as Charles and remember his friend John Troy was also from Rensselaer. There is also a Julia Wager, who I think is Julia Thayer, who remarried. I can not confirm that to my complete satisfaction. She is applying for widow's benefits for her husband, who was killed during the Battle of the Wilderness. That would place her husband and Charles in the same place at the same time. But, the letter is written prior to his being killed. It will happen soon, but not yet.

A final thought. This is a brother/sister letter. Maybe Julia and Rebecca are friends. Perhaps Julia is seeking information, and she encourages Julia to contact her brother for help with whatever the issue is. There had to have been some reason for Charles to mention Julia.

Sunday, May 22, 1864

Dear Mother,

I take the pleasure to write to you a few lines to inform you that I am still among the living. I have been in a battle. I came out alright. There was a great many killed. It was an awful sight. We shove the Rebels so they did not come back again. Well, Mother about ten o'clock in the night we came out of the battlefield to the rear and rested. In the morning we went on to the field and threw up breastworks. We got the breastworks done. We was ordered to report to Ginney Station (Guinea). You look that up on a map and see how far it is from Vernia Courthouse to Ginney Station. Well, it was an awful hot day. Some of the men got sunstroke. I was so tired when we stopped that I laid down in the road and went to sleep. Then as soon as the army stopped we was sent out on reconnaissance. Well, Mother, an order just came to move so I must stop.

Charles is referencing the Battle of the Wilderness. At this point, the family is faced with the reality of Charles' situation. He hasn't written for 47 days and can't complete this one.

We will refer back to the Captain's Diary.

Sunday, May 22nd
At one o'clock in the morning, we were ordered back over the road upon which we had advanced the day before and, after marching some distance, were halted until 4 o'clock P. M. and then sent to Bowling Green, where we camped near Harrison's stores. The distance traveled was not far from six miles, but why we were kept moving about in this way, no one seemed to know. (62)

Charles must have been writing his letter at 1 am.

This is the road that led to the Spotsylvania Court House.

The Battle of Spotsylvania Court House, fought May 8–21, 1864, was the second major engagement of the Overland Campaign during the American Civil War (1861–1865). After the Battle of the Wilderness (May 5–6), in which Union general-in-chief Ulysses S. Grant had tried to turn Confederate General Robert E. Lee's right flank and was pushed back, Grant refused to regroup or retreat. Instead, he continued to maneuver south toward the Confederate capital at Richmond, next meeting Lee at the strategically important hamlet of Spotsylvania Court House. There, the Union Army of the Potomac and the Confederate Army of Northern Virginia clashed for nearly two weeks, with the heaviest fighting occurring for approximately twenty-one hours from May 12 to May 13. In what some historians have called the most intense combat of the war, the two sides fought largely hand-to-hand inside Confederate entrenchments. The worst of it occurred at an exposed portion of the line Confederates dubbed the "Mule Shoe" and a nearby curve that came to be known as the "Bloody Angle." Bodies piled up five deep in a driving rainstorm so that blood mixed with water, and some wounded men drowned. (63)

Charles has now been in battle for fifteen of the last twenty-one days. In both battles, the fighting is fierce, with high casualties.

4th Artillery Regiment (Heavy), NY Volunteers Civil War Newspaper Clippings Clipped from Cohoes Republican.

CAMP IN FRONT OF HANOVER JUNCTION
May 25, 1864

Those who contemplate volunteering will be pleased to learn that men are wanted in the 4th N. Y. Heavy Artillery for the past two years on garrison duty near Washington, D. C., where they will have comfortable barracks, good fare, light duty, and good pay. Col. JOHN C. TIDBALL, late of the regular service, is in command. A number of Cohoes boys are already in the regiment and express themselves well satisfied and pleased with the service. "A word to the wise, &c. A letter from WM. FERGUSON, of the 4th N. Y. Heavy Artillery, received by his brother in this village, speaks in terms of unqualified praise of the conduct of the Cohoes boys in the recent engagements before Richmond. He says they fought like veterans.

Personal.—We are happy to learn that Seward F. Gould has been commissioned and mustered in as Captain of his old Company in the 4th Regiment N. TY. S. V. Heavy Artillery (Col. Tidball's Regiment) is now stationed at Fort Ethan Allen, near Chain Bridge, Va. Fourth Heavy Artillery.

    Those who have friends in the 4th N. Y. Heavy Artillery, which has been, for the past two years, doing garrison duty in one of the forts near Washington, D. C., will be interested to know that the regiment has been ordered to the front for infantry service. This will be good news to most of the boys, who are tired of the monotonous drill to which they have so long been subjected, and who have been sighing for active service. They will, in all probability, soon have an opportunity to test their nerve and skill. A considerable number of Cohoes boys* are in this regiment. The Invalid Corps are to take the place made vacant by the transfer of the artillery.**

*The 4th is a unit formed in Cohoes, but many from Waterford are in its number.
**The Invalid Corps, later called the Veteran Reserve Corps, was authorized by Secretary of War Edwin Stanton's General Orders No. 105 on April 28, 1863. It was a time during the Civil War when the Union was having difficulties filling the ranks of its enormous armies. Manpower needs were being addressed by Abraham Lincoln's Emancipation Proclamation of January 1, 1863, which called for the enlistment of African American soldiers, and Congress's Conscription Act of March 3, 1863, the first draft in United States history. The creation of the Invalid Corps was a third measure intended to expand the pool of available military manpower. By the end of the war, about 60,000 men, previously made "unfit for active field service on account of wounds or disease contracted in the line of active" but still "meritorious and deserving," served in the new branch of the Union Army. (64)

    In the above article, *The Cohoes Republican* mentions how the 4th have been doing garrison duty and how they have been wanting active service. They have experienced it now. Will it reflect in their letters?
    On May 25, 1864, the 4th Brigade of Heavy Artillery now officially began operation as an Infantry Regiment. They will see duty as both an Ar-

tillery unit and infantry at least once at the upcoming Battle of the Crater.

The Battle of the Wilderness was part of the Overland Campaign. It was conducted May 5 - 7, 1864. The cost to the Union Army was 17,500 casualties.

In March 1864, Lincoln named Grant general-in-chief of all Union armies. Grant immediately began planning a major offensive toward the Confederate capital of Richmond. The primary goal of this Overland Campaign was to engage Robert E. Lee's Army of Northern Virginia in a series of battles to defend the Southern capital, making it impossible for Lee to send troops into Georgia, where Maj. Gen. William T. Sherman was advancing on Atlanta.

Grant decided to make his headquarters with the Army of the Potomac, commanded by Maj. Gen. George G. Meade. He would concentrate on general strategy, while Meade would oversee tactical matters. By early 1864, the Union Army of the Potomac and the Confederate Army of Northern Virginia faced each other across the Rapidan River in central Virginia. The two armies eventually met in the dense woods known as the Wilderness. The fight would prove deadly for both sides, and after 48 hours of intense combat, neither was the victor. Despite the outcome, Grant did not retreat. To the relief of President Lincoln and the joy of his men, the general continued his advance toward Richmond. (65)

The fighting on the 7th was of a defensive character on both sides. Our battalion felled three or four acres of wood, threw up breastworks, got a battery in position, and lay behind it until dark.

Then we were ordered to fall in and marched all night, chiefly in a southeasterly direction. The woods were on fire on both sides of us the forepart of the night. This doubtless tended to prevent straggling, but many of the men were actually asleep while moving on. About midnight there was a brief halt to enable some batteries to overtake us. Every man was instantly asleep by the side of the road. Sunday morning, May 8th, found us on the heights of Fredericksburg, marching southward to support some batteries in position. (66)

Wednesday morning, May 4th, the men who had been aroused and had already prepared their breakfasts fell in line and moved with the light batteries, via Stevensburg, to Germanna Ford on the Rapidan River, which was crossed about 10 o'clock A.M. on pontoon bridges, the battalion halting on the heights above. The rebels made no opposition, though a long line of rifle pits and some small earthworks were found on the heights commanding the Ford. The weather had grown warm and pleasant; the men threw away their coats, blankets, and everything they could spare, covering the ground along the line of march from Culpeper with clothing and blankets.

Near Hanover Station, May 24, 1864

Dear Mother,

I received your letter and was very happy to hear from you. We had moved camp and got settled when the mail came in. Well Mother, the Lord has spared my life in the Battle, I did not get wounded but there was a great many killed in the Company. Oh Mother, as you said I have seen a great many hard sights. Oh, it is awful. Well Mother, I have marched a great many miles. We are now 25 miles from Richmond and maybe the next time you hear from me I will be in Richmond. I hope so. Every time the rebels make an attack on us, they get licked. I was in the battle on the 23rd. The rebs came in without any guard. 900 came in today and I don't know how many last night. They come in in flocks. They say, "a right smart army." I reckon we take a great many prisoner. Well Mother, it is getting dark and I will close for tonight. I will finish next chance I get. So good night. Oh, how i wish I could kiss you all. Will close for I mustread a chapter in the Bible. May the Lord spare my life to meet you all once more. I try to be a good boy, so does Westover. He sends his love to you. Mother, my paper is dirty and so am I. I will send you the likeness of a little boy I found on the battlefield.

The top of this letter states it is from Camp near Hanover. It is actually from Hanovertown or perhaps just somewhere in Hanover County. During the Civil War, Hanover County was a frequent battlefield as Union troops commanded by various generals attempted to fight their way to Richmond through the Confederate army. Note should be taken that Captain Brown had advised his men to police (bathe) themselves in the North Anna River on May 11th. It should further be noted that for Charles, civilized life is over. He lives in fields and forests. For the remainder of his time in the war, he has limited access to food, water, a change of clothes, and anything a person takes for granted on a daily basis. *Knowing* Charles, like I think I do, he availed himself of this opportunity to bathe, and it may have been his last.

Charles concludes this letter with, "I will send you the likeness of a little boy I found on the battlefield." The implications of this statement are endless. It could be as simple as it sounds. The possible scenarios and spiritual meanings of this statement are limited only by the mind of the reader.

Rhetorically, what moved Charles to send the picture of an unknown child to his mother that he had found on a battlefield?

Brown's Diary confirms Charles' writing.

Monday, May 23rd
At 5 o'clock A. M., we joined the wagon train as a guard and marched about twelve miles to Mt. Carmel Church, where we arrived at half-past eleven and were permitted to halt and boil our coffee. The Second Corps passed to our left and the Fifth Corps to our right, and with the latter Corps, we crossed the North Anna River, and in a short time, skirmishing commenced, and a battle opened

vigorously at about 5 o'clock, which lasted some two hours. We understand that Gen'l Hill's rebel Corps is in our front. The night was spent digging rifle pits and getting our troops into position.

May 25th, the next day, to Mother.

Wednesday, May 25, 1864

Well Mother, the morning has come again. Oh, how thankful we ought to be to the Lord. He gave us plenty to eat and drink. Oh, if we could only thank him enough for what he has done for me, Mother. Charles Westover told me to tell you he tries to do right. Mother, if you were here to look over the field and see the soldiers you would think that you were in a hornet's nest. Some a singing and talking, everything you can think of. On the night of the 23rd, about 5 o'clock in the afternoon the rebels came across the field in seven lines of Battle and drove our troops a little, was then they turned around and stood their ground and the artillery opened up on them with grape and canister and oh, to see them go. It was awful. You could not see no more of the Rebels. Seven Lines of Battle, we killed 900 Rebels on that one surge. Well, Mother, I must close for my paper is getting short, so I will close for the present, so goodbye, may the Lord have mercy on us all, til we meet again. Give my love to all.

This letter to Mother demonstrates the changes in Charles. It begins by thanking and praising the Lord for subsidizing and protecting him. Mentions, friend Charles Westover, trying to do right. Ends his letter to Mother, almost braggingly reporting on the killing of 900 Rebels. I believe we are witnessing a battle-affected soldier's change of outlook. Charles has been involved almost continually, for thirty days, in a life-and-death environment. In one moment, he is thankful to the Lord, and in the next, we killed 900.

For the only time in the comparisons of Charles' letters to Agustus' Diary, we find a possible aberration. They don't agree. Several possibilities exist. Augustus mentions a skirmish. Charles mentions a battle with artillery fire. Both did occur. Perhaps Charles was reassigned on the battlefield. But shouldn't Agustus be aware of that?

Maybe the transcriber entered the wrong date. I trust the accuracy of Charles' reports.

Charles has just spent nineteen of the last twenty-one days in battle. On June 1st, he writes to Sister. The next day will be the first of seventeen more days of the Battle of Cold Harbor.

Cold Harbor, after several days of inconclusive sparring at North Anna, General Grant maneuvered his men southward in yet another attempt to outflank General Lee's Army of Northern Virginia. On May 31, 1864, General Sheridan's cavalry seized a vital crossroads near Cold Harbor. By gaining possession of Cold Harbor itself, Grant would be able to maneuver his army between Lee and the Confederate capital of Richmond. Late on June 1, the Union VI and XVIII Corps launched an assault that met with partial success. A follow-on Federal assault was delayed twenty-four hours as Grant waited for the II Corps to arrive. At dawn on June 3, the II, VI, and XVIII

Corps attacked and were repulsed after briefly penetrating the enemy defensive line. Union casualties exceeded 7,000, while Confederate losses were 1,500. Cold Harbor pointed out once again the folly of frontal assaults against fortified positions. (67)

Camp near Hanover Courthouse,
Virginia, Wednesday, June 1, 1864

Dear Sister,

It is so long since I got a letter from you. I often think of you

and wish that I could see you but before long I think this cruel war will be over so the soldiers can return home to their friends. Dear Sister, I am about 9 miles from Richmond. I wish it was only one mile, I hope this month brings this war to an end, but I am afraid not. If you could be down here and hear the canons roar and the muskets, you would think the world was coming to an end. We got so nigh Richmond that they can hear the roar of the canon and we will be so nigh before long, they will smell the powder, I bet, or something else. Well, Uncle Smith is killed. He got killed the 19th of May. Charles Abby got wounded in the mouth. Uncle George got wounded at the Wilderness in the two day battle. Dear Sister, I must close I don't have time to write much. Write as often as you can. I am well and hope that these few lines will find you well. We are going to have a Siege Train, it is on its way to us now. Well I will close now, good-bye, God Bless you. May the Lord spare my life to meet you all again. My love to all.

In this letter, he rather matter-of-factly reports on the death of Uncle Smith. With another uncle, George was wounded in the Battle of the Wilderness. I don't know who they are. He also mentions his friend Charles Abby being wounded in battle, but there is no emotion in his writing. Save for "God Bless You, and may the Lord spare my life until we meet again."

We are going to have a Siege Train. What is a Siege Train?

The siege trains of the Civil War consisted almost exclusively of guns and mortars. Guns fired projectiles on horizontal trajectory and could batter heavy construction with solid shot or shell at long or short range, destroy fort parapets, and dismount cannon. (68)

General Grant devised a long-term plan to end the war. His plan is intended to cut down on casualties by reducing hand-to-hand fighting. He intends to cut off the supply lines to the Confederate Capitol in Richmond by stopping railroad transportation to Richmond and bringing in a Siege train with the requisite armaments to wear down Richmond from afar. With their supply lines removed, they will no longer be able to continue the war.

This will happen, but not before another seven months will pass.

June 10th

Dear Mother,

I received your most kind letter and was glad to hear from you. I am well and hope this letter finds you the same. It does me good to get a letter from home. When a soldier gets a letter from home how good he feels. You will see his laugh and some don't get any. Some ain't got no friends to write to. Oh, how bad I would feel if I had no Mother or Father to write to. I would hardly know what to do. Thank God, I have lots of friends to write to me. That is all that keeps a soldier in good spirits. Well Mother, there ain't much fighting going on. We went in on a Flag of Truce today. You could see the Rebels on their breastworks and our men on theirs. Once in a while our men would go halfway and the Rebels would too and exchange newspapers and run back to their breastworks. The Rebel breastworks ain't only 20 yards from ours. My Company is back in the rear. Ain't been in any battle since the 19th of May nor ain't likely to go in any for we are an Artillery Brigade. Our Colonel is Chief of Artillery. Mother, there ain't much news, if any, so I will close. Charles Westover sends his love to you and wants you to pray for him, and for me also. I will write in a few days again. Give my love to Grandmother and Grandfather and all the rest. May the

Lord spare our lives, until we meet again. Write as often as you want. Good-bye and a kiss.

Charly Shepard
Company H
Heavy Artillery

Charles states, "Ain't been in any battle since the 19th of May." His Company is supposed to be performing Heavy Artillery Duty. They were reassigned to Infantry Duty and have been switched back. Charles is still in battle, just not on the front lines with man-to-man combat. His letter does sound a little more relaxed.

He writes of sending in a Truce Flag.

For the Battle of Cold Harbor, The flag of truce occurred on June 7. The Union attacks ended midmorning on June 3 without any visible gains. The current National Park Service estimate is that Grant lost about 6,000 men that morning, most of them in one hour's time. A substantial number of badly wounded attackers lay where they fell, now between the lines, beyond the reach of aid and unable to help themselves. The purpose was to secure a temporary cease-fire in order to rescue wounded men. (69)

June 12th

Dearest Mother,

I received your most kind letter this morning and was very happy to hear from you. It is Sunday and it is just the same as any other day here. Well Mother, I was reading the Bible when the Sergeant came and threw a letter in my lap. Oh, you better believe I opened it quick. I was up most of the night working on breastworks. We were in the works so I had a chance to write a little. Dear Mother, I have written 5 or 6 letters home. I don't know the reason you don't get them. Mother your letter found me well and I hope this letter will find you the same. There ain't much fighting going on now. Charles Westover sends his love, he wants you to pray for him and he will pray for himself. Oh, Mother sometimes I feel so happy when I try to do a favor for some of the soldiers. Oh, if some of them would only read their Bibles and pray, how much better I would feel. I try to pray and read my Bible and do what's right. Dear Mother, there is a rumor in camp that we are going to march to Harrison's Landing. I must hurry up and cook some dinner. I will close. If we don't go I will write tomorrow again. Kiss Em for I will write her as soon as I can. Good-bye, my love to all. Tell Beck to send her picture and I will get it. Give my love to Bech and Father. God bless you all, good-bye.

                Your loving son
                Charles Shepard
                4th Artillery Brigade
                Company C

Charles has just been through a terrible period of the war. He is still safe. Not only has his faith been confirmed, but he wishes others would follow his lead in reading the bible.

This letter explains a dark period in the Shepard Family when they hadn't heard from Charles for an extended period. For unknown reasons, Charles' letters were sent from wherever he was but were not being received in a timely fashion. It should be borne in mind that previous mailings were from Fort Marcy. Now the mail is coming from the battlefield; apparently, it is not as smooth a flow.

Much of the Shepard family's discontent and apprehension concerning Charles' welfare during the war was that extended period when they received no letters. They, of course, had no knowledge that letters had been written but not delivered in a timely nature.

June 20th

Dear Father,

    I received your most kind letter and was glad to hear that you are well. Well Father, I have seen some tough times since our march from Cold Harbor. I will give you a little description of our march from Cold Harbor. We started Monday night, the 12th, about 6 o'clock and marched until 7 o'clock the next morning. We were about a mile from the Ciahcahominy River. There we cooked our breakfast, such as we had, then we were told we had two hours to rest. We then marched all day and most of the next night. Then we about four miles from the James River that we marched to the next day with good will. Then we was ordered to chop a road through the trees so the men could march through. That took us all day. Then we rested all day and night. The next day we went down to the river and helped load the boats with wagons, mules and artillery. We stayed a day and a night, then we marched up to Petersburg, here we are now. We gave the Rebels fits. The first time we came here, we drove them about half a mile. I hope this cruel war will end soon for it is awful. The Rebs will have to get out of the city or Grant will burn it down. We have got two of the railroads in our hands now. We will soon have the other and the city too. Well Father, I will close my letter for this time. Send me a paper, when you send it put in a couple of papers of *tobacco in it. They won't know the difference. Well, Father I will write in a few days again. So, good-bye, may the Lord bless you all. A good kiss to all.*

Charly Shepard
Co. H 4th NY
Artillery Brigade

A long letter with a lot of content. There is no embellishment in this writing. Every occurrence mentioned in this letter is supported by many sources. They marched for eleven hours. Then they cooked breakfast and rested for two hours. After the two-hour rest, they marched again, all day and into the night. The next day they march four miles to the James River. There they rested all that day and the next. They were assigned to chop down trees to create a roadway and rest again. After that, they report to the James River to help load boats. This is part of General Grant's preparation to lay siege to Richmond. They rested again. Then marched to Petersburgh.

Other than referring to the cruelty of the war, his writing is quite positive. He even seems to show some compassion for the Rebs when he hopes they leave town before Grant burns it down.

P38 The pontoon bridge over the James River. The II Corp, including Charles, was here to unload supplies.

Monday, June 12th, and Tuesday, June 13th. From the diary.

It is not very remarkable that the reaction from the strain of thirty-nine days under fire should make this day's march of about twenty miles seem to me particularly fatiguing.

A detail of a thousand men from the regiment was made this morning to go to the river near the Charles City Court House.

Camp near Petersburg
Friday, June 24, 1864

Dear Mother,

I now take the pleasure to answer your letter. You see that I commenced this letter with ink, but my ink give out. Well, Mother I am well and hope that this letter will find you the same. I am most played out. It is awful hot down here and it is awful dry weather. We ain't had no rain for over a month and if we don't get some before long, I don't know what we will do for water, it is awful hard to get water now. Well Mother, I have been in another battle. The 18th of June we made a charge on a Rebel Works and got repulsed but we gained a half a mile in ground. The boys fell like hailstones all around me. I expected to go at any minute, but I got through clear. We lost 5,000 men in that charge. Oh, it was an awful sight. Well Mother, they talk about sending us back to Washington in the Fort, I hope they will. Well you must try and read this letter because it ain't wrote very good. I will write in a few days again. Send me the Waterford paper and put a couple of papers of tobacco in it. Well Mother, I will close for this time. May the Lord *spare my life to meet once more. May the Lord bless you all. So, good-bye, a kiss.*

Your loving son, Charles Shepard

This letter is written four days after the above letter to Father. It is quite different, other than the request for the Waterford paper and the tobacco. He mentions his most recent battle, the one at Cold Harbor. Only four days have passed since Father's letter. In that letter, he has been marching for days towards Petersburg; in this letter, he is announcing a hope of marching to Washington, D. C. We know this doesn't play out. It was a common occurrence in Civil War-era encampments for rumors such as this to be spread. It was such a desired and hoped-for event that many wanted to believe it.

From the Captain's entries.

Saturday, June 18th

Although originally sent out merely to build the line, about midnight, an order was received directing us to hold it when built, and at three o'clock in the morning, this order was followed by another assigning us to a position in the front line in a charge to be made from our rifle pit at four o'clock. To men who had marched under a broiling sun all the day before and had worked all night like beavers with nothing to eat and little to drink, this last order was not particularly welcome.

I shall never forget the hurricane of shot and shell which struck us as we emerged from the belt of trees. The sound of the whizzing bullets and exploding shells, blending in awful volume, seemed like the terrific hissing of some gigantic furnace. Men, torn and bleeding, fell headlong from the ranks as the murderous hail swept through the line. A splash of blood from a man hit in the cheek struck me in the face. The shrieks of the wounded mingled with the shouts of defiance which greeted us as we neared the rebel works, and every frightful and sickening incident conspired to paint a scene which no one who survived that day will care again to witness.

Author's note. Charles' friend Asa Smith is wounded in this battle and hospitalized.

Monday, June 20th
The regiment was ordered to report to Col. Tidball, commanding the Artillery Brigade of the Second Corps, and on reporting, was ordered back to its camp. It is rumored that the Second Corps is to be relieved and sent to Washington or somewhere else, and we Heavy Artillerists fervently hope that there may be truth in the report

Sunday, June 26th
There seems to be no salvation for the "Fourth Heavy." Heretofore, though nominally brigaded with the artillery, we have not only supported the artillery and furnished men to fill up the batteries but have been detailed to guard wagon trains; to build roads and earthworks as engineers; to occupy breastworks; to do picket duty and make charges as infantry, and, in short, to perform every kind of military duty except that for which we were enlisted, but now, with the battalions again separated, we are infantry with no longer any disguise about it. General Pierce assures our battalion commander that the companies will have no picket duty to perform except in very urgent cases, but we know, of course, that that is all humbug, for in military operations, all "cases" are "urgent."

Monday, June 27th
Captain Eddy of Company B resigned today, and I would resign also were it not for the fact that I induced so many men to enlist in the battalion or the Eleventh Heavy Artillery, which was consolidated with the Fourth, and it would seem like deserting those men, instead of standing by them as I am in honor bound to do, though I do not

now command the company which I recruited. As expected, details from the battalion were sent out on picket in the afternoon.

Five days later, to Mother.

> Camp in front of Petersburg, June 29th
>
> Dearest Mother,
>
> I have got a half a sheet of paper and a poor lead pencil, so I will try and answer your letter. I was glad to hear that you was all well. I am well and I hope this dirty paper will find you all the same. Suppose you will have a fine time up north for the fourth of July. I would like to be up there to enjoy it with you all but, I think I would hide myself in the cellar if they fired any firecrackers for I have gotten tired of hearing such noise. Well Mother, we are in summer quarters in the woods. It is a nice place. We got a good chance to clean up. I am glad of it, I am so dirty that I hardly know myself. You can tell by this paper. I got Beck's likeness. It did me a great deal of good. Now, if I had Em's, and yours, and Fathers, I would be a hunky boy. Well Mother, I must close for my paper is getting short, send me some soon so I can write. Try and read this. God bless you, my love to all. I will write in a few days. I hope you will have a good time in New York. C. Shepard

Charles seems to acclimate well to whatever circumstance he is in. This series of letters from June 20 - 29 reflects a period of terrible battles where his life was truly in jeopardy. Yet, he attempts brevity in mentioning how dirty he is, the condition of his paper, and his writing instruments. At the same time, reports others around him were being killed and how they marched many miles in one direction and, soon after, in another direction. He is still looking forward to receiving their pictures (likeness) and expressing hopes for his mother to have a good time in New York.

Charles, in my mind, from the time I have spent researching his short life and analyzing his letters, I have come to the following conclusion. He was a very strong person physically, mentally, and spiritually. He seems to possess the ability to recover from or handle any challenge that is presented.

And on the same day, 1864

Dear Sister,

It is with pleasure that I now take the pleasure to set myself on the ground in the woods to answer your most kind letter and was glad to hear that you are all well. I am well and fat and I hope this letter will find you all the same. Well Sister, I am putting a little extra in my letter. It is what I wear on my hat. It is the 2 Army Corp badge. It is called a club. Well, we are a club and a dirty one too, You would think so if you would see us. We look as if we had been drawed through a knot hole then rolled through the dust and put in a kettle and boiled. The weather is most hot. Every five minutes I take off my shirt and wring it and put it back on. All we have to do when we cook our dinner is put it out in the sun. In a little while our dinner will be cooked. Oh, talk about your comforts, you don't get it here. I had a bully breakfast this morning, soft bread, a piece of pork, had to pan it through the spider so the maggots would not run away with the fire and the spider. Had a coffee strong enough to kiss a nigger. Then to settle my breakfast took one of Uncle Sam's pills. Charlie Bandwell got sunstroke yesterday.

Tell Em that Charles Westover is very sick and gone to the hospital. It is hard but it is honest, I have been a lucky fellow, had the Rebel bullet go through my hair. Oh, the varmint, if I could get a pop at him he would think that one of our nigger soldiers was after him. I saw the nigger corppass yesterday. They was a good lot of soldiers. I saw your brother, he asked me how you were. I told him you were well, I showed him your picture and he said it looked just like you. Well Beck, I have written enough nonsense so I will close. There ain't much news of any importance in our front, but we expect to go to Washington for the Rebels are there. Well try and read this letter, give my love to all. I will write in a few days so good-bye. I took a dress from a Rebel Home, I will send it when I get back to Washington.

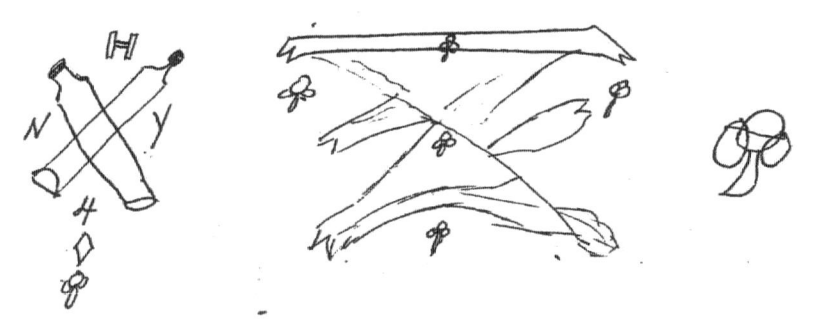

The drawing that Charles included.

The first portion of this letter to Rebecca contains so much hyperbole that I feel he is being facetious with her.

In the second part, he tells of a Rebel bullet going through his hair. We do find substantiation for that. He then goes into a derogatory description of the Colored Troops but at the same time praises them. Next, he says, "I saw your brother; "he asked me how you were." Has Charles gone metaphysical? He is her only brother. Is it an attempt at humor? Could it be a transcription error? Perhaps it is a close Waterford friend who is now in the military that is jokingly or affectionately referred to as Rebecca's brother. I don't detect any evidence of mental fatigue in his writing. Charles likes to joke around in his letters. I believe that is the case in this instance.

He apparently has obtained a dress from a Rebel house, which he will send when he gets to Washington.

"Well, Beck, I have written enough nonsense, so I will close." Perhaps that sums it up.

Six days later, another letter to Sister.

Petersburg, July 5, 1864

Dear Sister,

I now got a sheet of paper by trading my whiskey ration for it, so I will answer your kind letter and was glad to hear from you. I am well and hope this letter finds you the same. I suppose you all had a good time up north on the 4th. I hope you did. I had a good time in camp myself, hearing the firing of muskets and mortar shells at night. They go through the air at night. You would think it was a Roman candle. I don't like such Fourth of July's. I hope I will never see another in Virginia. Dear Sister if any of you want me to write, you must send me some paper. This is the last I will write until I get some paper for I can't get it for love or money. Charles Westover has gone to Washington, he is very sick. Tell Em, he fainted away. If he don't get good care, he will die. It is too bad, me and him and Charles Abby had always been together since we came out. Now Westover is gone and so is Abby, so I am the Lucky Boy. I have had good health. Well Beck, I think this outfit is going back to

Washington when our hundred days are up and that is Wednesday the 7th. I hope we will because it has been the worst hundred days I ever had or ever go through again. I bet. Well, Mother has gone to New York I suppose. Well, I hope she has gone and will enjoy herself for she works hard and wants a good rest. She is a good Mother. Well Sister, I will close. Kiss Em and Father for me, my love to all, good-bye, Your Brother

Hope is reignited in this letter. Charles mentions that the one-hundred-day mark is coming up. Usually, when a unit has been in battle for that long, they are relieved.

The next day, Father receives his letter.

Petersburg, July 6, 1864

Dear Father,

I received the Waterford paper and some tobacco. You put on too many stamps, two was enough. Well Father, I am well and hope this will find you the same. It is very warm here today. We all lay in the shade, a panting away. Well Father, what kind of a time did you have up north? I hope a good one. I suppose that Mother went to New York and you and Em and Beck stayed home. Well I had the pleasure of being a Picket, shooting all day and once in a while a canon and at night mortar shells and the stars fall. That was my fireworks. Well Father, I begged this paper off one of the boys and had to do hard work to get it. Father, you get the Harper's Weekly Newspaper and look where the Handcock Corps is crossing the James River it looks just like it. You will see Handcock in a chair just as he sat in that chair by the riverside, and the Battery that you see, my Company built that Battery. The picture looks as natural as you were there yourself. You will see a Rebel Soldier in a corner of a fence, dead, that was killed on the 19th of May. I took some things out of his haversack. All of those pictures look just the same as if you were there yourself. Try to get it. Well, I suppose the Easell Corps is up to Harper's Ferry, If he gets back to Richmond, he will be a smart man. The talk is we are going back to Washington in four or five days. We took 500 prisoners the other night. Well, I will close for this time. There ain't no news of any importance, so good-bye, my love to Em, Mother and Beck. I will write in a few days.

Your everloving Son,
Charles W. Shepard
Saratoga County

At this point, the contents of this letter to Father are a microcosm of his experiences to date. John Shepard does obtain a copy of *Harper's Weekly*. He reads the story and sees the pictures.

Petersburg, July 10, 1864

(written in the margin of the letter: This paper is dirty and so am I. I will bet you an arm, you can't read this.)

Dear Mother,

It is with pleasure I sit myself on the ground, under a big pine tree to let you all know I am well and in good health and fat as a pig. I hope these few lines will find you well. I am on Picket and its most time to be relieved. I enjoy the picket on Sunday, reading my Bible. I wish I was home to enjoy it instead of on picket. Well Mother, my friend Charly Westover, is very sick and has gone to *the hospital. He was very sick. It is awfully hot here. The flies bother me so I can hardly write. I hope you had a good time in New York. Oh dear, how the flies does bother me. They keep my hand a going all the time. Never mind, next winter should bring me out of this thing. I hope. So far, I am tired of it. I have seen enough of war to go home, settle down and be contented, I bet, along with every other man, I reckon. Well Mother, there ain't any news o fany importance. Most every morning the Rebels make a charge on our right lines. They think that we are gone, but they get slipped up on it. They think we have gone after Ewell. If the Rebel General ever gets back to Richmond, he's a smart man, if he don't get gobbled up it will be a wonder to me. We are going back to Washington in a few days. We think they will have to send us back. We thought we would go to City Point last night, but we ain't gone yet. Tell Father I got the paper with the tobacco in it. I must close now for it is time to be relieved. I hope this letter will find you all well and in good spirits. My love to Em, Beck, Father, GrandMother and Grandfather and all the rest of the folks. A kiss to all. Oh, how I would like to see you all, I will before many days. I will close, good-bye and God bless you all.*

Your Son, Charles
The Union Forever

The writing conditions are such that it is a wonder that he could write at all.

Now a war battle veteran, Charles seems to have gained the ability to relax, read the bible and write letters while on Picket Duty.

Once again, his writing is bolstered by the reports of Augustus Brown.

This statement offers some insights into the behavior of the Picketts, both north and south.

Notwithstanding the rough experiences the war entails, there are occasional incidents which save us from altogether losing confidence in human nature. For instance, today, at a point where the picket lines were not more than fifteen yards apart, the men on these lines agreed not to fire upon each other and at once got out of their burrows, exchanged papers, traded knives, tobacco, and coffee, and discussed politics.

Since the 2nd, we have lain in the rifle pits with the infantry, sweltering in the sun in the daytime and doing quite our share of picket duty at night. At midday, it is no uncommon thing to see the thermometer mark 110 degrees in what little shade there is. There has been no rain for weeks, and heat is killing more men than the "Johnnies."

Not having felt at all well for some time, I determined today to act on the advice of the surgeon and go to the hospital for a few days.

We will not have the privilege of the Captain's Diary until July 13th. Mother is the recipient of the next letter, on July 18th.

Petersburg, July 18, 1864

Dear Mother,

It is with pleasure I write to you to let you know that I am well and that this letter finds you the same. It is quite pleasant here this morning. When I first got up, it looked like rain. I was in hopes it would rain for we need it very bad. We ain't had no rain for a long time. In the road it is awful. Well, we had preaching in the camp today by our Chaplain. He preached a good sermon. He gave us all a paper to read. He is a good man. He talks to the soldiers and tries to do them good. We are going to be paid off days, I will send it all home. How does Em get along for money? She wont tell me rather she's got any or not. I hope she has enough until I get paid. What is the name?

Tell Em I think of the baby often. Oh Mother, if I ever get in Waterford, I'll know enough to stay there. I bet there will be a great many boys that will know how to appreciate a home once they get there. There was a boy in my Company the other night, the band was playing "Who Will Care For Mother Now?" and he commenced to cry.

He said, if it wasn't for that tune, I never would have enlisted. Poor boy. In one of our hospitals there was a boy who got wounded, he was dying. He called the chaplain to his side and told him to write to his mother and tell her that all was well, and then he died. Oh. how happy that mother must have been to know that her son died happy. May the Lord have mercy on our soldiers for there are a great many bad ones. Charlie Westover has gone to the hospital, he was very sick. He will go home on furlough when he gets better. Mother. I wish you would see that Emma gets everything she wants and when I come home, I will make it right. Mother. I will close for now, don't forget me.

Tell Em I forgot to put my picture in her letter, I will send it next time. Kiss the baby for me. Your Son, Charles.

Charles has been informed of the birth of his daughter and wonders what her name is. One has to admire Charles' confidence in his return. He does not state if I come home; it's when I come home.

Another letter was received three days later.

Petersburg, July 21, 1864

Dear Father,

I received a letter from you and I was happy to hear that you are all well. I hope this letter will find you all well. I am well and fat. Well Father, I seen John Halpin of the 115th Regiment, tell his father he is well. I will go see the rest of the Waterford boys. They are in the 18 Corps. They are about one mile from our camp. Night befor last, I was to work on forts. I seen Edward White, he is well. The Vanderwerken boys are well. Jerry Welch has gone to the hospital, he was sick. We have had a nice rain down here. Suppose you had some rain up north this time. I hope so. If you could see your son, you would hardly know me, fat, dirty and tall, I have grown like fun since I left home. A great many of the boys said I would cave in on the first long march but they got slipped up on it. I have led them very ones on marches and tuckered them out on our marches. They don't say any more about marching. Well Father. There ain't much news of any importance that I know of. I got the Waterford paper with the tobacco in it. Well I will close for this time, I got your picture, it is very good. My love to all, good-bye. Your Son,

Charles Shepard
Co. H 4th NYV
Heavy Artillery

The Edward White mentioned in this letter is a member of the 22nd N.Y, S. Infantry. That is the unit that was marched across the Union Bridge by 82-year-old John Cramer at the beginning of the war. Edward survives the war and returns to Waterford. Edward was married before the war. He and his wife Caroline had three children prior to his enlistment and three more upon his return. He appears on the 1890 Census, living alone. He does not appear in the 1900 Census. Charles was friends with the Vanderwerkens and John Halpin; it is likely he mentions White because he is from Waterford.

The Jerry Welch, who was sick and went to the hospital, was Jeremiah Welch. He enlisted in January of 1864, and by July of that year, he was in the Depot Field Hospital in Virginia. He died there of disease on July 13, 1864. Charles' letter was written on the 21st. He wouldn't have known of his fate at that time. Jeremiah was a Teamster on the towpath, as was Charles' father. That could be the reason he was mentioned in the letter, coupled with the fact that he was from Waterford.

Petersburg, July 25, 1864

Dear Father,

It is with much pleasure that I now take time to write you a few lines, to let you know I am well and I hope this letter will find you all the same, but not so hungry. Sunday morning, about 4 o'clock, we were called up to work on a fort. We did not have no time to get something to eat so we went and worked till noon. Then there was a loaf of bread fed to you. We came into Camp about 7 o'clock and we was so tired we didn't get anything till this morning, so I feel much better, I seen Edward White, William Coones and the two Vanderwerken boys, they are all well. Their Regiment is going to Washington in a day or two. They feel quite good over it, we are building a big fort for our Regiment. I was out in the front lines and I could see the Rebs walking about their works, looking in on our lines once in a while. They will get

a lot of them together and then our artillery will let fly on them. They get down quick. I came across Billy Johnso. He belongs to the 44th NY Regiment. He works for Ben Murry. Perhaps you don't remember him and John Timbrooke. They are all well. I came across someone from Waterford almost everyday. I seen John Halpin, tell his father he is well. It rained hard here last night. There ain't much fighting on our front. Along the 9th Corps the Pickets are firing all the time. They are undermining the Rebel Forts. I expect to wake up some fine morning and hear the greatest noise that I ever heard in my life. My Regiment still lays back in the woods. I should like to stay back until the war is over. Well. I suppose now that Atlanta has been taken by Sherman, I hope he will capture the whole Jojnson forces. I was sorry to hear that Uncle Abrams is dead, poor Aunt Rebecca. What will she do? I hope she can get North. Well Father, I will close for this time. My love to all, I will write in a few days. My love to you and all. Good-bye. Your Loving Son,
       Charles Shepard

 John Shepard, Charles' father in 1864, read this letter in real-time. I had the privilege of reading it through the historical prism of time. There is much to examine in this letter.

 First, let's discuss the people that Charles mentions in this letter. We have gathered information on people he knew, both new friends from within his regiment and old friends from Waterford. Taking into consideration that he is only nineteen, he apparently has many lasting relationships of friendship with varied contemporaries. We can reasonably assume that he was of exemplary character to have maintained such close contact and concern.

He mentions Edward White again, who we already met. He mentions again the two Vanderwerken boys, as well as William Coones. It is believed that William Coones is actually William Coons. We are dealing with letters that were transcribed and typed about one hundred years after they were written. The letters written after Charles leaves Fort Marcy and is in the field are written on whatever is available and not under ideal conditions. I found no William Coones or Coons in Waterford during this era. There was a William H. Coons who served in the same Heavy Artillery at the same time as Charles. He was from Ballston Spa. After the war, he was a farmer in Charlton. He married and had two children; he died in 1878.

In his quick mention of the Vanderweken boys, he writes of the possibility of their regiment returning to Washington, D. C. soon. This is a positive thought. In theory, once a unit has been in the field for one hundred days, they are taken out of action for a while. Charles' regiment has been engaged now since late April. They are approaching the one-hundred-day mark. They could soon be next for relief.

He mentions Billy Johnson. It appears that William H. Johnson was originally with the storied 77th Regiment, known as the Bemis Heights Regiment, out of Saratoga. He later is transferred to the 4th Heavy Artillery; he and Charles become wartime friends. Ben Murray is also mentioned. I can locate evidence of many Benjamin Murrays, however. I did not uncover any historical link to him and Charles being in the same place together. Obviously, they were; I just could not substantiate it. There was no evidence to support a candidate that I found. By no means am I claiming that Charles' letter contains errors. My research didn't lead me to confidently lay claim to the fact that I had uncovered the correct person.

The last person he writes of is John Tenbrook. John was in the same theatre of operations as Charley at the time of this letter. He is from Waterford and is likely a pre-war associate of Charles. His post-war story was a bit confusing. He survived the conflict and, by 1865, had returned to Waterford. He takes residence with his brother Henry Tenbrook Jr., who is employed as a bank teller. Prior to the war, he lived with his parents, Henry Sr., Mother Maria, along with brother Edward. Henry Sr.'s occupation was farming. Although twenty-four years of age in 1860, living with his parents, he claims no occupation. His new living arrangements leave much to make one wonder. Henry Jr. is listed as head of household at age twenty-eight. John is listed as residing there. He is now thirty and lists his occupation as a gentleman. Both he and his brother are unmarried. What makes the picture more confusing, they employ Fannie Goodrich, age forty-nine, as a live-in housekeeper for $600 per year. Also in their employ is twenty-five-year-old Ellen Malloy as a domestic servant with no pay mentioned. It just appears to be a living condition that would raise the eyebrows of mid-19th-Century Waterford. Making matters more mysterious is that John drops out of sight until April 2, 1918. On that day, he is buried in the Waterford Rural Cemetery at age seventy-seven. Between 1870 and 1918, I found no trace of him.

Charles, in the body of this letter, reports, "We are in sight of the Rebels!" He writes of undermining a fort and expects to wake up one morning to the loudest noise he's ever heard. John, as he reads this letter, likely has no idea what this represents. We will soon learn of the Battle of the Crater.

He mentions that he supposes Sherman has taken Atlanta. Sherman is in the process and will, but not until September 2nd; this letter is dated July 25th. Charles' awareness of what is happening and his accuracy in reporting events of the war in real time have always amazed me.

The mention of Uncle Abram and Aunt Rebecca. This is unsubstantiated. I believe that Uncle Abram is either John or Harriet's brother. Or was Aunt Rebecca a sister? Was Beck's named after her? At any rate, Uncle Abram is now deceased, and the hope is that Aunt Rebecca can come north. Uncle Abram may have been connected with the Confederate forces. He was from the South, but his affiliation was never outlined.

Lastly, in this letter, he reports he has gotten a rotten blow. Another of Charles' colloquialisms? My research of speech during that era offered two possibilities. Either he is ill, but in the letter, says he's fine, or he has done something wrong, and someone has reported him. I'm leaning toward the latter.

Petersburg, July 28, 1864

Dear Mother,

I received your most kind letter and was happy to hear from home. I am well and I hope this letter will find you the same. It has been very warm for the last 4 or 5 days. My Regiment has been building forts. We go out to work every day and we work ten hours until we get them done. Well Mother, I suppose that you know, my friend Charlie Westover is dead. He died on his way to New York, so Mr. Mayhew said. He got a letter from home that said he was dead. Well Mother, I can say one thing, he was a good boy, he read his Bible and was a good boy. He was liked by all in the Company. The last time I seen Charlie, I went out to tha ambulance and helped him in the wagon and bid him good-bye. I told him to take good care of himself and when he got better to write me. He said he would but I never got a letter so I thought he was worse. Poor boy, he died happy. The Lord only knows what will become of us. I trust in the Lord that my life will be spared to return home. Well Mother, I was out to work yesterday on the front and the Rebels threw a mortar shell in the breastworks the 118th Regiment was in and killed one man and wounded three others. Blowed one man 30 feet in the air, and the leg off another. It was awful, it was the worst thing I have seen since I have been out here. There is only a few of my Company in camp today. I got excused from duty today. The boys that I did tent with at Culpepr, I am the only one left. They are sick, in the hospital, killed or wounded. The 2 Army Corp is gone away for parts unknown. They was ordered to take badges off their caps and if any of them were taken prisoner not to tell what Corps they belonged to. Well Mother. I will close for this time. We expect to get 4 months pay any day. I will write to Em and Beck on my next chance.

This letter needs no editorializing from any writer; a century and a half later, it's still very clear. *"Dear Mother..........I am the only one left!"*

The final word on his friend Charles Westover. He died of disease, on July 18, 1864, at Davids Island, New York Harbor.

In the postscript, there is a word that the transcriber, Charles' great-grandson, could not read. ( ). In several exchanges with his sister Rebecca Becks, he mentions sending home his likeness. It is my belief that likeness is the unreadable and untranscribed word in this letter. In this letter, he states he had forgotten to include his likeness in Em's letter, so he did include it in his mother's. At this time, a picture of Charles, in uniform, was received at the Shepard home on Sixth St. in Waterford. Was there only one? Likely. It was intended for Emma. Did Mother give it to her? Did it ever make its way to Addie? Where is it now?

August 1, 1864

Dear Mother,

I received your most kind letter and was glad to hear that you were all well, but Em. I hope she is not very sick, quite a prize. I am glad it is so pretty as you tell about. I would like to see it myself. Kiss it for me 3 or 4 times. Well Mother, your letter didn't find me very well. I have been in another awful battle. Friday night my outfit was detailed to go up to a fort in the front.

The name of the Fort was Fort Tilton. You might see the name of that Fort in the papers for it done great damage. About 5 o'clock Saturday morning we were called up to get ready so while the Captain was waking the rest up I got up on the Fort and was looking down on the Rebel lines. Oh. Mother, I had been up there about a minute before I saw a Rebel Fort going up in the air. Oh. it was an awful fight, I tell you. The Fort hadn't been blown up a second, when the Artillery began to throw solid shot and shell from both sides. It was one of the hottest places I have ever been. It blowed up about 2000 Rebels. Oh, it was awful. Our men made a charge of their works drove them out. Then the Rebels masses their Troops together, drove them back. Well, we made another charge and did the same. There was charge after charge made on both sides. Oh Mother, there will be a many poor mother or wife hear of their sons or husbands got killed. It was one of the awful battles for the times that the Army ever saw. I suppose a good many of the Waterford boys is killed, wounded or taken prisoner. I haven't seen none of them yet, but as soon as I get time I will take a walk up that way to see if any of them, god forbid, any more of such cruel murdering. The dead was piled up in piles on both sides. Well Mother, the Lord has been good to me. He has seen me past a good many dangerous places. Well Mother, I will close for this time. My head aches. So you can name the baby among yourselves, I can't think of anything now. My love to Em, tell her to take care of herself and the baby. I will write to her, Father and Beck. So, good-bye. A good kiss for all and 6 or 7 for the baby.

Your Truly Son
Charles Shepard
Heavy Artillery
In your next letter put a little mustard in it, it goes good.

A lot of emotion in this letter. In the letters to Charles, the new baby is a topic in letters received.

Charles begins with the mention of Fort Tilton. I was not able to find a fort by this name in Virginia. There were and are forts by this name, but not here. Either Charles is mistaken, or perhaps it is a local reference.

He soon gets down to what's foremost in his mind; the battle that he has been both a witness to and a participant in. This is the Battle of the Crater. It was on July 30, 1864. Less than forty-eight hours have passed when Charles writes his description of the battle. In my own mind, I find it curious that this letter would be addressed to Mother. One would think that Father would be a more likely candidate to be informed of this event. From the many accounts that I have read of this battle, it was worse than Charles describes. Even General Grant telegraphed Henry W. Halleck, the Army Chief of Staff, calling it "The saddest affair I have witnessed during the war."

Some Military Historians have created a list of the Top Ten Blunders in Military History; the Battle of the Crater comes in as Number 2.

At the outset of this battle, Charles has a bird's eye view. He is with the Artillery Brigade looking down at the battle as the explosion occurs. He reports on line after line being formed to charge into the battle. His Company is one of those lines. They make charge, after charge, advancing and retreating. There were over 8,000 participants, and more than half were casualties. (Casualties include deaths, wounded, missing, and taken prisoner.)

It would not be in our best interest to attempt an explanation of all that occurred in this battle. An abbreviated thumbnail sketch is in order. In short, a Pennsylvania Regiment, composed of many coal miners, came up with a plan to dig a mine underneath the Confederate camp, fill it with gunpowder and blow it up. A plan was formulated. Part of that plan included the utilization of a company from the U. S.

C. T. (United States Colored Troops). After the explosion, they were to lead the charge, followed by others to easily defeat and overcome the shocked Confederates. The U. S. C. T. had trained for this event. The day before the event, for a multitude of reasons, the plans changed. They decided to use a different company. The company chosen was determined by lot. The General in charge of the "winner" got drunk and was not around for the attack. There were many other glitches in the execution of the plan. For those interested in the complete story, there are many excellent books on the battle. An online search will also supply a wealth of information.

Charles is now calling the war cruel murdering and writes of the piles of bodies he sees while searching for Waterford boys piled up from both sides. The realization of danger all around him seems not to have frightened him, but I believe he is now keenly aware of the importance of the here and now. Rightfully so, his head hurts, and he is unable to be involved in the baby's naming. Years ago, before I had an understanding of what Charles' experiences were. I would read these letters and think ill of Charles and his lack of interest in naming the baby. After several years of research and study, I no longer harbor any ill feelings towards Charles for his inability to offer a name for his daughter.

Put a little mustard in it. It comes good. An example of here and now.

Our final referral to Captain Augustus Brown will be this next piece. In Charles' letter, he writes, "The fort hadn't been blown up only a second before the artillery began to throw solid shot and shell from both sides."

The Captain reports. As soon as I saw the vast inverted cone of earth, fire, and smoke caused by the gigantic explosion, I gave the order, "Commence firing, No. 1 fire!" and before the noise of the explosion, or even the trembling of the earth, had reached us, No. 1 had sent a thirty-three-pound shell into a two-gun battery facing us, smashing through the parapet and opening the way for a shell from No. 2, which, aimed by Corporal O'Connor as a columbiad for want of a trunnion sight, sent its shell under the muzzle of an old-fashioned barbette gun doing duty as a field-piece, and dismounted it before it could fire a shot in our direction. Nos. 3, 4, 5, and 6 followed in rapid succession, and the order "fire at will" brought on an almost continuous roar. There was a rebel camp in plain sight over near "Fort Damnation," and when the first shell from my No. 6 dropped among the tents and exploded, it was amusing to see the "Johnnies" turning out in consternation and very few clothes, and skedaddling to cover. (70)

To Sister.

Petersburg, August 4, 1864

Dear Sister,

As I have one more sheet of paper and such good news I thought I would answer your letter today. I have written Father today and to George Steenburgh so I am pretty well wrote out. Well Beck, my Regiment is going to start for Washington in the morning. The boys are kicking up at a great rate. Such a noise you can't hardly write. I have not been well for the last 5 or 6 days, but I think I am well enough now. Going back to Washington is the best news I have had yet. Well Beck, I suppose you get to be Auntie. Well such things will happen. This is a curious world. Well Beck, I must close. My love to all. I will write a good long letter next time, so good-bye. My love to the baby and all of the rest. A kiss from your absent Brother.

C. Shepard

Before Charles was "wrote" out, he had written to George Steenburg. George was a fellow Waterfordian who lived on Fourth St. in Waterford. He was a neighbor of Caroline Shepard (unknown if Caroline was related to Charles), a widow who was a dressmaker. George, unlike Charles, who enlisted, was a draftee. He was single when he was drafted and survived the war. He married after the war. His wife's name was Amy, and they raised a son and a daughter. George and his brother David operated a carriage business in Waterford, making, painting, and repairing carriages. They were also wheelwrights. George lived until his 84th year and was buried in the Oakwood Cemetery.

Charles thinks they may next return to Washington D. C. He writes of the excitement in camp with the noise from the celebrations in camp making it difficult to write. He has not been well for the last five or six days. These are the days following the Battle of the Crater.

He concludes this letter by telling Becks that this is a curious world. No doubt, he still has the carnage he witnessed and participated in a few short days ago on his mind; and now he may be getting off the battlefield. He even mentions the baby.

On the same day, Augustus writes.

> *Thursday, August 4th*
> *Found myself quite weak and exhausted this morning and experienced some difficulty in walking, but I managed to keep up and around the camp. Companies A and M returned from Siege Train Landing today and joined the regiment, and an order was received again assigning us to the Second Corps. Lieut. Col. Alcock, now in command of the regiment, reported to our new corps commander, but nothing was done about breaking camp. It is rumored that the Second Corps is to be sent to Washington, though precisely why we are not informed.*

Interesting to note that both Charles and Augustus are not feeling well and that the rumor of going back to D. C. is rampant among the officers as well as the men.

The next day, he writes to Mother.

Petersburg, August, 1864

Dear Mother,

    I received yours and sisters letter yesterday and I was glad to hear that you was all well. I am well and enjoying myself. How I would like to see you all. I hope and pray that this cruel war will soon end. I sometimes think that the rebels will lick us for just about the time there is going to be a battle fought, you will see our officers all drunk. That was the reason we lost that fight the other day. Lord forbid such if we had good praying men to guide us. We would lick them every time. They will drink so musch they don't know what ginger is and don't know how to give commands. Our soldiers had a soft thing on the 30th of July, if we had sober officers to guide us. Well Mother, I ain't seen none of the waterford boys yet so I don't know if any of them was killed or not. I suppose there was because there was awful hard fighting where they was. The boys of the 115th Regiment, told me that George Cole and James Geddins was wounded and a prisoner. They saw them when they were taken. I was very sorry that C. Westover was dead. Well, he was a good boy, he was liked by all in the Company. I miss him since he left. I hardly know what to write. My thoughts don't come fast today so I will close. We are going to Washington. We expect to go any minute, so I may be in Washington when you hear from me again. So I will close for this time. I will write to Em and Beck the next chance I get. Kiss the baby for me. My love to Em. Beck, Father,

Aunt Fanny, Granmother, Father and my friends. You ain't heard nothing from Aunt Rebecca, poor soul? I hope she will get North, May the Lord bless us all and spare our lives until we can meet again. Your Truly and Loving Son,

C. Shepard

Send me some mustard in a letter

Another letter to Mother that research has given insights into the state of Charles' mind. I find this letter very revealing in its content. I made a past announcement concerning a presentation I made on Charles' war experience with family members in attendance when several said; it's like you knew him. In the eight years that I have been creating this, I do feel as though I knew him.

He starts out by saying he is well and he is enjoying himself. He is not in battle at this time. The date of this letter is August 5th. He has been in the field for ninety-one days. They think they are returning to D. C. They are not within sight of the Rebels for the first time in three months. This had to be a great relief and enjoyment.

He wants to see everyone. He wishes the cruel war would end. He is praying, and he has hope. At the same time, he laments the fact that he has doubts that the Union can win because the officers are always drunk. There is historical evidence of that being true. It was part of many problems at the Battle of the Crater. This statement was supported in Captain Augustus Brown's diary.

Charles uses another colloquialism here that I was not able to interpret, "they will get so drunk, they don't know what ginger is."

General Burnside was relieved of command for the final time for his role in the fiasco, and he was never again returned to command. To make matters worse, Generals Ferrero and Ledlie were observed behind the lines in a bunker, drinking liquor throughout the battle. Ledlie was criticized by a court of inquiry into his conduct that September, and in December, he was effectively dismissed from the Army by Meade on orders from Grant, formally resigning his commission on January 23, 1865. (71)

He mentions the welfare of the Waterford boys from the 115th Regiment. When he attempted to contact them, he came into contact with the piles of dead soldiers and discontinued his efforts.

He mentions George Cole and James Giddens.

George Cole was from Halfmoon. He enlisted on August 8, 1862. He was captured in his first battle at Harper's Ferry on September 15th and released on the 16th. (they were still doing prisoner exchanges in 1862) On February 20, 1864, he is wounded and once again captured in a battle at Oulstee in Florida. He was paroled to the Foster Hospital in North Carolina and released on May 2, 1865, and returned home.

James Giddens, of Waterford, was actually James Gittings. He enlisted on August 12, 1862. He, too, was captured at Harper's Ferry and fought at the battle at Oulstee. He was wounded and captured in that battle. After confinement in the infamous Andersonville Prison, he died there on August 25, 1865.

He misses his friend Charles Westover, and optimism for a return to D.C. remains high.

Prior to his admission to the hospital, this is Captain Brown's last diary entry.

Monday, August 8th
As there appeared to be no likelihood of an immediate movement of the Second Corps unless it might be to Washington, I concluded temporarily to accept the hospitality of Doctor Hoyt and went over to his hospital, and he at once put me to bed.

On August 5th and 8th, both Charles and Augustus write and make note of the potential for the Corps' next move is Washington, D. C. There is excitement, joy, and relief experienced by the belief and trust in this news. Not only in camp but especially so at the Shepard household. The II Corps has earned this relief, and they deserve it. They have done their one hundred days. The worst should now be over. The general feeling is that the war will soon be over. If relieved from the battlefield now, as scheduled, there is a good chance that they won't return. The II Corps and the Shepard Family must think; the nightmare has ended. Good news is anticipated.

The next and final letter was written on August 25, 1864. It is to Father. It is not the letter that was anticipated. It's worth reiterating here that it is only known when these letters were written. We have no idea when they were received. Letters that are written in the field during battle campaigns usually are received much later than their written date. At the time that this letter was received, it is imagined that the Shepard family did not anticipate that this was the final letter.

Reams Station, August 25, 1864

Dear Father,

I received your most kind letter and was happy to hear that you are all well. I am well and hope this letter will find you the same. Well Father, I have been on the go since the 12th and I am most played out. The 2 Corps left Deep Bottom Saturday night and marched all night. It rained and it was awfully muddy. We marched about 25 miles. We got to Petersburg Sunday morning about 7 o'clock. I was about done in. Well, we went in camp, I put my tent up and went to sleep. About 11 o'clock we heard the 5 corps had taken the Weldon Railroad. We was ordered to pack up. Well, we went down to the railroad about 4 miles and stayed there all night and had a good rest. In the morning we were ordered to go down to the railroad and tear up the tracks. We tore the tracks up for about 10 miles. I tell you the 2 Corps has seen tough times since the 12th. We are going back to today or tonight, then I will get a chance to write more. At least I hope so, well Father, I will tell you about a scrap that my Company and Company A got into and its a scrap I don't want to get into every day. Company H and A were sent out to support a Brigade of Calvary. When we got there we found them dismounted and in a line of battle. Well, our two Companies formed on their right and made a charge. We charged and drove them back about a mile, till we got in a nest of them. Then they drove us back. Oh, how hot it was. We lost 25 killed and wounded. Half our Company got sunstroke. I got back by the skin of my teeth. Well, I must close because I am afraid we will move. So. good-bye. I will write to Em, next chance I get. A kiss to all, 6 or 7 for the baby. Good-bye and God bless you all. Tell Em that John Troy is killed or a prisoner. C. Shepard

I need not tell you what you have just read. The family does not know that this is the last letter. They are in anticipation of news that Charles' Company has returned to Washington, D. C. At the time this letter was written, the regiment has been in the field over one hundred and twenty days. Now they are in a battle at a railroad. The battle is known as the Battle at Ream's Station.

I offer the following report from the New York Times.

New York Times, August 25, 1864
The Second Battle of Ream's Station
August 25, 1864

On August 24, Union II Corps moved south along the Weldon Railroad, tearing up the track, preceded by Gregg's cavalry division. On August 25, Maj. Gen. Henry Heth attacked and overran the faulty Union position at Ream's Station, capturing nine guns, 12 colors, and many prisoners. The old II Corps was shattered. Maj. Gen. Winfield Scott Hancock withdrew to the main

Union line near the Jerusalem Plank Road, bemoaning the declining combat effectiveness of his troops. (This is the date of Charles' last letter home. He talks of tearing up the tracks, 2 Corps seeing tough times, and what a tough battle it was.)

It is said that the Fourth New York Heavy Artillery, or a considerable portion of them, stood their ground on the left when our line gave way and, rushing to the guns of the battery nearest to them, worked it till the enemy came on and surrounded them, capturing a considerable portion of them along with the battery.

Union casualties were 2,747 (the II Corps lost 117 killed, 439 wounded, 2,046 missing/captured; the cavalry lost 145); Confederate casualties were 814 (Hampton's cavalry lost 16 killed, 75 wounded, three missing; Hill's infantry 720 total). Although the Confederates had won a clear victory, they had lost a vital piece of the Weldon Railroad, and from this point on, they would be able to transport supplies by rail only as far north as Stony Creek Depot, 16 miles south of Petersburg. From that point, supplies had to be unloaded, and wagon trains would have to travel through Dinwiddie Court House and then on the Boydton Plank Road to get the supplies into Petersburg. The South Side Railroad was the only railroad left to supply Petersburg and Lee's army.

One of the 2,046 missing/captured was Charles.

Grant and Meade were generally satisfied with the results of their operations against the Weldon Railroad, despite the tactical setback suffered by Hancock.

There can be little doubt that in the engagement, they outnumbered us two to one, for the men of the two divisions we had there were so exhausted by fighting, hard marching, and their laborious work on the railroad that their effective strength had been very materially reduced. The enemy will very naturally pique themselves on the capture of our breastworks and artillery, but if they are allowed to claim a victory, it is of a kind that they may pray to be excused from experiencing too frequently.

(Charles also mentions all of this in his last letter.)

What you have just read, the family was not privy to. How and when they would gain this information has been lost to time. It may not have been realized until March 25, 1865. Considerable time passes from the receipt of the last letter until the actual news is received, but that date is unknown to us.

The circumstances bring to mind the inaugural address of President Gerald R. Ford when becoming President after the resignation of Richard M. Nixon.

> *"My fellow Americans, our long national nightmare is over.*
>
> *Our Constitution works; our great Republic is a government of laws and not of men. Here the people rule. But there is a higher Power, by whatever name we honor Him, who ordains not only righteousness but love, not only justice but mercy. Thomas Jefferson said the people are the only sure reliance for the preservation of our liberty. And down the years, Abraham Lincoln renewed this American article of faith, asking, "Is there any better way or equal hope in the world?"* Inaugural address, Gerald R. Ford, August 3, 1974.

President Ford was stating the nightmare was over. For the Shepard family, their nightmare had begun with the receipt of Charles' most recent, albeit last, letter.

Was this Charler's last letter? It was the last letter the family received. Through the exchange of letters between Charles and his several family members, we see mention of Charles writing letters that the family may never have received or received late. He wrote nearly 40 letters between January and August of 1864. An average of more than one a week. Many of those letters were written under adverse conditions. We know, from reading these letters, that he continues to correspond with friends at home, new friends in the army, and other family members. He was an active letter writer. After this battle, they hear no more from Charles. It has never been determined when, by what method, and in what manner the family received notification. History tells us he was captured; the family is unaware.

Thoughts on the letters.

Now that he had been captured, one could anticipate that the letters would stop. This was an assumption that I quickly made. My assumption was wrong. Letters, indeed, could be sent from and received in prison. As seen in the following two examples.

P39 Mail sent by and received at the Salisbury Prison.

Charles was taken prisoner on August 25, 1864. He died in prison about January 25, 1865, some 150 days later. The possibility exists that he may have written. Mail service when Charles was at the fort was quite dependable. Mail service in the field camps was available. The battlefield mailings seemed to be the ones that would take some time to arrive. Mail from prison would be tricky. Postal service was not the same as it is today, and you have a nation at war with itself. In order to send mail, oftentimes, a flag of truce arrangement had to be established for the mail exchange to occur. In the latter stages of the war, this was extremely difficult to execute. I strongly feel that if Charles were able to obtain some paper and something to write with, he would send a letter. If so, it was never delivered. Obviously, the family could not correspond with him. They did not know where he was or if he was still alive.

The only documentation we can produce on Charles after he is taken prisoner is from his military record.

New York, U.S., Town Clerks' Registers of Men Who Served in the Civil War, ca 1861-1865	
Saratoga > Ballston-Wilton	
M John Harriet Shepard Teamster	Taken Prisoner August 25, 1864 at Ream Station went to Libby Prison then 3 Days 1 month on bell Isand and then to Salisbary and there he died Jan 22 1865

This document suggests a three-day stay at Libby Prison, one month at Belle Isle, and then Salisbury until his death, noted here as January 22, 1865. Conditions for all three of these camps were deplorable at the time that Charles was there. My belief is that it is highly unlikely that writing paraphernalia would be available, and if it were, getting it delivered would be a challenge.

My intuition from my self-claimed knowledge of "knowing" Charles, I am certain that his inability to contact his family weighed heavily on his psyche. Guilt, torment, and worry have probably clouded his mind. He likely has fears, but not for himself as much as for his family members.

As mentioned earlier, a lot of research was completed on Civil War Era Prison Camps, trying to solve the John Troy mystery. A common theme among those who survived was; those who died quickly were the lucky ones! This statement from survivors explains all one needs to know concerning prison life.

We know that Charles survived the prison experience for about 150 days. One should consider he entered prison from the battleground. He had been in an exhausting campaign, hard labor, and defeated in battle in the thirty-six hours leading up to his capture. They are now marched to the railroad, stuffed on a train, and transported to the Libby Prison. Charles never sees this newspaper, but it sums up the attitude at the time of the local press.

Richmond Dispatch, July 1864
Editorial on prisoners at Libby

We confess to a special delight in hearing of piles of Yankee corpses, no matter how long or high that pile. For prisoners are troublesome to guard and must be fed. But dead men attempt no escapes, create no disturbances, eat no food and cost no money.

At the Salisbury Prison, where Charles was incarcerated the longest, this description of camp conditions was reported.

The most painful period for the Salisbury prisoners was from October 1864 until their release in February 1865. Accounts from POW diaries indicate that the prisoners took in about 1,600 calories per day, whereas 2,000 calories were considered the minimum for survival. (72)

Charles arrived here from Belle Isle in early September when the prison was at its worst, and he almost survived. All the prisoners were freed about two weeks after Charles succumbed to starvation. Many of the surviving prisoners died after release and did not make it home. Many were scarred for life by their experiences at the prison.

On April 10, 1865, the following appeared in The Albany Express.

> **GEN. LEE AND HIS ARMY SURRENDERS TO GEN. GRANT.**
>
> **BOYS, DO YOU HEAR THAT?**
>
> Gen. Grant Proposes the Terms and Lee Accepts Them.
>
> **NOW, BOYS, A ROUSER FOR GEN. GRANT AND HIS HEROES.**
>
> **ONE MORE AND A TIGER.**
>
> P40

Many twists of fate came together to prevent Charles from joining the chorus of "Three Cheers and a Tiger!" What if?

What if Charles never enlisted? Charles enlisted, thinking that he would be drafted anyway. If he were to be drafted, he would receive no bonus. If he enlisted, his bonus would enable him to purchase the property on Sixth Street. We now know that if he hadn't enlisted, he would not have been drafted because Waterford had met its quota.

Charles had volunteered in a Heavy Artillery Unit. This unit was later reassigned as a Light Artillery Unit. They were being used as an Infantry Unit in several battles and were supporting a Calvary Unit at the time of his capture. What if they never lost their Heavy Artillery classification? Would he have survived the war? There were no Heavy Artillery personnel on the scene at Ream's Station. They were in the theater of activity but not captured.

What if the prison camps weren't such Hell Holes, Northern, and Southern alike? Charles nearly survived, imprisoned for 153 days. Surviving that long under unspeakable conditions demonstrated that he had the resolve necessary to overcome intolerable circumstances. Under even slightly better conditions, he might have survived.

Where is Charles today?

P41 The Federal Monument to the Unknown Dead is a granite obelisk that was commissioned by Congress in 1873. The government contracted Alexander McDonald of Mount Auburn, MA, to build the monument by December 31, 1876. The monument, measuring 50 feet tall with a base of 18 feet, was built to honor the unknown soldiers who died in the Salisbury Confederate Prison.

Recent historical research has led to a dispute over how many men are believed to have died during the last year or so of the war and are buried in the cemetery. The dead were buried in 18 trenches measuring about 240 feet long, located at the southeast end of the cemetery. Colonel Oscar A. Mack, the inspector of cemeteries, said in his report of 1870–1871, "The bodies were placed one above the other, and mostly without coffins. From the number of bodies exhumed from a given space, researchers estimated that the number buried in these trenches was 11,700. The number of burials from the prison pen cannot be accurately known." The figure of 11,700 was accepted for many years. However, the actual number of burials is probably lower, and it is doubtful we will ever know exactly how many unknown remains are buried there.

An estimated 3,000 to 4,000 soldiers were likely buried here after dying at Salisbury Prison. Even in the years immediately after the Civil War, the federal government was unable to verify the number of dead. (73)

Over the ensuing years, the cemetery has been erecting plaques to honor the memories of those whose interment here could be documented. The following is Charles' recognition.

> 1868 Roll of Honor #2862
> Sheperd, Charles W.
> PVT Co K 4th NY HA
> died 26 Jan 1865 of disease.
>
> Burial: Salisbury National Cemetery
> Salisbury, Rowan County, North Carolina, USA
> Plot: Unmarked Burial Site

P42

Note that we now have three dates of the death of Charles. A newspaper account states January 25th, but his Military Record states the 22nd, and the plague reads the 26th. The plague also reads Company K; he was always in Company H. It is a commonly held belief that he died of starvation.

Think back to the family's oral and written memories of the old man who came to the door many years after Charles had died, seeking forgiveness. This discrepancy in dates of death fits very well with the reason for John Troy's agony that he carried with him for the remainder of his days. It should be noted that the Shepard Family members he encountered were now Rebmans, but they were Charles Shepard's grandchildren who did absolve John Troy from his guilt.

Charles is also memorialized in the Soldiers & Sailors Park in Waterford, New York, on the Veterans Monument there.

P43 Author's; personal collection

Dear Mother.....I am the Only One Left

P44 Author's; personal collection

"Comrade dear: Thy march is ended, all thy suffering here below. Go with angel guides attended to the throne of Jesus — go."

"For on that celestial camping ground, thy bivouac is spread, and there — there, dear comrade, you shall rest till the angel sounds reveille for the dead."

"For almighty God is fair and just to all those who may seek his aid. Then let us rely on his judgment. If we do, we need not be afraid."

The prayer of James M. Bradford. Chaplain, Col. Lewis Buckley Post Ohio, GAR.* (74) *GAR Grand Army of the Republic.

The Grand Army of the Republic had a branch in Waterford; it was the General Phillip Sheridan Post.

Philip Henry Sheridan (March 6, 1831 – August 5, 1888) was a career United States Army officer and a Union general in the American Civil War. His career was noted for his rapid rise to major general and his close association with Lt. Gen. Ulysses S. Grant, who transferred Sheridan from command of an infantry division in the Western Theater to lead the Cavalry Corps of the Army of the Potomac in the East. In 1864, he defeated Confederate forces in the Shenandoah Valley, and his destruction of the economic infrastructure of the Valley, called "The Burning" by residents, was one of the first uses of scorched earth tactics in the war. In 1865, his cavalry pursued Gen. Robert E. Lee and was instrumental in forcing his surrender at Appomattox. (75)

The GAR was a national organization, a forerunner of The American Legion. They conducted an annual Encampment each year attended by tens of thousands of veterans. They would camp in fields as they had done during the war. Encampments were held throughout the country. There were several in Saratoga Springs, which was the smallest city to ever host an encampment. (76)

P45

WATERFORD G. A. R. IS REDUCED TO SIX

WATERFORD, May 23.—With the death of Hiram Coons, the roster of Philip H. Sheridan post of the Grand army is reduced to six members, Edward Laboy, John P. Davidson, Jerome Ball, W. John Lavery, Enos Jerome and James Cooney. They are arranging to participate in the Memorial day observance.

May 27, 1925

P46 The GAR was also somewhat of a Last Man's Club, as evidenced by this note in the Waterford Gazette.

P47

338   Russ Vandervoort

Two of the above-listed men appear here in the G. A. R's last appearance in Waterford. Leading the Decoration Day (Memorial Day) parade on Broad St. in Waterford, in front of the Town Hall. If Charles had been the "Lucky Man," he claimed to be in his February 8, 1864 letter and survived, I'm sure he would have been a part of this group.

Let's use some of Charles' words in our closing.
As Charles stated in a series of letter closings.

> "My head is all gone now;
> I can't write anymore,
> I've talked enough foolishness!"

BIBLIOGRAPHY/END NOTES

(1) Paraphrase of a quote by Laura Holloway, Founder and Chief of The Storyteller Agency.

(2) Jenks, Leland Hamilton (1927). The Migration of British Capital to 1875. Alfred A. Knopf. pp. 66–95

(3) Richard Hildreth, Banks, Banking, and Paper Currencies (Boston: Whipple & Damrell, 1840), p. 9

(4) David Rice Whitney, The Suffolk Bank (Boston: Privately printed, 1878)

(5) History of Saratoga County N. B. Sylvester

(6) History of Waterford Sidney Hammersley

(7) Hudson River Maritime Museum Blog Post

(8) Gazetteer and Business Directory of Saratoga County, N. Y. 1871

(9) Minutes of Knickerbocker Engine Co. No. 1 1847, courtesy of Waterford Historical Museum and Cultural Center

(10) Saratoga County Heritage p 501

(11) Waterford Historical Museum and Cultural Center

(12) Minutes and records of Knickerbocker Engine Company 1847, courtesy of Waterford Historic Museum and Cultural Center

(13) Sylvester, N. B. History of Saratoga County

(14) Adjunct Report United States Civil War

(15) Waterford Historical Society

(16) Quote of Louis VanDervoort Jr. *Canal Canaries and Other Tough Old Birds*

(17) Records of Knickerbocker Engine Company 1849 courtesy Waterford Historical Museum and Cultural Center

(18) Shannon, Fred Albert, The Organization and Administration of the Union Army

(19) General Order No. 94, Civil War

(20) John Cramer (id: C000867)". *Biographical Directory of the United States Congress*

(21) Wikipedia Sanitary Commission Civil War

(22) https://www.civilwaracademy.com/elmira-prison.html

(23) The Adams Express Company 150 Years www.adamsfunds.com/wp-content/uploads/adams_history

(24) "The Civil War and Reconstruction" by Randall and Donald

(25) From the history of Mosby's Rangers, see 43rd Battalion, Virginia Cavalry.

(26) History of the 4th Brigade N. Y. S. Heavy Artillery pgs 40 - 41

(27) Jump up "Barney, John." *National Park Service - Soldiers and Sailors System*. Retrieved 9 February 2015

(28) History of the 4th Artillery Regiment (Heavy), NY Volunteers

(29) Civil War Newspaper Clippings NYS Military Museum Wayne Mahood "Tiger at Morton's Ford" The Civil War Times Volume 41

(30) This content appears as part of the Civil War Trust's Overland Campaign Battle App®

(31) The Diary of Captain Augustus Brown

(32) North Anna Campaign May 23-26, 1864 BY Gordon Rhea

(32) ibid

(33) Battle of Spotsylvania Court House by Gregory A. Mertz Encyclopedia Virginia

(34) Burying the Dead at Spotsylvania–1864 By Donald Pfanz

(35) U.S. War Department. The War of the Rebellion: a Compilation of the Official Records of the Union and Confederate Armies, U.S. Government Printing Office, 1880–1901

(36) HISTORY OF THE CANAL SYSTEM OF THE STATE OF NEW YORK NOBLE E. WHITFORD CHAPTER VI. THE CHAMPLAIN CANAL.

(37) 22nd Regiment New York Volunteer Infantry Civil War Newspaper Clippings June 17, 1863

(38) Davis, William C., and the Editors of Time-Life Books. *Death in the Trenches: Grant at Petersburg*. Alexandria, VA: Time-Life Books, 1986. ISBN 0-8094-4776-2 pgs 52 - 53

(39) Lyrics & Music by Charles Carroll Sawyer

(40) William Tecumseh Sherman. (n.d.). BrainyQuote.com

(41) The Photography Book, Phaidon Press, London 1997. ISBN 0714836346

(42) On the Canal," Whitehall Times, Wednesday, 31 December 1986

(43) Canal Commissioner's Report 1865

(44) The Waterford Gazette July 1860

(45) Tindall, Dr. William (1918). "Beginning of Street Railways in the National Capital"

(46) Adjutant General's Reports Civil War

(47) American Battlefield Trust

(48) ibid

(49) Christmas during the Civil War Corporal J. C. Williams, Co. B, 14th Vermont Infantry, December 25, 1862

(50) Lt. Col. Frederic Cavada, writing about Christmas 1863 in Libby Prison

(51) Charles Shepard Military Record Ancestry.com

(52) Troy Daily Times, January 26, 1865

(53) American Lung Association Early research and treatment of tuberculosis in the 19th Century

(54) Charles Shepard Military Record Ancestry.com

(55) Brown, Augustus Cleveland. *The Diary of a line officer, by Captain Augustus C. Brown, Company H, Fourth New York Heavy Artillery.* [New York, 1906

(56) https://encyclopediavirginia.org/entries/culpeper-county-during-the-civil-war/

(57) New York Government Museum.dmna.ny.gov:newspaper-clippings

(58) The Diary of Captain Augustus Brown PGS 139 - 141

(59) Fourth New York Heavy Artillery, First Battalion, Major Thomas D. Sears. 143 - 146

(60) Excerpt from Captain Augustus Brown's Diary, April 15, 1864.

(61) Captain Augustus Brown's Diary, May 20, 1864

(62) The Diary of Captain Augustus Brown, May 22, 1864

(63) Mertz, Greg. "Spotsylvania Court House, Battle of" Encyclopedia Virginia

(64) Lande, R. Gregory. "Invalid Corps." Military History 173 (June 2008): 525–28

(65) From American Battlefield Trust, the Wilderness

(66) Captain Augustus Smith's Diary, Pgs 168 - 171

(67) The United States Army History, Campaigns of the Civil War, 1864-1865

(68) Siege artillery in the campaigns against Richmond, with notes on the 15-inch gun, including an algebraic analysis of the trajectory of a shot in its ricochets upon smooth water. Author: Abbot, Henry L Page 156

(69) American Battlefield Trust-The Flag of Truce at Cold Harbor

(70) Diary of Captain Augustus Brown's final entry

(71) Battle of the Crater. (2023, March 30). In *Wikipedia*

(72) Encyclopedia of North Carolina

(73) https://www.cem.va.gov/cems/nchp/salisbury

(74) Akron Beacon Journal, May 2016, Akron, Ohio.

(75) Wikipedia, General Phillip Sheridan

(76) April 30, 2015, by Jerome Orton

Picture credits

P01 New York State Library

P02 Michon Collection

P03 Chris Valcik Collection

P04 Waterford Villages Archives

P05 Michon Collection

P06 New York State Museum of History and Art

P07 Michon Collection

P08 Hart Cluett Museum, Troy, New York

P09 Richard Herzog Collection

P10 Poughkeepsie Journal May, 1862

P11 Albany Argus April 13, 1861

P12 Waterford Historical Museum and Cultural Center

P13 Regimental History, 4th Brigade Heavy Artillery NYSV

P14 Wikipedia

P15 ibid

P16 History of Adams Express Company

P17 From the history of Mosby's Rangers, see 43rd Battalion, Virginia Cavalry

P18 Regimental History, 4th Brigade Heavy Artillery NYSV

P19 ibid

P20 Journal of Civil War Cooking Utensils

P21 Wikipedia

P22 Harper's Weekly June 1864

P23 ibid

P24 ibid

P25 Johnson Song Publisher, Philadelphia

P26 National Park Services

P27 Poughkeepsie Journal

P28 ibid

P29 National Park Services

P30 The Fayetteville Observer August 2, 1865

P31 Waterford Historical Museum and Cultural Center

P32 John and Helen Anderson Collection

P33 History of the 4th Brigade Heavy Artillery NYSV

P34 Library of Congress

P35 ibid

P36 Wikipedia

P37 Diary of Captain Augustus Brown

P38 Regimental History of the II Corp

P39 Swanne Auction Gallery

P40 Albany Albany Express April 10, 1865

P41 Library of Congress

P42 Salisbury National Cemetery

P43 Author's

P44 Town of Waterford

P45 Waterford GAR, Phillip Sheridan Post

P46 Waterford Gazette May 30, 1925

P47 Saratoga County Historian's Office